Reshapi
Liturgical Tradition

Ecumenical and Reformed

Jonathan Hehn
Martha Moore-Keish

Reshaping the Liturgical Tradition: Ecumenical and Reformed

Edited by Jonathan Hehn and Martha Moore-Keish

Copyright © 2021 The Order of Saint Luke

ISBN 978-1-878009-78-4

First edition, February 2021

Cover photograph by Andrew E. Kimble

OSL Publications
810 Fries Mill Rd.
Franklinville, NJ 08322

OSLPublications.org

This book has been typeset using the font Garamond.

CONTENTS

ACKNOWLEDGMENTS

Thank you to all the following people whose feedback, advice, and expertise made possible the completion of this book, especially Daniel Benedict, OSL from Order of Saint Luke Publications; members of the Reformed Pre-Meeting of the North American Academy of Liturgy, whose advice not only guided this project but helped initiate it; several colleagues at the University of Notre Dame, including Hansol Goo, Brad Gregory, and Todd Walatka; the library and archives staff at the Boston University School of Theology; Marney Ault Wasserman for her contributions to chapter seven; as well as Elsie McKee of Princeton Theological Seminary and Bryan Spinks of Yale Divinity School for their contributions to chapter nine.

Thanks are due most especially to the editors' spouses, Kelly and Chris, and to all whose support during the writing and editing process has made this book possible.

I. PREFACE

by Jonathan Hehn, OSL

<u>Introduction and Background</u>

In February of 2019, the noted liturgist, professor, ecumenical activist, and Presbyterian pastor Horace Thaddeus Allen, Jr. died in his longtime home of Brookline, Massachusetts. From 1978 until his retirement in 2003, Horace was Professor of Worship at the Boston University School of Theology. He also served for several years as the Director of Worship and Music for the Joint Office of Worship for the United Presbyterian Church in the U.S.A. and the Presbyterian Church in the U.S., denominations which would merge in 1983 to become the current Presbyterian Church (U.S.A.), known colloquially as the PC(USA). Before joining the staff of the Joint Office of Worship, Horace served for several years as the warden of Iona Abbey, a prominent center of ecumenical liturgical and musical thought located in Scotland. Among his other achievements and his renown as a teacher, Horace was perhaps best noted in ecumenical circles as one of the fiercest proponents of the Common Lectionary, and its successor, the Revised Common Lectionary (RCL), which he helped create as a member of The Consultation of Common Texts (CCT). Through his work on the CCT, his tireless efforts for reform within the Presbyterian Church (U.S.A.), and his long tenure

i

as a professor in a United Methodist seminary (Boston University School of Theology), Horace had a broad and significant impact on the worship life of the ecumenical Church.

In the months before Horace's death, I had been in conversations with a handful of colleagues in the PC(USA) about the need for a new pedagogical liturgy resource for Presbyterian seminarians. We agreed that the published resources for teaching liturgy in Presbyterian seminaries were less than ideal and increasingly dated, but we were divided on what any future publications should look like. Nearly all mainline denominational seminaries are populated by students who come from a variety of denominational backgrounds; this creates a responsibility on the part of professors to address, to the extent possible, what Horace would call the "particularities" of each student's denominational tradition, oftentimes over the course of just a one-semester introductory class on worship. However, one could argue that there is an equal or greater responsibility on the part of the Presbyterian seminaries more broadly to pass on knowledge about, and to form their students in, the distinctives of that tradition, especially when Presbyterians still form the majority, or at least the plurality, of their students. At the crux of our disagreement on the shape of future pedagogical resources was how to achieve the balance between these two responsibilities.

A key moment in these conversations came in January of 2019, during the annual meeting of the North American Academy of Liturgy in Denver, Colorado. During that meeting, a group of Presbyterian members of the Academy held a memorial service for Chip Andrus, a fellow Academy member who had died in September of 2018. After that service, I expressed to my colleague David Gambrell a desire for a new generation of scholars and practitioners to take up the work of liturgical reform both within the PC(USA) and ecumenically. The fervor of the liturgical movement in the middle of the twentieth century, marked especially by the Second Vatican Council, had produced a large number of dedicated liturgical reformers who had accomplished a great deal within the Church. I shared with David my concern that, as this first generation of post-Vatican II reformers was dying out, there needed to be a new generation of folks taking up their mantle and carrying their work forward into the future. I was completely unaware that Horace T. Allen Jr., one of the most important of this first generation of reformers, would die less than a month later.

Horace's death was a catalyst for this current book project in a few ways. First, it galvanized my resolve to create a book that could serve as an academic resource for both Presbyterian liturgical scholars and those working in the wider Church. Second, it suggested an obvious shape to the book, a Festschrift. As an edited volume of chapters by various authors, it would offer the opportunity to embrace a range of views on liturgical renewal, something a standard textbook such as I had been discussing with colleagues prior to Horace's death could not have offered. Third, a Festschrift would also provide the chance for a number of younger scholars to carry forward the work of liturgical reform through their contributions to the book, thus satisfying, in a way, the desire I had expressed to David Gambrell just a month before. Moreover, in reaching out to potential authors, I discovered that some former students of Horace's from Boston University had actually already been pondering a Festschrift honoring his legacy for some time. Knowing this gave me confidence that such a book could indeed be a fruitful and worthwhile endeavor.

It quickly became clear, during the many hours of conversation with colleagues and publishers about the book, that this work would benefit greatly from having two co-editors rather than myself as sole editor. I have thus been very grateful to my colleague, Martha Moore-Keish, for agreeing to co-edit the book with me. Her expertise and work in the area of Reformed worship with particular interest in ecumenism has enabled me to focus my work on the Presbyterian-specific portions of the book, sections 2 and 3, while she has edited the first section entitled "Liturgical Ecumenism." Martha also provided invaluable feedback on my own chapter, and has been generous with her wisdom and guidance about the process of creating a book such as this one.

Significance and Subject Matter

Festschrifts in a person's honor are by their nature unique. *Reshaping the Liturgical Tradition* seeks to honor Horace's legacy by helping bring forward the pioneering work by him and others of his generation to foster the renewal of Presbyterian worship and the worship of the ecumenical Church. It is one of only a small handful of volumes to address the topic of Presbyterian worship in an academic manner in recent years, a fact which alone speaks to the importance and timeliness of its publication. Much about worship has changed since the Second Vatican Council, of course, both within Presbyterianism and within the Church ecumenical. Many of the chapters in all three sections of the book seek to address some of these recent changes as a way of carrying forward Horace's legacy of work.

Reshaping the Liturgical Tradition is also one of the only published works to address the history of Black American Presbyterian worship traditions. Like many Christian denominations in the United States, the Presbyterian Church is one which has been marred by racial divisions, especially between African-Americans and Americans of European descent. Despite, or perhaps due to, this division, the number of black Presbyterians has remained small over the course of American history. And while they represent a greatly important minority group, and the oldest significant minority group of Presbyterians in America, there has been until now no study of black Presbyterian worship traditions. Lisa Weaver, Assistant Professor of Worship at Columbia Seminary, and herself a person of African-American descent, has contributed this important chapter to the book. A more recent and numerically larger minority group within the Presbyterian Church globally is Korean Presbyterians. The worship practices of this group have thankfully already been well-represented in academic publications. Part of this is due to the sheer number of Korean Presbyterians worldwide. To give some anecdotal perspective, the number of Presbyterians in South Korea alone is roughly four times the total number of all Presbyterians in the United States. While there remains relatively little academic work on the worship practices of Korean-American Presbyterians, we decided early on to approach a Korean author about writing on worship practices in Korea itself. This was for two reasons. First, Horace Allen was well known for his teaching of Korean liturgy students, both at Boston University and in South Korea. Second, Korean worship traditions in North America have been largely imported from Korea over the course of the twentieth century, and the Korean traditions themselves stemmed largely from models adapted and somewhat enculturated from North American and Australian missionaries in the century prior. Seung Joong Joo, a former doctoral student of Horace, has written a chapter which speaks to some of that exchange.

Finally, the book's focus on liturgical ecumenism pushes forward that important facet of Horace's work, in a time when there is an emerging new sense of ecumenical cooperation among many Christian traditions. Such cooperation has manifested itself in a number of concrete ways, including the publication of the Common Lectionary (1983) and its successor, the Revised Common Lectionary (1992). Horace was a member of the Consultation on Common Texts, which created the (Revised) Common Lectionary, and after its creation he was a tireless advocate for its use. The group of authors for the book itself speaks to the same spirit of liturgical ecumenism championed by Horace, comprising writers from the PC(USA), United Church of Christ, United Methodist Church, American Baptist Church, United Church of Canada, Presbyterian Church of Korea, and the Evangelical Lutheran Church in America. We have chosen February 5, 2021 for a publication date, exactly two years after Horace's death. In addition to this symbolic timing, the creation of this volume happened in the fiftieth year after the release of the *The Worshipbook*. In addition to being the first Protestant denominational service book published in the wake of the Second Vatican Council, *The Worshipbook* was also the subject of Horace Allen's dissertation and the primary resource he helped promote while he served in the Joint Office of Worship beginning in 1970.

In short, by bringing together some of the foremost scholars and influencers of the ecumenical liturgical movement, as well as those within the Presbyterian tradition, this new collection of essays promises to make an important contribution to the way that teachers and leaders of worship understand the liturgical renewal movement of the twentieth century while honoring and urging forward the legacy of Horace Allen's own work. Each of the contributors to this new book is connected to Horace in some way. Some are his former students, some close colleagues. Others are his successors in one way or another, carrying his work forward or holding positions of leadership that Horace himself once held. Its primary audience is intended to include academic theologians, teachers and students of liturgy, and ecumenists with an interest in worship. We hope that it will be also useful for, and find a secondary audience with, liturgical practitioners and lay people interested in worship and ecumenical studies.

Photo of Horace T. Allen, Jr. from the Horace T. Allen Collection,
Boston University School of Theology Archives, Boston University. Used by permission.

II. INTRODUCTION

by Barbara Thorington Green

I will start this book introduction, in the style of Horace Allen, with a memory: In the late 1990s I sat in many classrooms under Professor Horace T. Allen, Jr. One day we were talking about heresies in the early Church when I heard him present an idea:

> The determination of what was seen as heresy,
> what was labeled heretical,
> depended upon
> who had leadership,
> who was in power,
> at the time.
> Things that were considered heretical at one time
> might be declared orthodox at another.

These are probably not his exact words, but this is what I heard and remember. Perhaps this insight about heresies freed Professor Allen to take his own visions seriously, whether or not they coincided with the present attitudes of his church. Perhaps it was this freedom that encouraged him to boldly (and slyly?) insert a suggestion in an early version of the Presbyterian *Worshipbook*; a suggestion for a "systematic selection of scripture readings for worship throughout the year." He presented this idea, often associated with Catholicism, in the major worship resource of a Reformed denomination that professed and practiced complete freedom for text and form selection, at the total discretion of clergy.

His style of teaching through first person narratives, and this thought that leaders could legitimately think 'outside the boxes' of present realities, gave his students a sense of the fluid nature of work steeped in tradition. Such fluidity is demonstrated in this book, which is filled with stories and insights from a variety of his students and colleagues who consider collectively a wide array of subjects. I can almost hear his signature 'ha' as he notes each significant idea.

This Festschrift is written to recognize the life and work of Professor Horace T. Allen Jr., Professor of Worship at the Boston University School of Theology. Professor Allen's passion for ecumenism was the impetus for much of his work. Perhaps he is best known for his prominent role in creating and encouraging the use of the Common Lectionary. This resource has effectively guided churches of many denominations to focus on the same texts on any given Sunday. It opened the door for clergy (and laity) scripture-based discussions within and across denominations, enhancing the possibilities of broader thinking and respect for one another. His ecumenical interests also encouraged his involvement in the sacramental and liturgical renewal movements of the twentieth century. I write this introduction as one of his past students who also had the opportunity to work for him.

Professor Allen's ecumenical passions developed early in his adulthood, perhaps beginning with the second World Council of Churches Assembly, held in 1954. He attended as a twenty-one-year-old youth steward. It is rumored that he wandered about gathering autographs of various leaders and that he brought home (swiped) the Ecumenical Patriarchate of Constantinople's sign. (Many of us who knew him can visualize both of these activities). He was convinced from that time his ministry would have an ecumenical focus.

The Rev. Dr. Horace Thaddeus Allen, Jr. died on February 5, 2019, just short of his eighty-sixth birthday. The chapters of this festschrift are written by former students and colleagues. While they share some details of Professor Allen's life and work, they also share the on-going work of sacramental and liturgical renewal which he inspired. I believe he would appreciate each one *and* have suggestions of what we could think about more deeply.

A timeline falls short in telling the story of this passionate, enthusiastic, somewhat eccentric, brilliant professor with visions and wandering thoughts; yet it does give a framework for and a synopsis of his life.

> March 8, 1933: Born in Uniontown, Pennsylvania to Dorothy and Horace T. Allen Sr. (Elder in the Presbyterian Church) with a sister Dorothy.

> 1954: Bachelor of Arts degree from Princeton University.

> 1954: Attended the World Council of Churches Assembly in Evanston, Illinois, coming home convinced his life work would involve ecumenism.

> 1957: Master of Divinity degree from Harvard Divinity School.

> 1957: Ordained in the Presbytery of Philadelphia.

> 1957-62: Pastor, Spring Creek and Frankford Churches, Renick, West Virginia.

> 1962-65: Assistant Pastor, Towson Presbyterian Church, Towson, Maryland.

> 1966-67: First Warden at Iona Abbey, Argyll, Scotland.

> 1967-68: Minister at St. James Presbyterian (Presbyterian Church of England), Bristol, England.

> 1968-1980: Doctor of Philosophy student, Union Theological Seminary in New York City.

> 1970-1975: First Director of the Joint Office of Worship, United Presbyterian Church in the U.S.A. and the Presbyterian Church in the U.S.

1975-1997: Presbyterian representative to the Consultation on Common Texts, co-chairing the English Language Liturgical Consultation.

1985-2003: Professor of Worship at Boston University School of Theology.

1983: The Common Lectionary, which he was instrumental in developing, is published.

1991-1998: President of the Mercersburg Society.

1992: The Revised Common Lectionary (RCL) is published.

2003-2019: Professor Emeritus at Boston University.

2012: Awarded the Massachusetts Council of Churches' Forrest L. Knapp Award for his ecumenical work, commitment to robust common worship, and his leadership in creating the RCL.

February 5, 2019: Joined in the music of the heavens.

<u>I remember …...</u>

Professor Allen loved sharing his life stories with students. Often his classes were filled with wandering story telling. Lecturing was not his style. We gained insights as we listened to first hand reports of his adventures in his theological/liturgical/pastoral work, his meetings, and his experiences. There was often a chuckle and a bit of self-deprecation. I remember one day he came into his office passionately expressing dismay with words something like:

I know so many people,
I have been so many places,
I have participated in so many projects.
Me,

> Horace Thaddeus Allen Jr.
> How did this happen?
> I still can't believe it.

In the passion of the moment, he even spoke his full name. I realized then it was as if the stories he told in our classrooms came compulsively out of what he saw as the incredulous nature of his life.

In the midst of storytelling, Professor Allen would often come to a word or phrase he would then put on the board so he could share his insights and stir up ours. I recall three in particular:

Liturgy

He explained liturgy as the "work of the people," taking worship out of the sole hands of the clergy. My developing thought: A leader would need to know the people as well as the faith to encourage worship that children, women, and men of today could unite deeply in with their hearts, their souls, and their minds.

Sozo

This is the Greek word often translated as "to save" in our scriptures. Professor Allen shared that it also can be interpreted as healing. My developing thought: perhaps we all need to keep the 'L' in salvation, remembering the salve that comes to soothe and to heal brokenness, the balm in Gilead.

Lex orandi, lex credendi

This connection indicates that our liturgies (worship) reflect our theology (beliefs) and our theology grows out of our liturgies. My developing thoughts: this stresses the critical theological as well as liturgical development of our worship leadership, and this connection indicates the formative power of our worship in the living beliefs of our congregations. In a way, Professor Allen's description of liturgy comes out of this connection.

I am not sure Professor Allen always realized where his wandering thoughts and insights might lead his students. These words are just a sample of how his instruction 'happened' through one story or another.

Professor Allen's life stories included lessons in pastoral care. When serving in West Virginia, he visited an older couple of European heritage. Just before he left their home, they brought him their large Bible and asked him to read from it. He discovered it was written in German. Two things came to his mind, first, that they didn't even realize the dilemma (probably they couldn't read), and second, that he didn't want to embarrass them. He turned to what was probably Psalm 23 and recited it in English, the language they all knew. Another lesson in caring came as he told us that (at least for a while) he spent Sunday afternoons with a colleague visiting the Children's Hospital in Boston. They would go to the chapel, pray with any who came, and they would also go through the prayer box, praying for all the concerns that had been left there. We heard real stories of pastoral liturgy.

While I was working for Professor Allen, at his suggestion, we gathered worship/liturgy professors from the Boston area once a month at Boston University for a meal and sharing time. Horace made this time a joy. His enthusiasm for seeing each person was obvious. His stories, chuckles, and witty remarks added life and pushed our thinking. These were truly ecumenical meetings with appreciation and respect for one another, reflecting Professor Allen's own attitude. He saw the importance of coming together, sharing life and work situations without finding fault with one another.

Long before I had heard of The Rev. Dr. Horace T. Allen, Jr, I and many benefited from his work. In 1990 I entered the ministry as a local pastor in the United Methodist tradition; my mentor told me a few clergy had started meeting for 'lectionary' studies' to prepare for Sunday worship. I searched out a group. They were using the 'Common Lectionary' for guidance, and a few years later we switched to the 'Revised Common Lectionary'. We were all United Methodists, but I soon discovered ministers of various denominations were using the same readings and gathering for their own 'lectionary study' groups. Without these resources, these weekly gatherings of clergy would not have happened. These gatherings created support groups as well as providing a space to hear and consider various interpretations of the scriptures. I did not realize I was being guided by the insights, leadership, and energies of a man I would later be gifted to study under and work for.

I would be remiss if I didn't share some of the personal ways I benefited from Professor Allen's guidance while I was a student. During my time at Boston University, I received a grant to complete a study of Holy Communion. My plan included interviews with several of the 'big' names in the liturgical renewal movement. Unbeknownst to me, these leaders were invited that year to speak in Professor Allen's classes and lead worship at Boston University. He arranged for me to have time with each of them and at each interview he appeared with a camera so I could have a photo record of each event. After the study was completed, Professor Allen saw to it that Daniel Benedict, OSL, received a copy. Benedict was at that time the Director of Worship Resources for the General Board of Discipleship of the United Methodist Church. He was establishing a study committee to create a United Methodist Holy Communion resource. My experiences with that committee, and other groups that I then was privileged to participate in, gave me many new experiences and connections. Later, Professor Allen suggested I present a paper at the North American Academy of Liturgy in the seminar on Eucharistic Prayer. I was afraid he would be embarrassed by my quite feminist presentation, but instead, after the presentation he walked across the room, placed a kiss on my cheek, and gave me a gift. Under his tutelage I am now a long-time member of that Academy.

Closing Thoughts

I am not convinced that Professor Allen was aware of the tremendous formative powers of the Revised Common Lectionary. It brought scripture new life and opened new doors for clergy interactions and ecumenism. Many churches that once had a minimum of scripture read on a Sunday, now use two or three texts. Many who once ignored the psalms now find worship would be bereft without them. Clergy who have gathered to discuss the texts together are more likely to have their preaching and teaching grow out of broader interpretations of the "scriptures for the week." There are groups of laity as well as clergy who gather regularly to investigate the coming scripture readings. The Bible has been brought to new life as it has become more central to worship.

People have become more aware of the shape of the scriptures and the significance of "Hebrew scriptures", "Gospels," "Epistles," and "Psalms." Worshipers have discovered that the same scriptures are used in various churches. The realization that various denominations are using the same readings helps people connect to and respect one another, lowering our fears and skepticism of each other.

Professor Allen's ecumenical interests contributed to the creation and introduction of the (Revised) Common Lectionary. His ecumenism thrived through his participation in the liturgical renewal movement. Professor Allen saw a concreteness, a realness, in his ecumenical focus on faith, worship and liturgy. He declared and lived a 'reformed catholicity' that did not disparage the faith journeys of others and yet did not denounce his own.

Horace Allen had two other interests that must be noted: First, he loved music, especially classical music, particularly Bach. He kept his double bass in his office. Last, but not least, he loved trains. He could provide hymns on his train whistle, he had a model train at his home, and he always traveled by train if possible.

Professor Allen had particular characteristics. We might start with his brilliance, his enthusiasm or his dedication, but I believe none of these would have been as effective without his humble humor, his eccentricities, and his first-person story telling. Professor Allen was a professor of liturgy who professed his beliefs and practices of theology and worship in his own unique style. He had human frailties, he carried burdens, yet his passions and even his willingness to be impish or even devious in order to accomplish his goals helped him achieve amazing accomplishments, accomplishments which his students and colleagues are now carrying into the future.

Section 1

Liturgical Ecumenism

1. MAGNIFYING PARTICULARITY:

HORACE T. ALLEN'S MODEL
OF ECUMENICAL LITURGICAL FORMATION
AT THE BOSTON UNIVERSITY
SCHOOL OF THEOLOGY

by Mark W. Stamm, OSL

Horace T. Allen, Jr. was both a committed ecumenist and a Presbyterian leader, an Evangelical Catholic in the deepest sense of the term. In this chapter, I will draw upon various sources, including interviews, to explore the manner in which he practiced that vision at the Boston University School of Theology, where he taught liturgy and led worship for a quarter of a century. For Professor Allen, an ecumenical vocation meant not the search for an indistinct and inoffensive *praxis* of the lowest common denominator, but rather a deep respect for ecclesial particularities. Along with that respect came commitment to discern and promote arenas of convergence; chief among these were the three-year lectionary[1] and efforts focused on the reconciling of liturgical texts, in

---

[1] Horace Allen began writing about the Catholic three-year lectionary and Protestant reception of it well before release of Common Lectionary (1983) and Revised Common Lectionary (1992). Except for times when it may be necessary to distinguish

particular the Consultation on Common Texts (CCT) and the International Commission on English in the Liturgy (ICET). For many years, these institutions gave him cause for deep optimism, yet that optimism ended in significant disillusionment. I write this piece as something of an insider, having been Allen's doctoral student and chapel assistant during the early 1990s.

Ecumenical in the Mercersburg Way

What do we mean when we say "ecumenical?" For some, including some seminary professors and directors of seminary chapel programs, "ecumenical" becomes a synonym for a liturgical *praxis* that we might better name "non-denominational," one aspiring, it seems, to an idealistic liturgical usage that leaves behind denominational particularities and in some forms even excludes classical theological-liturgical language such as the Triune Name: Father, Son, and Holy Spirit. Many offer such revisions in the name of inclusivity and, as noted, to avoid giving offense. Horace Allen worked from a different understanding. His ecumenical *praxis* reflected that of the Mercersburg Theology,[2] a mid-nineteenth century movement led by John Williamson Nevin, himself a Presbyterian, and his Reformed colleague, Philip Schaaf, who together served as the faculty of the small German Reformed seminary located in Mercersburg, Pennsylvania. The Mercersburg Theology began with Nevin's critique of American revivalism as it was embodied in the New Measures formulated by Charles Grandison Finney. Perhaps ironically, Finney also was a Presbyterian, albeit nominally so. Finney's liturgical method was essentially Restorationist, insisting that "set forms of prayer" were an "absurdity"[3] and thus should be rejected. As he viewed it, such forms, as well as the ecclesiology that supported them, were disposable and could be endlessly reshaped to fit the perceived needs of local communities. This viewpoint remains attractive to many contemporary

---

one from another, I will use the term the Lectionary when referring to any of the three-year lectionary systems.

[2] During my time as Allen's doctoral student, he served as President of The Mercersburg Society.

[3] Charles Grandison Finney, *Lectures on Revivals of* Religion, 1835 (Old Tappan, New Jersey: Fleming H. Revell Company, n.d.), 111.

Protestants. According to Mercersburg, that viewpoint is based on an erroneous understanding of the Protestant Reformation, that it represents a repudiation of the Western Catholic tradition. Theoretically, such a repudiation allows leaders to develop worship forms simply by consulting scripture and relying on their creativity, perhaps ascribing the results to the movement of the Holy Spirit. In contrast, the Mercersburg theologians insisted that Protestantism should be understood as an organic development of the Western Catholic tradition, including its liturgical forms and creeds. Nevin wrote,

> Protestantism has no valid mission in the world, any farther than it is willing to build on this old foundation. Its distinctive doctrines are of no force, except in organic union with the grand scheme of truth which is exhibited in the ancient creeds …[4]

While the need for ongoing discernment and reform was presumed, the Mercersburg theologians insisted that the Holy Spirit that shaped and inspired the first Christians was present throughout the development of the Western Catholic tradition, and the same Spirit continued to shape the work of Catholics and Protestants to this day. Thus Schaff wrote the following, which expresses the fullness of the Mercersburg ecclesiology:

> … Catholicism and Protestantism, do not, separately taken, exhibit the full compass of Christian truth; and we look forward accordingly, with earnest longing, to a higher stadium of development … that shall be neither one nor the other … The realization of this evangelical Catholicity or churchly Protestantism, forms more and more clearly the great problem of the current age.[5]

In his work at Boston University, Horace Allen embodied such an "Evangelical Catholicity," both in his own ecclesial commitments and in his work with others. In each case, ecclesial particularities were honored,

---

[4] Nevin, "Early Christianity" in *Catholic and Reformed*, 227.

[5] Philip Schaff, "What is Church History, A Vindication of the Idea of Historical Development, 1846," in *Reformed and Catholic: Selected Historical Writings of Philip Schaff*, ed. Charles Yrigoyen, Jr. and George M. Bricker (Pittsburgh, PA: The Pickwick Press, 1979), 114.

including his own, and deep commitment to Holy Scripture was the foundation upon which all of it rested.

An Ecumenical Vision Rooted in Scripture and Lectionary

I am increasingly aware of the extent to which Allen's commitments and manner of teaching have influenced my work, now at the beginning of my third decade at Perkins. In early February of 2020, around the February 5th first anniversary of his death, I was privileged to preach a three-part sermon series, that is, of a peripatetic nature. Specifically, the series occurred in three different locales—consecutive Sundays in two different United Methodist congregations and a Thursday midday service in Perkins Chapel. This series afforded me an opportunity to engage the three readings from the Sermon on the Mount that the Lectionary offered during Year A 2020: Matthew 5:1-12 on February 2, Matthew 5:13-20 on February 9, and Matthew 5:21-37 for our chapel service on February 13. I much enjoy engaging the in-course readings that the Lectionary offers during Ordinary Time, and find it bewildering that some prominent critics insist that such use of scripture makes Lectionary use incompatible with addressing the needs of congregants.[6] As another prominent Presbyterian scholar, Thomas Long, has taught, one can place any question in dialog with the scriptures, and one should do so.[7] The criticism notwithstanding, an Evangelical Catholic methodology will always put the scriptures first, and that was Allen's way. As I will note later, Allen taught preaching by example, and in particular he reveled in the exegetical commitment required for in-course reading and preaching during Ordinary Time. Because he taught me to love such work, I never thought that my scholarly vocation had been misplaced when I spent the first six years beyond my doctoral work as the pastor of a local congregation, preaching and leading worship on a weekly basis.

---

[6] Adam Hamilton, *Leading Beyond the Walls, Developing Congregations with a Heart for the Unchurched* (Nashville, Tennessee: Abingdon Press, 2002), 90-91.

[7] Thomas G. Long, *The Witness of Preaching*, 2nd ed. (Louisville, Kentucky: Westminster/John Knox Press, 2005). Note, for example, his suggestion that one "view the text through many different 'eyes'" (86-87).

We do well at this point to document Allen's optimism regarding the possibilities inherent in the three-year lectionary as expressed in his *A Handbook for the Lectionary*, published in 1980, toward the beginning of his service at Boston University. He concluded the introductory materials with the following. Note its lyrical, almost prophetic tone:

> "Separated" sisters and brothers are discovering a deep commonality around the Holy Scriptures. We Reformed Christians believe that those Holy Scriptures are the hidden bedrock beneath "one Lord, one faith, one baptism." An ecumenism that starts there will not end there.[8]

When he wrote those two sentences, Common Lectionary (published in 1983) and Revised Common Lectionary (published in 1992) still lay in the future, along with much work on the development of consensus liturgical texts. All of that would stand at the center of his teaching and witness during the Boston University years. With all of that in mind, note several things about what Allen wrote here. Notice how he used the phrase "'separated' sisters and brothers," drawing it from the 1964 Vatican II document, *Unitatis Redintegratio* (Decree on Ecumenism).[9] I hear him saying it in an almost playful sense, as if to say, "separated for now." Further, notice that he self-identifies as a Reformed Christian, and not as a Protestant. That is, he did not see himself in the spirit of "protesting," but in the spirit of reform. But more than anything else, again notice its lyrical, prophetic tone. Many of us who experienced Allen's work—his teaching, his preaching his presiding—would agree with the summary expressed by his student and teaching assistant, James Olson, a United Church of Christ pastor and member of the Evangelical Catholic Order of Corpus Christi.[10] Olson remarked, "I always got the

---

[8] Horace T. Allen, Jr., *A Handbook for the Lectionary* (Philadelphia: The Geneva Press, 1980), 41.

[9] Unitatis Redintegratio (Decree on Ecumenism), Second Vatican Council of the Catholic Church, 1964. http://www.vatican.va/archive/hist_councils/ii_vatican_council/documents/vat-ii_decree_19641121_unitatis-redintegratio_en.html.

[10] The Order of Corpus Christi is a religious order formed to embody the liturgical and spiritual values of the Mercersburg theology. One can be a member of both the Mercersburg Society and The Order. http://www.orderofcorpuschristi.org/.

sense that Horace believed what he was saying and doing."[11] Another former student, Episcopal priest Beth Maynard, found that Allen's work expressed "an accountability to the tradition, an obedience to it."[12] In other words, his presiding was not about him and his leadership; it was about the Church, both in its overall unity and in its particular forms.

But what about the playful sense that I allege in the preceding paragraph? Numerous students and colleagues remember it, even as part of his ecumenical pedagogical method. United Methodist pastor Doressa Collogan remarked, "He was an elfin creature with a brilliant mind,"[13] and that aspect of his personality was shown especially around the Feast of Fools, something of a liturgical farce that he orchestrated in Marsh Chapel every Shrove Tuesday. While at times little more than silly—there was usually a duet that involved Allen's wooden train whistle and the organ--even these services reflected his Reformed liturgical sensibilities, the commitment to maintain a proper distinction between the one God whom we worship and the means that Christians have developed for doing that work. As a matter of biblical and theological integrity, he believed that we needed to spoof the liturgy. For example, on one Shrove Tuesday he came into Marsh Chapel pulling "a little red wagon that was carrying a big Bible." He turned to student David Dismas, and in a conspiratorial whisper, said, "The Little Entrance."[14] Later a bishop in the Independent Sacramental Movement, at the time the liturgy that Rev. Dismas and his church were following included some aspects of Eastern Rite usage, and so even the joke was ecumenically focused. Allen's jokes were often shared, many times in class, often told on himself. In a pair of stories that I heard him tell, he described visiting Rome and buying a pair of red socks,[15] an anecdote that he told in close proximity to this quip: "When the pope dies, Horace packs his bags." As to the latter, I

---

[11] Rev. Dr. James Olson, interview with author, February 28, 2020.

[12] Rev. Beth Maynard, interview with author, February 11, 2020.

[13] Rev. Doressa Collogan, interview with author, January 7, 2020.

[14] Bishop David Dismas, interview with the author, February 28, 2020. "The Little Entrance" refers to the entrance procession of the Gospel book in Byzantine rite churches.

[15] Red is the color of socks worn by Roman Cardinals.
https://www.meschaussettesrouges.com/en/gammarelli-socks/54-red.html.

cannot remember if he attributed it to a Catholic or a Protestant colleague, and it is altogether possible that he simply made it up.

As with all of Allen's quips, one needed to listen through them to their (sometimes) deeper point. These were jokes, yes, but they point to the fact that Horace Allen perceived himself as a Reformed Christian, and if he was protesting against anything, perhaps it was against the Protestant rejection of the Catholic way. Again, he was an Evangelical Catholic, Reformed according to his understanding of the Mercersburg Theology. That commitment included a willingness to express his own denominational particularity, not for its own sake, but as a contribution to the emerging whole.

Ecumenical Generosity Rooted in His Own Identity

As already noted, Horace Allen's *praxis* of ecumenical liturgical formation was rooted in his own strong identity as a Reformed Christian in the Presbyterian tradition, and so when he arrived at Boston University in 1978, his "career shifted from denominational work (which he never entirely left)" to his work as Professor of Worship at the School of Theology.[16] That short parenthetical phrase "which he never entirely left" is telling. Those who knew him never doubted that was a Presbyterian, and indeed he had been one from the cradle. He had embraced a vocation as scholar-pastor for the whole Church, yet again, particularly for his church. As such, he took up a vocation similar to that which James F. White and Hoyt L. Hickman exercised within The United Methodist Church, advocating for liturgical reform in light of the Second Vatican Council and its *Constitution on the Sacred Liturgy*. Beginning in 1970, Allen "was engaged as the first Director of a new (Presbyterian) Joint Office of Worship and Music," charged with promoting its newly published text, *The Worshipbook* (1970),[17] to pastors and churches.

---

[16] "In Memoriam, Horace T. Allen, February 5, 2019," obituary by Taylor W. Burton-Edwards, OSL, Secretary, The North American Academy of Liturgy and Chair, The Consultation on Common Texts.

[17] *The Worshipbook: Services.* Prepared by the Joint Committee on Worship for the Cumberland Presbyterian Church, the Presbyterian Church in the United States and The United Presbyterian Church in the USA (Philadelphia: The Westminster Press, 1970).

According to his fellow Presbyterian liturgical scholar Arlo Duba, he focused not only on matters of practice, but also on the theology that supported it.[18] As Duba noted, "This was a gargantuan task which could not, in any conceivable scenario, be entirely successful,"[19] but, he insisted, Allen tried and succeeded more than could have been predicted. Duba recalls the enthusiasm with which Allen engaged the task:

> Allen became the "popularizer" of the work of the committee(s) for which he was the spokesperson ... He brought to the office a contagious enthusiasm and a rich background, both in theology and in music ... It would have been rare to have been in the Northern or Southern Presbyterian denominations and not have known Allen.[20]

My own experience with Presbyterians who were serving at that time confirms Duba's assessment that Allen was widely known, both for his brilliance and for his eccentricities.

While he remarked on a "flamboyance ... that often surprised, sometimes shocked," Duba focused more directly on a consistent teaching agenda that his students of later decades easily recognize:

> He was a peripatetic troubadour-teacher ... Wherever he went he insisted that the Lord's Day and Lord's Supper go together, that the Psalms should be sung, that the sacrament of Baptism should permeate all liturgical theology and practice, warning about the dangers of jettisoning Trinitarian "Father-Son" language, insisting that children should not be dismissed from morning worship and that all the baptized should be welcomed at the Lord's Table.[21]

And one could continue the description, even to what Duba calls "artistic expression," specifically Allen's "colorful vestments and lavish

---

[18] Arlo D. Duba, *Presbyterian Worship in the Twentieth Century, with a focus on the Book of Common Worship* (White Sulphur Springs, West Virginia: OSL Publications, 2012), 30.

[19] Duba, *Presbyterian Worship,* 30.

[20] Duba, *Presbyterian Worship,* 30.

[21] Duba, *Presbyterian Worship,* 30-31.

use of music and water." A United Methodist pastoral colleague of mine, well known for his multi-colored liturgical robe, attributes the inspiration for that vestment to lectures that Allen delivered at the July 1971 Summer Institute of Theology held at Union Theological Seminary in Virginia.[22] In like manner, I remember Allen's action during the 1991 Boston University Easter Vigil in which he removed the liner from the Robinson Chapel[23] baptismal font and performed the *asperges* throughout the assembly, not finishing until the bowl was empty.

My point here is that Allen brought a well-formed and particular liturgical-theological *praxis* into work at Boston University and he retained it throughout his quarter century of service there. Indeed, I was his student, in the midst of dissertation writing, when the Presbyterian *Book of Common Worship*[24] was published in 1993. That version of the BCW presented a significant evolution in that it reflected the Post-Vatican II ecumenical liturgical consensus as well as deeply held Presbyterian values. I remember his pointing to it as vindication of his life's work. Again, he had brought that very clear and particular perspective with him to Boston University, and he had maintained it consistently. Rather than being a hindrance to his ecumenical method, that identity was the source of its strength and generosity. I will provide a series of examples.

Invoking John Calvin among the Methodists

Among the ironies of Horace Allen's life is the fact that this cradle Presbyterian, further shaped by service among the Scottish Presbyterian neo-monastic community at Iona, then served for more than two decades at the Boston University School of Theology, the first to be

---

[22] Rev. Guy W. A. Camp, III, interview with author, June 3, 2020. According to the institute brochure, Allen's lectures were titled "Worship—In Tradition and Contemporary Life."

[23] Robinson Chapel was another of the Boston University worship spaces, this one in the basement of Marsh Chapel.

[24] Presbyterian Church (U.S.A.) and the Cumberland Presbyterian Church, *Book of Common Worship* (Louisville, Kentucky: Westminster/John Knox Press, 1993).

established among the thirteen United Methodist seminaries.[25] Contemporary Presbyterians reading this text may not realize the intense negative reaction of many Methodists to the very mention of John Calvin, a reaction that relates directly to John Wesley's critique of double predestination.[26] Listening to some Methodists, one might assume that the whole of Calvin's *Institutes of the Christian Religion* was devoted to that one topic, but Allen did not let us Methodists get away with allowing John Wesley to read our Calvin for us. Rather, he would openly—and, it seemed, proudly--discuss Calvin, and that in classrooms often filled predominately with United Methodists. There were, of course, others there as well. Roman Catholic doctoral student and Jesuit priest, Thomas Scirghi recalls presenting Allen with a signed copy of John O'Malley's book *The First Jesuits*.[27] After reading it, Allen told him, "You know, Thomas, if you were to substitute Calvin's name for Ignatius of Loyola, the book would read very much the same."[28] Perhaps that was something of an overstatement, but nonetheless it demonstrates that Horace Allen brought Calvin and his theological heritage along with him and that unapologetically, yet not as some manner of zero-sum game, as if receiving the wisdom of one tradition required the rejection of another.

Wednesdays in Muelder Chapel, Teaching United Methodists Their Own Rite

Many students from that era fondly remember Allen's leadership of the thirty-minute Word and Table service held Wednesday afternoons in

---

[25] The Newbury Biblical Institute, established in 1839 in Newbury, Vermont, eventually moved to Boston and in 1869 became the founding school of Boston University. https://www.bu.edu/sth/about/our-history/

[26] See John Wesley, "Predestination Calmly Considered," in *John Wesley*, ed. Albert C. Outler (New York: Oxford University Press, 1964), 427-72.

[27] John W. O'Malley, SJ, *The First Jesuits* (Cambridge, Massachusetts: Harvard University Press, 1993).

[28] Rev. Dr. Thomas J. Scirghi, SJ, conversation with the author, January 2, 2020, and e-mail to the author, June 12, 2020. John O'Malley directed Scirghi's licentiate thesis at Weston School of Theology in Cambridge, Massachusetts. O'Malley and Allen knew each other through the Boston Theological Institute, a consortium of graduate theological schools in the Boston area.

Muelder Chapel, the small worship space located on the third floor of the School of Theology building. Muelder Chapel had chairs sufficient for about thirty persons, a lectern and an altar set against the wall, a small organ, and copies of the then newly released *United Methodist Hymnal* (published 1989). An icon of the Rev. Dr. Martin Luther King, Jr., Boston University alumnus and martyr of the Church, was affixed to the wall at congregation's left, overlooking the altar.

There was never a printed bulletin for those Wednesday services. Rather, we followed the Service of Word and Table I as printed in *The United Methodist Hymnal* (pp. 6-11). He would direct us to page six and we would begin with the Greeting printed there, "The grace of the Lord Jesus Christ be with you ..." etc.[29] Then, he would announce and lead a hymn, after which we would return to page six for the opening prayer (the classic Collect for Purity), and the prayer for illumination. As to the latter, he taught us that it reflected a tradition practiced by John Calvin. The service would then continue with one lesson from the Lectionary for the following Sunday and a short sermon based on that text. Then would follow intercessions, and the full Service of the Table, including invitation, confession and pardon, passing of the peace, The Great Thanksgiving, and communion. The service closed with the dismissal. Although the full service lasted but thirty minutes, nothing essential was omitted. He taught us many things through those Wednesday services, but particularly the following: (1) a strong model of biblical preaching based on the Lectionary; (2) that United Methodists possessed the equivalent of a prayer book rite; and (3) that pastors should make use of that rite. Not only did we use it, but regular attenders soon discovered that we were memorizing key portions of it. And so a Presbyterian minister of Word and Sacrament was teaching his United Methodist students the shape of their own rite and that quite specifically.

While not all of us were United Methodists, "Word and Table I" also reflected an emerging ecumenical consensus both in its general shape and its consistent use of materials held in common with other churches.[30]

---

[29] "A Service of Word and Table I," *The United Methodist Hymnal* (Nashville, Tennessee: The United Methodist Publishing House, 1989), 6.

[30] Specifically, "Word and Table I" uses ELLC texts for the sursum corda, the Benedictus, the memorial acclamation, and the Lord's Prayer. See English Language Liturgical Consultation, *Praying Together* (Nashville, Tennessee: Abingdon Press,

While ecumenical in those key aspects, "Word and Table I" remained a United Methodist rite,[31] and we were worshiping in a chapel housed within a United Methodist related institution. By using it in that setting, Allen was modeling respect for local ecclesial particularities. He presumed, it seems, that one should expect to encounter a United Methodist liturgy within a United Methodist chapel, yet with some local adaptations such as the icon of Dr. King, whom the School of Theology claimed as its own. Dr. Allen was quite aware of Dr. King's presence—indeed the icon gazed from the side wall perpendicular to the altar—and from time to time, it would become a matter of informal discussion following the Wednesday services. For example, Doressa Collogan remembers him pointing out the prison bars depicted in it,[32] and I have similar memories.

Engaging Liturgical and Ecclesial Particularity Through Mystagogical and Narrative Teaching

Note the pedagogical method that Allen employed during those Wednesday services—he was teaching a pattern of liturgical leadership first by demonstrating it and then by reflecting on the same, a mystagogical process and not just the imparting of theoretical concepts. Of course, mystagogical teaching reflects on particular acts of worship as done in specific living communities. Such teaching was second nature to Allen. Dr. Abraham Smith, now Professor of New Testament at Perkins, and thus my colleague, earlier served on the Boston University faculty with Allen. He remembers the explanations of ritual action that occurred during Marsh Chapel services, which, said Smith, Allen often delivered "from memory." These often deepened Smith's experience of the

---

`1988). I am thankful for the signed copy of *Praying Together* that he gave me, complete with the inscription, "with affection and the compliments of 'The Chair,' Horace." He was both committed to the work and proud of his role as co-chair.

[31] Note, for example, the relative uniqueness of the phrase "ate with sinners" within The Great Thanksgiving. See *The United Methodist Hymnal*, p. 9. See James F. White, "Word and Table I: An Historical and Theological Commentary," video recording of an address delivered at the Convocation of the Order of Saint Luke meeting at the St. Joseph Retreat Center, Greensburg, Pennsylvania, October 16, 2000. 1:23.35 through 1:24.02.

[32] Collogan interview, January 7, 2020.

event.[33] Such explanations were part of a wider circle of teaching and learning rooted in ecclesial praxis.

During the spring term of 1992, Allen audited Smith's course on the Gospel According to Luke. At that time, Dr. Smith was Assistant Professor of New Testament on the Boston University faculty, and he marveled that "an experienced, senior level professor would come to his class to learn from him."[34] Given my current position and experience, I understand Smith's sentiment now more than I would have then. Since, however, I was a student of Allen's at that time, I am able to relate my own memories of his enthusiasm at taking that class. He would make references to the class during those Wednesday sermons and also during the course on the Liturgical Year that I took with him that same spring, and I doubt that Smith had a more enthusiastic student. Allen's auditing of the class on Luke was part of a larger cluster of events that spring, which happened to be part of Lectionary Year C, with Luke as the primary Gospel. For part of that spring, Allen was serving as the interim preacher at the Fifth Avenue Presbyterian Church in New York City. That term, he was also teaching the course "Preaching the Lectionary," with Beth Maynard as a student in it. She remembers him discussing decisions that he had made for those sermons, and so particular sermons became material for reflection, yet not as generic homiletical models.[35] She remembers him discussing the sermon that he preached during his first Sunday there, with him demonstrating how he had worked a number of personal items into it. While he often taught with such stories, that was not his usual preaching style; but he did it, Maynard related, to establish a badly needed rapport with a church that was in the midst of a difficult transition. Quoting Allen directly, he did it "to give them as many hooks as I could."[36] Thus church and classes were part of the mystagogical circle--both the class he was taking and the ones he was teaching--and the method was typical for him. Sometimes it was done in class, but often in more impromptu settings like those referenced by Professor Smith.

---

[33] Dr. Abraham Smith interview with author, February 20, 2020.

[34] Smith interview, February 20, 2020.

[35] Maynard interview, February 11, 2020.

[36] Maynard interview, February 11, 2020.

Maynard remembers one of the services in Muelder Chapel "when (following the usual pattern of anticipating lessons for the following Sunday) we were celebrating Palm Sunday on a Wednesday."[37] He had brought palm branches and had given them to people during the passing of the peace, but he had still more in hand. As he moved to the altar at the end of the peace, "seemingly on an impulse ... he scattered them on the floor of the chapel."[38] Thus the branches were there on the floor when the assembly came forward for Communion. In a conversation following that service he asked those who remained, "Would each of you tell me why you think I did that?" Various responses emerged and those across an ecumenical range, including Maynard's Anglican perspective, that, via the palm branches "we were acknowledging the presence of Jesus as we come to the altar." She recalled that others spoke to equally valid understandings, reminding her "that gestures have almost infinite possibilities for interpretation."[39] Here again, along with the numerous stories that Allen told, again one finds a mystagogical and narrative way of teaching rooted in the *praxis* of the Church.

His stories could be disjointed and thus a source of frustration to some students. What did the Presbyterian circuit that he had served in West Virginia have to do with the Iona community where he had served as warden under Donald MacLeod? And furthermore, what did any of that have to do with the Fifth Avenue Presbyterian Church and the latest meeting of the Consultation on Common Texts, especially when one was trying to prepare responses for one's Board of Ordained Ministry review? Sometimes it was difficult to tell, but it was the way he taught. As James Olson insisted, "Horace was not a lecturer, and really didn't even like teaching that way, but he was a pastoral storyteller, and he never really left being a pastor. He was conveying a love of the liturgy and a regard for it, and that's what he drew out of us."[40] Again, for Allen, the liturgy was lived, and never just an academic subject, and "that's what he drew out of us, what he wanted us to learn."[41]

---

[37] Maynard interview, February 11, 2020.

[38] Maynard interview, February 11, 2020.

[39] Maynard interview, February 11, 2020.

[40] Olson interview, February 28, 2020.

[41] Olson interview, February 28, 2020.

An Episcopalian Who "Felt Seen"

Beth Maynard recalled that "she felt seen" by him,[42] but not in an uncritical manner. For Allen, ecumenical discussion went well beyond mere acceptance. For the Liturgical Year course he encouraged her to research and write a paper on the history of the Good Friday rite in *The Book of Common Prayer* 1979, which, at the time, was early in its second decade of use. While previous versions of the BCP had included lessons and collects for Good Friday, there had previously been no distinct Good Friday rite. As Maynard recalls it, within the paper she discussed her claim that the rite forbids Eucharist on Good Friday.[43] She recalled that Allen received that assertion, yet in his comments he stated why he thought having the Eucharist on that day could be a good idea.[44] Note here not just ecumenical expression, but ecumenical dialog, with particular differences engaged.

Not surprisingly, one of Maynard's most poignant ecumenical memories comes not from class, but from a chapel service, this time a service in Marsh Chapel. While Allen led the small Muelder Chapel services on Wednesdays, he also provided oversight for the larger School of Theology chapel services that took place on Tuesdays and Thursdays in Marsh Chapel, the university's primary worship space. Like most (if not all) seminary chapel directors, he was usually present for the services, sometimes leading, sometimes pleased with the services, at other times annoyed by them. On this particular occasion in the spring of 1993, graduating students had been invited to share a stanza of a favorite hymn, that as a way of testifying to their experience of God's work during their time in seminary. Beth observed that such testifying was "a very Methodist thing to do, but not what we Episcopalians do ... I needed a

---

[42] Maynard interview, February 11, 2020.

[43] Note that the Good Friday rite in the 1979 *BCP* does include rubrics for administering Holy Communion from the reserved sacrament. *The Book of Common Prayer* 1979 (New York: The Church Hymnal Corporation, 1982), 282. Commenting on that rite in the 1979 *BCP*, Marion J. Hatchett wrote, "This edition of the Prayer Book revives the tradition of prohibiting the celebration of the Eucharist on Good Friday and Holy Saturday." *Commentary on the American Prayer Book* (San Francisco: Harper Collins, 1995), 234.

[44] Maynard interview, February 11, 2020.

prayer and a ritual action,"[45] an alternative that would reflect the piety of her denomination. Thus she chose a collect from *The Book of Common Prayer* (1979)—interestingly, one included both in the Good Friday rite and in the Easter Vigil[46]—and then she went to the university registrar's office to obtain a copy of her transcript. When it was her turn to speak, she walked to the front of the assembly, offered the prayer, put the transcript in her copy of the Prayer Book and placed both on the altar. Then she bowed to the altar, and following that, turned and bowed to the assembly; but that is not the end of the story. 'Later in the day," Maynard said, "Horace sought me out to tell me that an Episcopal Church doctoral student had been in the service that day." According to Allen's report, that student said, "I never thought I would see such a sterling example of Anglican piety in Marsh Chapel.'" [47] These stories show Allen's ecumenical sensitivity as well as his pastoral method in seeking her out in order to tell the story.

An Independent Sacramental Movement Priest and "A Tridentine Mass" in Marsh Chapel?

Another example comes from David Dismas who wrote, "(Dr. Allen) supervised my studies but allowed me to find my own way. He always treated me as a partner in the enterprise and often asked me questions about how I approached the liturgy even as he shared his own insights."[48] A particularly striking example—albeit somewhat chaotic—came toward the end of Dismas' time at the school, when "we celebrated a service as close to the Tridentine Mass as possible ..."[49] Over the years, School of Theology services in Marsh Chapel had reflected a wide range of

---

[45] Maynard interview, February 11, 2020.

[46] *BCP* (1979), 280, 291. "O God of unchangeable power and eternal light: Look favorably on your whole Church, that wonderful and sacred mystery; by the effectual working of your providence, carry out in tranquility the plan of salvation. Let the whole world see and know that things which were cast down are being raised up, and things which had grown old are being made new, and that all things are being brought to their perfection by him through whom all things were made, your Son Jesus Christ our Lord. *Amen.*"

[47] Maynard interview, February 11, 2020.

[48] Bishop David Dismas e-mail with the author, February 13, 2020.

[49] Dismas interview, February 28, 2020.

ecclesial-liturgical particularities, including a Mar Thoma Eucharist and a healing rite from The Order of Saint Luke, and these were scheduled on the assumption that the liturgies celebrated were those followed by persons who were part of the school. In contrast, during my time on the chapel committee we received a request to hold something like a Society of Friends service, but Dr. Allen denied it because no one in the community represented that tradition. But this Mass belonged to the community in which Father Dismas was ordained, and so it was done, even with Horace as concelebrant. There was, however, one major exception. No incense was used, because, as Dismas related, Allen had numerous Korean doctoral students and they tended to associate incense with ancestor worship.[50] It would appear that nothing much else was omitted from this mass, because it lasted an hour and forty minutes, a rather significant miscalculation given that an hour was allotted for the Tuesday/Thursday services. Nevertheless, says Dismas, "Horace allowed us to teach each other," and perhaps in this case the community learned, yet again, that ecumenical work can be as messy as it is meaningful.[51]

Ecumenical Cooperation Manifested in "The Horace and Tony Show"

While his ecumenical partnerships allowed him to navigate within Roman Catholic contexts and among other churches that maintained an active dialog with the values of the liturgical movement—as he noted, sometimes there was little difference among the emerging ritual texts of the various mainline churches, even Roman Catholics[52]—Horace Allen also showed a sometimes surprising ability to work with free church Christians. The matter of the free churches was something of a contested point among the Mercersburg theologians. Indeed, Nevin used the pejorative term "sects" to describe churches and movements that believed they could build a theology and ecclesiology by relying on the

---

[50] Dismas interview, February 28, 2020

[51] Dismas interview, February 28, 2020.

[52] Horace T Allen, Jr., "The Ecumenical Context of the Proposed Book," *Prayer Book Renewal*, ed. H. Barry Evans (New York: The Seabury Press, 1978), 101.

Bible alone.[53] More particularly, Nevin rejected the enthusiasms of "the anxious bench," insisting that "Finneyism" was Pelagian.[54] Schaff, on the other hand, took a more nuanced view, insisting that even they held a place in the emerging church, that "every single denomination, every Christian people" has "something to contribute to (the) great result,"[55] that is, to the Evangelical Catholic whole. Within the School of Theology, this latter attitude was shown in the teaching partnership that Allen cultivated with Dr. Anthony C. Campbell, a National Baptist elder and Preacher in Residence for Boston University.[56] Campbell and Allen, each something of an outsized personality, led the Boston University Preaching Forum, an introductory preaching course for first year masters level students that students dubbed "The Horace and Tony Show."[57] Maynard remarked on the "seemingly unlikely rapport and appreciation that existed among them."[58] Theirs was serious work, if also entertaining, and ecumenical in the particularized manner described throughout this chapter.

---

[53] John Williamson Nevin, "The Sect System" (*The Mercersburg Review*, 1849), in *Catholic and Reformed, Selected Theological Writings of John Williamson Nevin*, ed. Charles Yrigoyen, Jr., and George H. Bricker (Pittsburgh, Pennsylvania: The Pickwick Press, 1978), 129-173.

[54] John Williamson Nevin, *The Anxious Bench* (Chambersburg, Pennsylvania: Publication Office of the German Reformed Church, 1844), in *Catholic and Reformed, Selected Theological Writings of John Williamson Nevin*, ed. Charles Yrigoyen, Jr., and George H. Bricker (Pittsburgh, Pennsylvania: The Pickwick Press, 1978), 98.

[55] Philip Schaff, *What is Church History, A Vindication of the Idea of Historical Development*, 1846, in *Reformed and Catholic: Selected Historical Writings of Philip Schaff*, ed. Charles Yrigoyen, Jr. and George M. Bricker (Pittsburgh, PA: The Pickwick Press, 1979), 143.

[56] Campbell was another of my mentors at Boston University, who taught me in class and in the years following, taking it upon himself to give me an ongoing tutorial in the worship of African American congregations. Each year, he was the primary preacher for Marsh Chapel Sunday worship during July and August, and he hired me to work as his liturgist during the summers of 1992 and 1993. When I attended some of his revival service appearances in the Boston area—somewhat at his demand—he would introduce me as his liturgist, thereby setting me up as his foil for the query that he would then put to the congregation, "What's the difference between a liturgist and a terrorist?" Since he taught me much and since he often bought dinner, I was willing to play straight man.

[57] Note Maynard interview, February 11, 2020. Andy Keck e-mail to the author, May 26, 2020.

[58] Maynard interview, February 11.

Andy Keck, a deacon in The United Methodist Church who now serves as Executive Director of Strategic Initiatives for Perkins School of Theology, recalls the following classroom exchange that occurred sometime during the 1991-92 school year:

> There was certainly the novelty of having two professors, who couldn't be more different in some ways, who highly respected and esteemed one another, disagreed respectfully, but were often amused at how much they did agree.

> As to the lectures, I recall that Allen often provided "the content" that was then enlivened with stories from Campbell. There was a bemusement with one another whenever the other strayed out of character with Allen telling the occasional story or Campbell expounding at length on some salient point.[59]

As I have demonstrated, Allen could hold his own as a storyteller. Be that as it may, Keck continued,

> I do recall one class considering "ritual." One of my classmates was adamant that there was no ritual in his tradition. Interestingly, Professor Campbell was the inquisitor – having the student recount step by step what happened in a typical worship service. And he then asked, "Is this the pattern you have every Sunday?" Moving from inquisition to proclamation, with Horace beaming alongside him, Tony proclaimed, "You, sir, have a ritual. It just isn't written down."[60]

And so, the ecumenical work continued, even if playfully expressed, and again, in no way was it merely a bland and inoffensive praxis of the lowest common denominator.

---

[59] Rev. Andy Keck e-mail to the author, May 26, 2020.

[60] Keck e-mail, May 26, 2020.

Reflections on a Significant Disillusionment

To this point, I have demonstrated how an ecumenical optimism like that expressed in Allen's 1980 *Handbook for the Lectionary* was a defining characteristic of his two and a half decades of service at Boston University, both his work in the classroom and in various iterations of the chapel program. Recall what he wrote there:

> "Separated" sisters and brothers are discovering a deep commonality around the Holy Scriptures. We Reformed Christians believe that those Holy Scriptures are the hidden bedrock beneath "one Lord, one faith, one baptism." An ecumenism that starts there will not end there.[61]

I suggested that one should notice the tone implied in that statement, as well as its content. I hear not a dispassionate scholar standing at a distance from his work, but rather an enthusiastic prophetic voice. He taught as one who believed, thereby reflecting the ecumenical stance expressed by John Wesley in his sermon "Catholic Spirit." Quoting 2 Kings 10:15 (KJV), Wesley wrote, "Is thine heart right, as my heart is with thine heart? ... If it be, give me thine hand."[62] As I have argued, Allen extended both heart and hand in a variety of directions, some of them surprising. The development of the three-year lectionary (eventually Revised Common Lectionary), the Consultation on Common Texts (CCT) and the International Commission on English in the Liturgy (ICEL) stood as bedrock expressions of his ecumenical commitment.

By acknowledging his passionate commitment to that ecumenical vision, one can then better comprehend the sharp disillusionment that he expressed in May 2002, near the beginning of his final year at Boston University. New Catholic standards for the translation of liturgical texts had been instituted with the release of *Liturgiam Authenticam* and that

---

[61] Horace T. Allen, Jr., *A Handbook for the Lectionary* (Philadelphia: The Geneva Press, 1980), 41.

[62] John Wesley, "Catholic Spirit," in *John Wesley*, ed. Albert C. Outler (New York: Oxford University Press, 1964), 94.

development, according to some sources, led to some significant Catholic absences from the spring 2002 meeting of ICEL.[63] While some cited other reasons for their absence, problems presented by *Liturgiam Authenticam* had been looming for some time, and thus Allen remained unconvinced. These developments contributed to the speech he delivered that May 9, somewhat ironically, at "… Rome's Centro Pro Unione, a center of ecumenical study sponsored by the Graymoor Friars."[64] Allen began where he so often began, with the Lectionary, noting his debt to the Catholic Church that had brought Protestants back to their first principles about use of scripture. He said, "Who would have thought that 450 years after the Reformation, Catholics would be teaching Protestants how to read scripture in worship?"[65] Nevertheless, as Allen viewed it, agreement on Lectionary was related to so much more, including the use of consensus liturgical texts, all of which now seemed under threat. This realization led to his now widely circulated conclusion: *Liturgiam Authenticam* signaled that "the entire ecumenical liturgical conversation and dialogue is over -- finished, dead, done."[66] Some, like Catholic Liturgical historian Robert Taft, insisted that Allen may have overreacted to this setback, asserting that, with Catholics, ecclesial progress can be as difficult to unwork as it is to accomplish in the first place.[67] Nevertheless, Allen believed that the effects of *Liturgiam Authenticam* on the ecumenical liturgical movement ultimately were tragic ones, and his well-known line—"finished, dead, done"--has become his enduring legacy of lament. At more than a decade's remove, I have encountered it quoted in two key places, from prominent Lutheran scholar Maxwell Johnson during his 2014 Vice-Presidential address to the North American Academy of Liturgy,[68] and

---

[63] John L. Allen, Jr., "Liturgist Says Ecumenical Dialogue Is 'Dead.'" *National Catholic Reporter Online* (24 May 2002),
http://www.natcath.org/NCR_Online/archives2/2002b/052402/052402i.htm

[64] John L. Allen, Jr., "Liturgist Says Ecumenical Dialogue Is 'Dead.'"

[65] John L. Allen, Jr., "Liturgist Says Ecumenical Dialogue Is 'Dead.'"

[66] John L. Allen, Jr., "Liturgist Says Ecumenical Dialogue Is 'Dead.'"

[67] John L. Allen, Jr., "Liturgist Says Ecumenical Dialogue Is 'Dead.'"

[68] Maxwell E. Johnson, Vice-Presidential Address: "*Sacrosanctum Concilium*: A Liturgical *Magna Carta* Then and Now," *Proceedings of the North American Academy of Liturgy, Annual Meeting*, Orlando, Florida, June 2-5, 2014, 13.

by the widely-published Catholic scholar-priest Paul Turner in his *Whose Mass Is It?*[69]

What shall we make of it, of this lament from the vantage point of nearly two decades and now on this side of Horace Allen's death? As his research assistant James Olson pointed out, the ecumenical setback was part of a difficult set of events that occurred within several months of each other across 2002: his teaching partner and friend Tony Campbell died in September of that year, and that occurred a little more than a month after the death of close faculty colleague Dr. Pratheia Hall. All of those losses overshadowed the end of Allen's tenure at Boston University[70] and may have been a large factor in his withdrawal from active participation in liturgical renewal circles like the NAAL.

Again, what shall we make of it? We should note that every reformer's vocation is often beset by difficulties and setbacks, as both John Calvin and John Wesley knew well[71] and disillusionment appears to be an occupational hazard. Perhaps such is the case especially among those who advocate for the liturgical and sacramental renewal of the Church and even more for those whose imagination toward justice has been shaped by those same streams of sacramental renewal.[72] Almost inevitably, it seems, texts revised or reframed to reflect advances in liturgical theology are then pulled in conservative directions, as people read the new rite according to the presumptions of the older one. For example, even with references to a moment of consecration now

---

[69] Paul Turner, *Whose Mass Is It? Why People Care So Much About the Catholic Liturgy* (Collegeville, Minnesota: The Liturgical Press, 2015), 63.

[70] Olson interview, February 28, 2020.

[71] Both suffered banishments of a type, with Calvin exiled from Geneva and Wesley barred from the pulpits of many English churches. Both, one might well imagine, suffered the misapplication of principles by their theological heirs.

[72] I remember Horace's first book recommendation to me, A. G. Hebert's text *Liturgy and Society, The Function of the Church in the Modern World* (London: Faber and Faber Limited, 1935). Hebert presents a robust account of strong sacramental *praxis* as foundation for a sacramental way of life. Hebert's book was long out of print, but, even in those pre-Amazon.com days, I was able to find it and read it in the months before moving to the Boston area. But those who see classic liturgy's relationship to a vision for justice find even more ways to end up with a broken heart.

removed from our eucharistic rites,[73] pastors often go looking for just such a moment—"Could it be the epiclesis? Yes, it must be the epiclesis"—and thus that venerable petition, well recovered by the scholars, ends up misunderstood in a way that contemporary liturgical reformers did not intend.[74] Or, consider weddings and the old patriarchal giving away the bride, intentionally omitted from many contemporary wedding rites. Many simply reinsert it, with little thought as to whether or not it is authorized. Or consider pietisms of various kinds, Catholic and Protestant, that further exert their influence, pulling the Church away from the strong consensual and ecumenical center that Horace Allen loved so deeply. That pietism may express itself in a romanticism about the pre-Vatican II priesthood and Latin mass or in the mistaken understanding that a person attuned to the work of the Holy Spirit could not possibly do such listening in dialog with the Lectionary. All of these factors erode liturgical progress, and sometimes just when key goals seem within reach.[75]

Equally frustrating are those matters that one simply cannot control, such as the politics of the Vatican or those of The United Methodist Church. As a United Methodist with my own Evangelical Catholic leanings, I am not certain, given possible dissolution of the denomination, that either the progressive or conservative wing of the Church would provide an optimal landing spot. Then on top of all that, throw the uncertainties of the COVID-19 crisis into the mix. All of these developments affect liturgical *praxis* in ways large and small; and so, these

---

[73] Note that "The Order for the Administration of The Sacrament of Holy Communion" in the Methodist *Book of Hymns* (published 1966) references "The Prayer of Consecration" (830.15) but there is no such designation in "A Service of Word and Table I," *The United Methodist Hymnal* (published in 1989), 6-11. It is presumed that the entire Great Thanksgiving is consecratory, not some part of it.

[74] See argument in Louis Weil, *Liturgical Sense, the Logic of Rite* (New York: Seabury Books, 2013), 82-83.

[75] Even so, experience suggests that some of the claims made by liturgical reformers—such as Allen's claim that 70% of Protestants were using the three-year lectionary—seem exaggerated when one examines them at ground level, and perhaps especially when one realizes that, at least among many United Methodists, "using the Lectionary" can mean that they are using any one of the four readings (including the Psalm), with perhaps the Epistle serving as sermon text one week, the Old Testament on the next, and so on. Let it suffice to say that this is not the pattern Allen and the framers had in mind.

days I find myself wondering, among other things, what Horace might have said about virtual liturgies in which only the leaders were present, not to mention the calls for online communion.

A Beginning Step Forward

Given the inevitable setbacks juxtaposed to the uncontrollable, the anger that Horace Allen felt over the fallout from *Liturgiam Authenticam* is understandable. How does one begin to move forward in the wake of such disillusionment? Imagine, if you will, a reading of Psalm 137 in light of failed liturgical reform, or perhaps worse, as juxtaposed to the COVID-19 crisis. There the crisis goes much deeper than threats to the previously shared words of the prayers, much deeper than disruptions in shared readings of the Lectionary. Now, we may wonder whether we can sing together at all, and so the very universe seems to mock the Church, saying "Sing us one of the songs of Zion!" (Psalm 137:3, NRSV). How do we respond? First, we may weep, saying "How shall we sing? (Psalm 137:4, NRSV)" and then anger or bitterness may follow (see Psalm 137:7-9). More than once I have witnessed a creeping bitterness among fellow liturgical reformers who seem to think that the Church has betrayed them, or perhaps worse, simply ignored their work. Given the disappointments I can sympathize with their disillusionment.

How shall we respond when such times of disillusionment beset us? No simple answer presents itself, but one could begin a response with "the assurance of things hoped for, the evidence of things not seen" (Hebrews 11:1, NRSV). Such faith would be followed by soulful lament expressed within communities that understand it. When combined with a sense of history, such faith can help contemporary reformers remember that the Church rarely adopts their vision in its entirety, but that false starts and setbacks are inevitable. Calvin argued for weekly Eucharist in Geneva, and Wesley urged his followers to practice constant communion, yet neither movement consistently reached that goal during their founder's lifetime, and such a full eucharistic *praxis* has emerged only sporadically since then. Nevertheless, the witness to such a full eucharistic way persists among both Presbyterians and Methodists, and perhaps especially among their liturgical studies professors; but one also finds it among some of their students, even if not among a majority of them. Difficult as it may seem, liturgical reformers must come to know that such faithful witness is good and right for its own sake regardless of any wide-ranging legacy of reception.

2. YEAR D:

THE LECTIONARY,
CONGREGATIONAL FORMATION,
AND EXCLUDED TEXTS

by Heather Josselyn-Cranson, OSL

Horace Thaddeus Allen was a gifted storyteller with a playful sense of humor. Given his presence at so many of the ground-breaking developments in the twentieth-century liturgical movement, he had an embarrassment of riches from which to illustrate points or share liturgical principles in a witty, narrative fashion. Like many of his students, I was drawn by his humorous, nevertheless true, tales. My favorite, which sparked my imagination more than any of his others, was the story of Year D.

According to Horace, those who were developing the Revised Common Lectionary needed to find a way to encourage local congregations to commit to using the lectionary, so that these churches would then provide feedback to further the efforts at revision. Horace and his colleagues imagined a carrot: if a congregation promised to use the three-year lectionary cycle three times, for a total of nine years, then after submitting its feedback, the congregation would receive – in an unmarked envelop – Year D. This secretive lectionary featured all of the

Biblical texts that were suppressed from years A, B, and C: stories of violence from the Old Testament, psalms that were considered too challenging, and the entire book of Revelation with its inscrutable imagery.

In addition to being a wonderful and funny story, this tale reminds us of the fact that the Revised Common Lectionary does not include the entire Bible. While laughing at Horace's whimsical joke, we are forced to consider the question of which texts feature in the lectionary – and therefore in Christian worship. We are also led to consider on what grounds these decisions should be made. It seems appropriate, in honor of Horace's abiding love of the lectionary, his deep scholarship surrounding the use of scripture in worship, and his whimsical story of Year D, to ponder these questions, as well as to imagine the contents of the mythical Year D itself.[1]

Horace Allen's Work on the Lectionary

Even before his work with the Revised Common Lectionary, Horace Allen was concerned with the use of scripture in weekly Christian worship. At the same time that the Second Vatican Council was meeting, Horace created a systematic schedule of Biblical readings throughout the year to be included in the 1970 Presbyterian volume *The Worshipbook*. In 1975, he joined the North American Consultation on Common Texts as the Presbyterian representative. By 1983, Horace and his colleagues had created an ecumenical three-year lectionary, which was first issued for

---

[1] Horace Allen has not been the only liturgical scholar to consider the idea of a fourth year in the lectionary cycle. Timothy Slemmons, a professor of homiletics and worship, published a book entitled *Year D: A Quadrennial Supplement to the Revised Common Lectionary* in 2012. Whereas Slemmons's volume is a serious and scholarly attempt to restore a larger portion of the Biblical canon to congregational preaching and worship, Horace's idea arose out of the humor inherent in creating a lectionary out of unexpected or even inappropriate Biblical texts. One final difference between the two lectionaries is their date of origin: Slemmons's volume is not yet a decade old. Horace, on the other hand, began to hand on his story of the unmarked envelope in the early 1990's and eventually, as to one untimely born, he shared it also with me.

trial use and finally released under the name of the Revised Common Lectionary in 1992.

Since that time Horace has written extensively in explanation and in defense of the Revised Common Lectionary (RCL). He wrote as an apologist for the concept of a lectionary to his own Presbyterian denomination in the 1980 *A Handbook for the Lectionary*, even before the Common Lectionary had been completed. Once it was, he crafted the Introduction to the 1983 volume *Common Lectionary: The Lectionary Proposed by the Consultation on Common Texts*. An example of his defense can be seen in his chapter "Using the Consensus Lectionary: a Response" in *Social Themes of the Christian Year: A Commentary on the Lectionary*, in which he counters arguments against the lectionary, arguments that we will explore in depth later.

In the *Handbook*, Horace notes, disarmingly, that a lectionary is "simply an ordered selection of readings appointed for liturgical use on specific occasions in the church year."[2] Yet this "simple" device has great power; Horace abandons his preferred mode of transportation[3] to borrow an image from Karl Barth to describe that power:

> The Christian community in its worship… manifests itself as that ship, making its perilous way across the deep, from the death and resurrection of its Lord to his return and victory. As Holy Scripture is the sole testimony to this journey's origins and endings, so the use of calendar-lectionary for the regular and weekly reading of that testimony in the community has become a kind of chronometer for that journey through time.[4]

The Lectionary as Formative for Congregations

In his writing and in his teaching, Horace shared his appreciation for the formative power of the lectionary. A committed ecumenist, he

---

[2] Horace Allen, *A Handbook for the Lectionary* (Philadelphia: Geneva Press, 1980), 12.

[3] Horace Allen was enamored with trains and travel by rail.

[4] Allen, *Handbook,* 12.

reflects this understanding in a text from the Catholic Introduction to the Lectionary of the Mass that he included in his Introduction to the 1983 Common Lectionary:

> The Church is nourished spiritually at the table of God's word and at the table of the eucharist; from one it grows in wisdom and from the other in holiness. In the word of God the divine covenant is announced; in the eucharist the new and everlasting covenant is renewed.[5]

as well as in a quotation from the forefather of his own Reformed tradition:

> Calvin contends, "Wherever we see the word of God sincerely preached and heard… there we cannot have any doubt that the Church of God has some existence." If this is so, a system of some sort for the choice of Scripture to be read and expounded would be essential.[6]

Elsewhere in his writings, Horace describes this formative function of the lectionary as a "catechetical" property, indicating how scripture in worship both forms and informs members of the congregation.[7]

Readings from the Bible, itself already understood as a holy book, receive even more validation from the treatment they receive within the liturgy. The liturgy places scripture in a position of special authority: at the Sunday service scriptures are proclaimed by a congregational leader to the congregation, read from a position of heightened visibility and audibility, elaborated upon in the subsequent sermon, and referenced by both hymns and prayers throughout the service. Not only are scripture readings given additional validation by their presence in the liturgy, but these may be the only verses from the Bible that many people in the

---

[5] Introduction to the Lectionary of the Mass, quoted in Horace Allen, "Introduction," in *Common Lectionary: the Lectionary Proposed by the Consultation on Common Texts* (New York: Church Hymnal Corporation, 1983), 15-16.

[6] From John Calvin, *Institutes of the Christian Religion,* quoted in Horace Allen, *A Handbook for the Lectionary* (Philadelphia: Geneva Press, 1980), 34.

[7] Horace T. Allen, Jr., "Lectionaries – Principles and Problems: A Comparative Analysis," *Studia Liturgica* 22 (1992): 71.

congregation encounter each week. Therefore, the choice of scripture readings that appear within the lectionary is vitally important. Unless congregations follow the practice of reading in course, or *lectio continua*, then decisions must be made about which texts will be offered to the congregation. Indeed, Horace recognizes the great power that preachers wield in making these choices. He begins his apologetic work on behalf of the lectionary in *A Handbook for the Lectionary* by assuaging the defensiveness of Presbyterian pastors who may feel curtailed by using a lectionary. He affirms "the freedom of the minister of the Word in choosing texts to be read and preached," while suggesting that the lectionary is a useful tool to help pastors make available to their congregations "'the full message of scripture'" as they are required to do by the Presbytery.[8]

In this acknowledgement, Horace points to a key question when it comes to the creation and use of a lectionary: how should the decision regarding which texts to include be made? Given the length of the Bible, most Christian congregations do not, in fact, encounter "the full message of scripture," in a literal sense, in weekly worship, even over the course of many years. A lectionary shapes a congregation's experience with the Bible by placing only certain portions of it before the congregation, at greater or lesser frequencies. Who has the right to determine which parts of the Bible the congregation should encounter, and which parts they should not? How should such determinations be made?

The Principles and Structure of the RCL

The Revised Common Lectionary, of which Horace was a creator and passionate supporter, arose as an ecumenical Protestant revision of the Mass Lectionary developed as part of the liturgical revisions of the Second Vatican Council. Liturgical leaders from many denominations, as members of the Consultation on Common Texts, collaborated on the Common Lectionary, followed by its Revised iteration. These scholars followed several of the principles adopted by the creators of the 1969 Catholic lectionary. A central principle of both lectionaries is that the choice of biblical readings would depend largely on the calendar of the

---

[8] Allen, "Lectionaries," 11-12.

Church's celebrations of the two great Christological feasts of Christmas and Easter. The theological import of the Incarnation and the Resurrection would determine, to a large degree, the scripture readings for the time of preparation as well as the time of celebration for each of these feasts, a time which in total runs approximately from the beginning of December to the end of May.[9]

This Christological focus of the Mass Lectionary is mirrored in the way the Revised Common Lectionary privileges the New Testament over the Old. Of the three weekly readings that the RCL offers, two always come from the New Testament, while only one usually comes from the Old Testament.[10] Even that Old Testament lesson is replaced by a passage from the New Testament book of Acts during the eight weeks between, and inclusive of, Easter and Pentecost.

Within the New Testament canon, the RCL places the four Gospels in a pride of place that the other books in that testament (epistle and history and apocalypse) do not share. Not only does one of the three weekly readings always come from a gospel, but that reading anchors each of the other readings during the Christmas and Easter cycles mentioned above. During that period of the year, the other readings are chosen for their relationship to the gospel reading for the day, making the gospel reading a driving force for the entire day's scripture readings. Even during the year's ordinary time,[11] apart from the Incarnation and Resurrection cycles, the gospel reading is always listed last, in the place of greatest importance.

Furthermore, the lectionary distinguishes between the four gospels themselves. The synoptic gospels, Matthew, Mark, and Luke, each anchor one of the three years of the Revised Common Lectionary. Their narrative structures and pragmatic approaches to describing Jesus' ministry made them especially suitable for liturgical use in the eyes of the

---

[9] The celebration of Pentecost, which marks the end of the Easter Season, can occur anytime between May 10 and June 13, depending on the date of Easter.

[10] In the Revised Common Lectionary, the psalm is understood as a response to the first reading and not as a reading in its own right.

[11] In his classes, Horace was always quick to point out that "ordinary" here is not a synonym for "boring," but instead a reference to *ordinal numbers*, as these Sundays are usually referred to as (for example) the fifth, or twenty-second, Sunday after Pentecost.

lectionary creators. John's gospel is fractured into separate readings and used to supplement the other gospels on their years but is not read continuously during its own year the way that the synoptics are. Less of John also appears in the RCL than of the synoptics, although this is not immediately obvious. There are 879 verses in John's gospel, of which 276 are not used in the lectionary, meaning that roughly two thirds of the gospel is read in worship over the course of the three-year cycle. That fraction is similar to what we find in Luke's gospel: there are 1151 total verses, of which 362 do not appear in the lectionary, again resulting in roughly two thirds of the gospel appearing in Christian worship. But of the 362 "missing" verses from Luke, 200 of them are similar or identical to verses found in Matthew and Mark that appear in the lectionary at other times. Since the synoptic gospels include so much repeated and borrowed material, omitting parts of each of them that are covered by the others ensures that the stories still have a place in congregational worship. The 276 "missing" verses from John's gospel, by contrast, are unique to that gospel and cannot be replaced by stories from the other evangelists.

In addition to privileging the New Testament and especially the synoptic gospels, the Revised Common Lectionary also distinguishes between other books in the Biblical canon, featuring some prominently and obscuring or silencing others. Books such as Leviticus, Judges, and Nehemiah appear in the Old Testament readings only a handful of times over the three-year lectionary cycle. Books such as 1 and 2 Chronicles and Ezra appear not at all. Even in the New Testament, 2 and 3 John and Jude have been excluded from the Epistle readings in the lectionary, while there are only six pericopes from the book of Revelation to be found in the three-year cycle.

Criticism of the Revised Common Lectionary

Scholars have critiqued the Revised Common Lectionary, or its predecessor the Common Lectionary, usually from one of two perspectives: its treatment of the Old Testament and its neglect of the stories of women in the Bible. Such criticisms reveal much about the RCL and the assumptions behind it, and so are worth considering closely.

James A Sanders offers a complete and coherent example of the complaint that the Revised Common Lectionary has minimized the voice of the Hebrew Bible in Christian worship. His chapter summarizing this complaint, "Canon and Calendar: An Alternative Lectionary Proposal," appeared in *Social Themes of the Christian Year,* where Horace Allen was assigned the task of writing a response to this critique. Sanders identified five areas of concern, at least three of which directly relate to the use of the Old Testament in the lectionary: the use of calendar rather than Biblical canon as a lectionary frame; the relative weight given to the New Testament over the Old Testament; the Christocentric, rather than Theocentric, approach inherent in the lectionary, the preponderance of stories from the first century of the common era rather than from other times; and the privileged approach of *lectio selecta* rather than *lectio continua.*[12]

It may be that Sanders' third point, the Christocentric nature of the lectionary, drives all of the others. Being Christocentric, the lectionary naturally adopts the traditional Christian calendar anchored by the two great Christological feasts of the Incarnation and the Resurrection. Likewise, a system that affirms the importance of Jesus Christ in God's saving actions will naturally reflect that importance in the frequent use of scriptural texts that tell about Christ's life (gospels) and explore the meaning of Christ for the lives of his followers (epistles). Favoring the gospels and epistles in this way, it naturally follows that the majority of the readings in the RCL will tell stories set between the birth of Christ and the growth of the early Church, stories that take place in the first century C.E.

The question of whether or not the RCL is too Christological is a valid one. Yet there are reasons suggesting that the lectionary must, of necessity, be firmly Christ-centered. Horace, in his rebuttal to Sanders' critique, notes that the lectionary was designed not to exist on its own but to be employed in services of Word and Table, worship in which the readings and sermon move inevitably to the eucharistic table and a sacramental encounter with Christ. Given this purpose and liturgical

---

[12] James A. Sanders, "Canon and Calendar: An Alternative Lectionary Proposal," in *Social Themes of the Christian Year,* ed. Dieter T. Hessel (Philadelphia: Westminster Press, 1983), 257-263.

setting, a Christological focus is not out of place and is possibly unavoidable.

In his response, Horace also mentions the absence of Old Testament readings during the season of Easter. He writes that while this reduces the number of Hebrew Bible pericopes that appear in the lectionary, it also prevents these readings from being read and understood in an overly typological way. Such a typological reading would dismiss the original meaning of the text and diminish the congregation's encounter with the reading on its own terms. This temptation would be even more inviting than usual for some Christian preachers during the Church's celebration of Christ's resurrection. In defending the lectionary's stance toward the Old Testament, Horace also extolls the RCL plan for semi-continuous readings from the Old Testament between Pentecost and Advent. This swath of time, which makes up roughly half the calendar year, allows preachers to follow the Old Testament narrative of the patriarchs and matriarchs in Year A, of David and Solomon in Year B, and of the prophets, especially Jeremiah, in year C.

Certainly, however, it must be admitted that the Revised Common Lectionary uses less of the Old Testament than it does of the New. While roughly 50% of the New Testament appears at least once within the three-year cycle of the RCL, only 20% of the Old Testament appears.[13]

Turning from the topic of the Old Testament to that of the way women are portrayed, Marjorie Proctor Smith offers a representative voice of the feminist critique of the Revised Common Lectionary. She studied the Common Lectionary at great length in order to write "Images of Women in the Lectionary," a comprehensive and concrete survey of all feminine imagery in the predecessor to the Revised Common Lectionary. More broadly, she has considered how the lectionary functions in ways that might help or hinder the causes of equality and liberation.

These broader thoughts can be found in Procter-Smith's *In Her Own Rite: Constructing Feminist Liturgical Tradition*. In this work, she posits that

---

[13] See Walter Deller, "Lectionary, Church, and context – the disaster of the *Revised Common Lectionary*, " *Liturgy Canada*, 11, no. 1 (Michaelmas 2005): 3, http://liturgy.ca/wp-content/uploads/2014/10/LitCan_Oct_05.pdf

"much of the content of the change instituted by the liturgical movement [including the lectionary] has been a recovery of biblical typologies and the ability to think typologically."[14] Traditionally, Christian typological thinking presumes that characters and actions in the Old Testament prefigure characters and actions that appear in the New Testament. A contemporary practice of typological scriptural reading would not necessarily read the Hebrew Bible through the lens of the Second Testament. The inclusion of multiple stories from scripture each week makes possible the comparisons that naturally lead into a typological understanding, one that recognizes and emphasizes the patterns connecting Biblical stories. Proctor Smith communicates a nuanced appreciation of typological thinking. On the one hand, she finds that it frequently perpetuates "unreflectively androcentric and patriarchal" understandings of the Bible.[15] On the other hand, she finds that typological scriptural interpretation, when engaged in imaginatively, is one way to combat the false objectivism and dry doctrinal character of much twentieth-century American Protestant worship. She believes that a typological approach to scripture, and to liturgy as a whole, can help congregants perceive a life-giving dialogue between different scripture passages as well as between the Bible and their own lives. She affirms the possibility of a feminist typology for understanding scripture, one that is dialogical and that starts with communal experience and women's lived realities.[16]

When turning to the Common Lectionary in search of biblical texts with which to engage in dialogue, Procter-Smith combed the lectionary for texts that included women, that placed women in central roles, and that showed women in a positive light. What she found was discouraging: only one fifth of all CL readings involved women or ideas concerning women, however oblique, and only one eighth of these readings showed women playing a significant role. In general, and especially in the Old Testament readings, women were "included as they relate to… male

---

[14] Marjorie Procter-Smith, *In Her Own Rite: Constructing Feminist Liturgical Tradition* (Akron, Ohio: OSL Publications, 1990), 105.

[15] Procter-Smith, "Rite," 107.

[16] Procter-Smith, "Rite," 109-110.

characters [such as Abraham, Jacob, and Moses] but are not regarded as actors in their own right."[17]

Procter-Smith also noted, given her understanding of the typological and dialogical approach to scripture that the lectionary encourages, that scriptural texts about women are interpreted differently based on the other texts with which they are paired. As an example of how this works, she noted that the Genesis story of the creation of Eve is partnered with a gospel text from Mark about divorce and children, demonstrating a hermeneutical "identification of women with marriage and family."[18] After her exhaustive study of the Common Lectionary, Procter-Smith called for the inclusion of more biblical pericopes including women, but "texts which reduce women to wombs, to chattel, or to sexual objects must be excluded on the principle that such denigration is itself a violation of the promise of life and hope given in the resurrection."[19]

In fact, it seems as though the creators of the Revised Common Lectionary heard the arguments of Procter-Smith and other scholars. Several "denigrating" texts were removed from the Common Lectionary during the revision process, while other, more positive texts featuring women in the Bible were added.[20]

An area of critique that rarely finds voice is the question of violence, or the lack thereof, in the Revised Common Lectionary. The RCL largely excises the more violent or pessimistic stories from its representation of the scriptures, and few scholars question this approach. Indeed, this decision seems part of a general approach to Christian worship evident throughout the later part of the twentieth century. This approach suggests that people come to church to reinforce positive feelings, and elements of worship that might introduce negative thoughts and emotions ought to be omitted. We see this in the marginalization of

---

[17] Marjorie Procter-Smith, "Images of Women in the Lectionary," in *Women: Invisible in Church and Theology*, ed. Elizabeth Schussler Fiorenza and Mary Collins (Edinburgh: T&T Clark, 1985), 57.

[18] Procter-Smith, "Images," 57.

[19] Procter-Smith, "Images," 60.

[20] My thanks to Mark Stamm, who pointed out the omission of Ephesians 5:21-33 and Ezekiel 36:24-28 and the inclusion of Luke 13:10-17 and Matthew 13:33, in the Revised Common Lectionary.

prayers of confession and in the rise of the identification of music with doxology, or "praise," to the exclusion of other, more somber purposes. We see this, too, in the way that people who have encountered deep tragedy or pain often report feeling unwelcome in worship, out of touch with the cheery pleasantness that is expected at church.

Thus there seems to be general, though tacit, approval of the way that the RCL has avoided many of the violent texts found in the Bible. But just as Marjorie Procter-Smith has questioned the androcentrism and patriarchy within the lectionary, so, too, she is willing to confront the sanitized version of the scriptures within the RCL. Indeed, she links the concepts of violence and feminism:

> We need such [violent] stories for two reasons. First, stories of the betrayal, rape, abuse, and murder of women are certainly part of the biblical heritage that is ours. But such stories are also, alas, part of stories of women today. In any congregation, a significant percentage of the women present will know first-hand about such violence. The rest of us will at least know what is [sic] is to fear it. To tell such stories is necessary, not only in order to mourn the women in the stories and those like them who have been victims, but also to ensure that such victimization does not continue. But there is also a second reason for reclaiming these tales. It is because at the very heart of the Christian proclamation is also a tale of betrayal, and abuse, and murder, and the apparent silence of God. To identify the sufferings of women with the sufferings of Christ is not to subsume or to legitimate the sufferings of women but to recognize that the abuse is blasphemy and an offense against God. It is to claim, simply, that women are daughters of God.[21]

To extend Procter-Smith's argument, all people need to hear the stories of suffering and pain in the scriptures, both because they will resonate with our own stories, and because these stories, when connected

---

[21] Procter-Smith, "Images," 60-61.

to the story of Christ's own passion, show us that all abuse of others is sinful and an affront to God.

Elsewhere in her writings, Procter-Smith indicates that drawing attention to the difficult stories of the Bible is crucial, as well, in order to be honest about what the Bible contains, and about how it has been used and abused as a weapon. She notes that violent scriptural texts are "a formative part of our common heritage," and that including these passages in the lectionary will allow communities to recognize, and lament, "the human cost of hostile texts."[22]

There is a growing message from liturgical scholars, in response to the focus on positivity mentioned earlier, that Christian worship must make room for lament, confession, grief, and even anger, not just in the scripture readings.[23] Honest and authentic worship requires acknowledgement of the full spectrum of the human experience. We are gaining an understanding that sorrow, guilt, frustration, and confusion should not be abandoned at the door to the church but instead brought into the sanctuary, in the search for resolution and healing.

Given this message of encouragement for the inclusion of a broader range of emotions, stories, and responses in worship, what might it mean to invite difficult scriptural texts back into the sanctuary? Or to put it in Horace's terms, what might Year D look like?

---

[22] Marjorie Procter-Smith, "Lectionaries – Principles and Problems: Alternative Perspectives," *Studia Liturgica* 22 (1992), 96.

[23] Some justifications for the inclusion of these in Christian worship can be found in Don Saliers's *Worship Come to its Senses* (which names the importance of truth); John Witvliet's *Worship Seeking Understanding* (Ada, Michigan: Baker, 2003) (which considers the psalms of lament); Michael Card's *A Sacred Sorrow: Reaching out to God in the Lost language of Lament* (Colorado Spring: NavPress, 2014); Debra and Ron Rienstra's *Worship Words: Discipling Language for Faithful Ministry* (Ada, Michigan: Baker Academic, 2009) (also affirming the importance of lament); William Dyrness's chapter in *A More Profound Alleluia: Theology and Worship in Harmony*, ed. Leanne Van Dyk (Grand Rapids: Eerdmans, 2004) (which explores the role of confession); and Walter Sundberg's *Worship as Repentance: Lutheran Liturgical Traditions and Catholic Consensus* (Grand Rapids: Eerdmans, 2012) (which considers repentance from Lutheran and Catholic perspectives).

Year D

The lectionary that I have constructed, following Horace's description of this hypothetical document, shares many underlying principles with the RCL upon which it is based. Year D follows the Christological organization of time of the traditional church year, and it makes use of the Old Testament – Psalm – Epistle – Gospel structure of the RCL. As does that lectionary, Year D incorporates thematic linkages between the readings, especially during the seasons of Advent, Christmas, Lent, and Easter, while usually adopting a semi-continuous structure for Old Testament and epistle readings during Ordinary Time. In Year D, however, these principles are held more loosely: the Revelation readings during Lent, for example, are continuous as they count down toward Easter, and the epistle readings during Ordinary Time after Pentecost occasionally work in relation with the gospel readings for the day. Finally, Year D also substitutes readings from Acts for Old Testament readings during the season of Easter.

There are also differences in structure between the Revised Common Lectionary and Year D. One major difference is that while the RCL includes two different options for the Old Testament reading during Ordinary Time, one that links thematically with the Gospel reading and another, preferred, option that works semi-continuously through the Old Testament, Year D includes only the second of these two options. Thus all of the Ordinary Time readings in Year D are sequential: during Ordinary Time after Epiphany, the readings come from 1 and 2 Chronicles, and during Ordinary Time after Pentecost they begin in Genesis and end in the book of Joshua.

Another difference between the two systems has to do with how to account for the varying amounts of Ordinary Time, especially following Pentecost. The variable date of Easter, when combined with the fixed date of Christmas, means that there can be as many as twenty-seven Sundays following Trinity Sunday before Advent, or as few as twenty-two. The lectionary must include enough readings for the maximum number of Sundays in Ordinary time, and must also direct users which readings to omit when there are fewer Sundays. The RCL instructs that the omitted readings should come from the beginning of the season. This results in a certain amount of violence to the concept of the semi-continuous Old Testament readings. For example, when Easter falls late during Year A, the congregation may hear the creation story in Genesis 1 on Trinity Sunday, and the next week jump to the Genesis 22 account of Abraham's sacrifice of Isaac. While such an approach might be used with Year D, it is not required nor presumed. Users of this lectionary might just as easily begin with the readings for the first Sunday after Trinity Sunday, and continue as far as possible, skipping to the Reign of Christ readings on the last Sunday before Advent. Both methods of coping with the variable amount of Ordinary Time are possible.

In addition to these principles, there are additional assumptions that form Year D. The first of these is that to the greatest extent possible, only scripture texts that do not appear in the RCL should constitute this lectionary. In some instances, this has meant including books of the Bible that are entirely absent from the Revised Common Lectionary, such as 1 and 2 Chronicles (which appear in Ordinary Time after Epiphany), Ezra (in Lent), Obadiah (in Advent), Nahum (also in Advent), 2 and 3 John (in Ordinary Time after Easter), and Jude (in Ordinary Time before Advent). Elsewhere, Year D includes readings from biblical books that were minimally present in the RCL. The most extreme example of this can be found in the book of Revelation, of which only small portions of five of its twenty-two chapters appear in the RCL. In Year D, there are twenty-six separate lessons from Revelation.

In some instances, verses that appear in the RCL are incorporated into Year D, usually with an expansion of the pericope. For example, the Revised Common Lectionary includes Genesis 3:8-15 in year B as an Old Testament reading paired thematically with the gospel reading for the day. These verses include the interaction between Eve, Adam, and God, and the cursing of the serpent. The Year D use of this story expands upon what we find in the RCL, incorporating both the beginning parts of chapter 3, with the conversation between Eve and the serpent, and the later parts of the chapter, where God curses both Eve and Adam, and sends them out from the garden. A New Testament example of this principle can be found on Easter Sunday. On Sundays in Year A, Matthew 28:1-10 is one option for the gospel reading (the other coming from John 20). This reading tells of the visit to the tomb by the two Marys and their encounters with the angel and Jesus. In Year D the reading for Easter Day extends through verse 15, including the attempt by the chief priests and Roman guard to cover up the resurrection.

A second assumption in the creation of Year D is that not all of the better-known biblical stories need to be included for the sake of continuity. This lectionary rests on the ability of cultural memory, or the preacher's work in the sermon, to connect particular stories to various trajectories throughout the Bible. For example, Year D includes the story of Noah's drunkenness and the curse of Canaan. It does not, however, include the story earlier in Genesis of the building of the ark and the flood. Several weeks later, it includes the story of Joseph and the wife of Potiphar, but it does so without having first shared the story of Joseph and his brothers. In order to make room for those readings that do not appear in the RCL, Year D skips over connective material that already appears in the RCL and that might be familiar to those in the congregation.

The inclusion of texts that don't appear in the RCL results in a broader – and therefore different – palette of scripture than what is found in the three-year lectionary. This difference can be considered through four different lenses: the way Year D features women, violence, well-known matriarchs and patriarchs, and eschatological texts.

The texts of Year D include a large number of Biblical passages featuring women. Within its first readings alone, from the Old Testament and the book of Acts, we find Eve, Cain's wife, Sarai, Hagar, Lot's daughters, Rebekah, Leah, Rachel, Dinah, Tamar, the wife of Potiphar, Zipporah, regulations for purification after childbirth, Michal, the Queen of Sheba, Sapphira, and Rhoda. This means that 16 out of 64 weeks, or one out of four, feature women prominently in the first reading of the week's texts. Recalling Marjorie Procter-Smith's three criteria in her study of the Common Lectionary, we should go beyond noting where women are included to also see if these women are shown to be active agents in their own stories, and if they are portrayed positively. In most of these readings, the women do indeed play crucial roles in the text. But not all of the texts show these women behaving in positive ways. Eve is tricked by the serpent; Lot's daughters rape their own father; Rebekah deceives her husband in order to help one of her children and hurt the other; and Leah and Rachel use conception as a means to compete with each other. Year D also shows us the detrimental, often tragic, effects of a patriarchal society upon individual women. We see this in the awareness of Leah and Rachel that their status in society depends upon their ability to procreate; in the horror of Dinah, who is forced to marry her rapist and then witness his murder by her brothers; and in the machinations of Tamar, who is left to ensure her own survival when her husband's family neglects her. Here, we see that showing more women of the Bible reveals more of the challenges of women's lives, and a greater variety of responses to those challenges.

In addition to including more texts that feature women, Year D also includes more of the violence that is found in both testaments of the Bible. We see the hurt that people inflict upon themselves, such as the suicides of Saul and Judas in 1 Chronicles 10 and in Matthew 27, as well as upon others, such as Abraham's rout of Kedorlaomer's army in Genesis 14 and the Levites' slaughter of their kindred in Exodus 32. We see violence attributed to God by the prophet Nahum and by the author of Revelation. Occasionally, there is death that borders on the inexplicable, as in the description of Uzzah's death in 1 Chronicles 13. Such texts can be uncomfortable in that they hold a mirror to the often many forms of violence in contemporary society. Reading of the reality of slavery in Egypt, in Exodus 5, might help modern American congregations reflect on the legacy of slavery in our own country. Hearing the story of bloody revenge in Genesis 34 may prompt us to reconsider our own responses to those who harm us.

While not an intention of Year D, a curious effect of this collection of readings is that it shows us more nuanced, and less flattering, sides of the Biblical patriarchs and matriarchs. With the notable exception of the story about David, Bathsheba, and Uriah in Year B of the RCL, we largely find Old Testament readings that make God's earliest followers seem especially holy and faithful. Year D provides several contradictory accounts. In Year D, we find Adam and Eve quick to pass blame, Noah embarrassingly drunk, Abraham willing to prostitute his wife for his own safety, Rebekah and Jacob scheming to steal a blessing, Moses killing an Egyptian and later instructing the Levites to kill thousands of Israelites, Saul committing suicide, and David forfeiting the lives of his people in order to count them in a census. Such stories show us a far more human, and less holy, side of the patriarchs and matriarchs, one that ultimately may be beneficial for congregations. The "people in the pews" often hear lessons from the Old Testament about characters who heard God speak and followed God's will unerringly. It is difficult to make connections with such perfect characters, and thus a distance is created between those people in the biblical accounts and the people in the church hearing about them. Revealing the imperfections of these biblical characters can make it easier for congregants to relate to them, allowing them to forge bridges between the world of the Bible and the world in which they live. Rather than disassociate themselves, as "imperfect," from the "perfect and holy" characters in the readings from scripture, congregants may begin to understand that God worked through flawed humans in the past, and God continues to do so in the present. Thus a fuller portrait of the patriarchs and matriarchs can help modern congregants to see themselves as participants in God's ongoing work.

Given the inclusion of so much of the book of Revelation, it is not surprising that Year D has a decidedly eschatological slant. This approach appears in times of the year when the RCL also features eschatological texts, but it extends to other times of the year as well. Advent texts from Revelation, 2 Timothy, and 2 Peter continue this perspective throughout all four Sundays of Advent, paired with Gospel texts about John the Baptist and prophetic texts from the Old Testament. The letters to the seven churches in Revelation 2-3, letters that promise a second coming of Christ, anchor the readings during Ordinary Time after Epiphany, while the opening of the seven seals, together with the ominous events that happen in Revelation 6, provide an anticipatory structure to Lent. Triumphant texts from Revelation 14 and 19 appear during Easter Season as well. In the Revised Common Lectionary, scripture texts at the end of Ordinary time turn toward eschatological themes in preparation for the beginning of Advent, usually beginning in the month of November. This turn happens as well in Year D, but it begins earlier in the year. Starting on the 20th Sunday of Ordinary Time, we hear the parable of the faithful manager from Luke 12, describing the return of Christ in metaphor. From this Sunday, which might occur as early as late September, until the last Sunday of Ordinary Time, the gospel readings present warnings of coming persecutions and parables about the end times.

Conclusion

At its best, Year D offers to the Church the recognition that God's followers are not now and never have been perfect. We see in Year D familiar Biblical characters acting in ways as frequently selfish as they are faithful. We see a broader cast of women, some of whom are treated unjustly while others engage in such treatment themselves. We see human beings acting out in violent behavior, sometimes at the instigation of a God who seemingly approves of this violence. And we see a world in need of, and restlessly waiting for, the end times. In many ways this expands upon the glimpse of the Bible we find in the Revised Common Lectionary, a view that encourages a positive view of humanity, of our Biblical forebears, of the world, and of our ability to affect this world. Such an expansion may be needed, especially now. The past several years have given humanity many reasons to despair: a growing loss of civility and cooperation, human blindness to the looming ecological crisis, and a resurgence of racial hatred and violence, to name but a few of those reasons. It may be time for a clear-eyed look at the role of the Bible that the lectionary affords. We may now be in need of honest reckoning rather than of rose-tinted inspiration. Year D may offer congregations the opportunity to see the problems they face in the biblical record, to recognize that God's followers have always failed, and yet to know that such failure has not made them any less God's children.

But this conclusion comes with a caveat: all of the qualities that make Year D different from the Revised Common Lectionary also make it more challenging for preachers. Biblical texts that feature clear moral lessons or encouraging advice can stand on their own before congregations. Biblical texts that display characters with mixed motives, or violence that goes unpunished, or morally ambiguous situations require more explanation. For these texts, preachers must help congregations to understand the cultural and literary roots of the Biblical books. They must accompany the congregation in its struggle to understand God's presence and activity in stories shadowed by nuance. And they may even have to confront questions of scriptural interpretation: when a congregation begins to wonder why God instructs Abraham or Moses to kill so many people in readings from Genesis or Exodus, that question may result in an examination of what it means for scripture to be "inspired" by God or to be called "the Word of God".

These are not light tasks to lay upon the shoulders of pastors, for whom preaching is only one of many responsibilities. Despite all of the ways that Year D (or a more expansive use of scripture in worship) might benefit twenty-first century congregations, one must imagine the labels "caution" and "use with care" written on the unmarked envelope of Horace's humorous tale.

A YEAR D LECTIONARY

by Heather Josselyn-Cranson, OSL

Date	Old Test.	Psalm	Epistle/ Revelation	Gospel
Advent I	Nahum 1:2-8 Avenging God	Psalm 109	Rev. 12:1-6 Woman gives birth	Lk 1:5-25 Zechariah
Advent II	Obadiah 10-15 No gloating, Yom YHWH	Psalm 44	2 Tim. 3:1-9 End Times	Lk. 1:57-66, 80 John's birth
Advent III	Amos 9:8-15 Warning and promise	Psalm 53	2 Peter 3:1-7 Last days, water	Lk. 3:7-20 John Preaches
Advent IV	Micah 2:8-13 Good king coming	Psalm 61	Rev. 22:7-11 Coming soon	Lk. 7:18-35 Are you the one?
Nativity	Leviticus 26:1-12 God will walk among us	Psalm 117	Gal. 4:8-11 No special seasons	Lk. 2:1-7 No room
Christmas I	Isaiah 16:4b-5 Throne in love	Psalm 110	Heb. 2:1-9 Jesus Lower than angels	Mt. 1:1-17 Genealogy
Christmas II	Leviticus 12:1-8 Purification after birth	Psalm 119:25-32	Heb. 3:1-6 Jesus highest	Lk. 2:22-35 Pierce soul
Epiphany I	Deut. 10:12-22 Fear God and benefit	Psalm 108	Rev. 1:9-18 Jesus	Mt. 2:1-18 Herod. Kings, and Innocents

Epiphany II	1 Chronicles 10:1-14 Saul's Death	Psalm 142	Rev. 2:1-7 Ephesus	Jn 3:22-36 John's testimony
Epiphany III	1 Chr. 11:10-19 Mighty Men	Psalm 144	Rev. 2:8-11 Smyrna	Mt. 14:1-12 John's death
Epiphany IV	1 Chr. 13:1-14 Lethal Ark	Psalm 119:81-88	Rev. 2:12-17 Pergamum	Mk. 3:7-12 Casting out demons
Epiphany V	1 Chr. 15:1-3, 25-29 David danced	Psalm 21	Rev. 2:18-29 Thyatira	Mk. 5:1-20 Legion and pigs
Epiphany VI	1 Chr. 21:1-17 Census and plague	Psalm 39	Rev. 3:1-6 Sardis	Mk. 7:5-23 Hypocrites
Epiphany VII	1 Chr. 28:1-10 Build the temple	Psalm 119:169-176	Rev. 3:7-13 Philadelphia	Mk. 9:14-29 Healing a boy
Epiphany VIII	2 Chr. 5:1-14 Dedicating the temple	Psalm 134	Rev. 3:14-22 Laodicea	Mk. 10:17-34 Rich young man
Epiphany IX	2 Chr. 9:1-12, Queen of Sheba	Psalm 25:12-22	Rev. 4:1-11 Worship	Lk. 6:1-11 S Sabbath and healing
Transfiguration	Isaiah 57:14-21 High and lofty, contrite	Psalm 18:1-19	2 Tim. 2:20-21 Noble purposes	Mt. 17:1-13 Transfiguration
Ash Wednesday	Isaiah 30:19-22 Away with idols	Psalm 88	James 5:1-6 Cries of poor	Mk. 11:12-25 Cleaning temple
Lent I	Ezra 1:1-11 Return to Jerusalem	Psalm 102	Rev. 6:1-2 First seal	Mt. 13:53-58 Lack of faith
Lent II	Ezra 3:1-7 Rebuild the altar	Psalm 87	Rev. 6:3-4 Second seal	Mt. 17:14-23 Healing and prediction
Lent III	Ezra 3:8-13 Rebuild temple	Psalm 101	Rev. 6:5-6 Third seal	Mt. 12:1-14 Healing on Sabbath
Lent IV	Ezra 4:1-5 Opposition	Psalm 11	Rev. 6:7-8 Fourth seal	Lk. 11:37-54 Woes
Lent V	Neh. 1:1-11 Prayer and confession	Psalm 119:145-152	Rev. 6:9-11 Fifth seal	Mt. 10:17-23 Speaking when arrested
Passion Sunday	Isaiah 48:1-6, 16-19 Stubborn people	Psalm 56	Rev. 6:12-17 Sixth seal	Mt. 26:1-13 Anointing
Maundy Thursday	Deut. 16:1-8 Passover	Psalm 55	Heb 6:4-12 Don't fall away, taste	Mt. 26:17-30, 47-56 Meal and Judas
Good Friday	Ezekiel 22:1-12 The Bloody City	Psalm 141	Rev. 8:1-5 Seventh seal	Mt. 27:1-10; 45-56 Judas' death; Jesus' death

Easter	Acts 3:1-10 Peter heals	Psalm 57	Rev. 11:15-19 Seventh trumpet	Mt. 28:1-15 Resurrection and cover up
Easter II	Acts 5:1-11 Annanias and Sapphira	Psalm 75	Rev. 14:1-5 Lamb and 144,000	Mk. 16:9-14 Lack of faith
Easter III	Acts 5:12-25, 33-42 Human or divine origin?	Psalm 115	Rev. 14:6-13 Angels	Jn 5:19-27 Eternal life
Easter IV	Acts 8:1b-24 Simon the magician	Psalm 7	Rev. 19:1-10 Worship	Jn 7:25-36 Is Jesus Christ?
Easter V	Acts 10:1-33 Cornelius	Psalm 104: 1, 10-24	Rev. 19:11-16 Rider on horse	Jn 8: 31-47 Children of Abraham
Easter VI	Acts 12:1-19 Persecution and Prison	Psalm 58	Rev. 20:1-6 First resurrection	Jn 16:17-33 Joy will come
Ascension	Acts 13:44-52 Good news to Gentiles	Psalm 119:49-56	Heb. 8:1-6 Jesus high priest	Jn 8:21-30 Jesus going away
Easter VII	Acts 18:1-17 Corinth	Psalm 129	Rev. 21:10-14, 17-21 City	Jn 12:44-50 Not to judge but save
Pentecost	Isaiah 44:1-5 Pour out Spirit	Psalm 68:11-19	Romans 7:1-6 New way of the Spirit	Jn 15:18-27 World hates Spirit
Trinity Sunday	Deut. 4:9-14 Remembering God	Psalm 119:41-48	1 John 5: 6-12 Trinity and testimony	Lk. 10:21-24 Those who see what you see

Ordinary II	Gen. 3:1-24 Snake and curse	Psalm 38	2 John Walk in love	Mt. 6:22-24 Darkness and money
Ordinary III	Gen. 4:1-16 Cain	Psalm 3	3 John Show hospitality	Mt. 7:1-6, Judging, pearls and swine
Ordinary IV	Gen. 6:1-8 Nephilim	Psalm 119:17-24	Heb. 12:4-13 Endure discipline	Mt. 7:13-20 Narrow gates and good fruit
Ordinary V	Gen. 9:18-29 Noah drunk	Psalm 119:65-72	James 4:4-12 God not world	Mt. 8:14-22 Healing, foxes' holes
Ordinary VI	Gen. 12:1-20 Abram Egypt	Psalm 140	Heb. 12:4-13 Discipline	Mt. 8:28-34 Demons and pigs
Ordinary VII	Gen. 13:1-18 Lot leaves	Psalm 119:89-96	Heb 3:12-19 No rest w/o faith	Mt. 11:20-24 Woe Korazim
Ordinary VIII	Gen. 14:1-24 Lot captured	Psalm 18:20-50	1 Thess. 4:1-8 Live holy	Mt. 12:22-37 Healing not of Satan
Ordinary IX	Gen. 16:1-16 Hagar	Psalm 6	Heb. 6:13-20 God's promise	Mt. 12:38-45 Asking for a sign
Ordinary X	Gen. 17:9-27 Circumcision	Psalm 119:57-64	Titus 3:1-5 Saved by mercy	Mt. 15:1-9 Washing hands
Ordinary XI	Gen. 19:1-29 Lot and Sodom	Psalm 59	2 Peter 2:1-10a False teachers	Mt. 16:1-12 Pharisees/Sadducees
Ordinary XII	Gen. 19:30-38 Lot's daughters	Isaiah 38:10-20 (Cant. of Hezekiah)	2 Peter 2:17-22 Sinners	Mt. 18:1-9 Children and eye gouging
Ordinary XIII	Gen. 27:1-40 Isaac's blessing	Psalm 120	2 Tim. 2:22-26 Teach gently	Mt. 19:1-12 Divorce
Ordinary XIV	Gen. 29:31- 30:24 Leah and Rachel	Psalm 107:1-3, 10-16	James 1:2-16 Temptation	Mt. 19:16-30 Rich young man
Ordinary XV	Gen. 30:25-43 Jacob gains	Psalm 64	James 2:18-26 Faith and deeds	Mt. 20:20-28 Sit at right and left
Ordinary XVI	Gen. 31:1-3, 17-55 Jacob leaves	Psalm 119:113- 120	James 4:13-17 Plan humbly	Lk. 5:33-39 Old and new wine
Ordinary XVII	Gen. 34:1-31 Dinah	Psalm 94	1 Peter 3:1-12 Wives submit	Lk. 8:16-21 Mother and brothers
Ordinary XVIII	Gen. 38:1-30 Judah and Tamar	Psalm 119:153- 160	Heb. 10:26-39 Don't keep sinning	Lk. 8:40-56 Girl and woman healed
Ordinary XIX	Gen. 39:1-23 Potiphar's wife	Psalm 35	Heb. 5:11-14 Milk and solid food	Lk. 9:1-9 Instructions to disciples
Ordinary XX	Ex. 2:11-25 Moses kills, is married	Psalm 28	Heb. 3:12-19 Belief	Lk. 12:42-48 Faithful manager

Ordinary XXI	Ex. 3:16-4:17 God and Moses	Psalm 12	Titus 2:1-8 Teaching women and men	Lk. 13:22-30 Narrow door
Ordinary XXII	Ex. 5:1-21 Slavery	Psalm 10	1 John 5:13-21 No sin	Lk. 21:20-24 What to watch for
Ordinary XXIII	Ex. 11:1-10, 12:29-30 Firstborn	Psalm 135	1 John 4:1-6 Test spirits	Lk. 19:11-27 Parable of 10 minas
Ordinary XXIV	Ex. 19:1-19 Sinai	Psalm 18:1-19	1 John 3:11-15 Love don't murder	Mt. 24:1-3, 9-14 End times
Ordinary XXV	Ex. 32:1-4, 19-35 Killing	Psalm 136:1-3, 10-26	1 John 3:4-10 Children of God	Jn. 16:1-4 Coming persecution
Ordinary XXVI	Lev. 25:1-12 Jubilee	Psalm 119:121-128	1 John 2:3-14 Live in light	Mk. 12:1-12 Parable of tenants
Ordinary XXVII	Num. 14:1-23 Grumbling	Psalm 119:73-80	1 John 2:15-27 Warning	Mk. 12:18-27 Marriage in heaven
Ordinary XXVIII	Num. 22:4b-6, 21-35, 23:16-26 Balaam	Psalm 83	Jude	Mk. 13:9-23 End times
All Saints (to be used on November 1)	Dan. 3:1-30 Fiery Furnace	Psalm 118:1-14	Heb. 10:32-39 Persevere	Mt. 13:10-17 Who sees and hears?
Reign of Christ	Josh. 1:1-9 God sends Joshua	Psalm 60	Heb. 4:1-13 Entering rest	Lk. 9:18-27 Who do they say

3. BREAKING THE WORD:

FROM BIBLE TO LECTIONARY[1]

by Fritz West

<u>Two Commitments</u>

Horace Allen's efforts to introduce, develop, and promote the three-year lectionary system, finally in the form of the Revised Common Lectionary (hereafter RCL), brought into conversation two of his commitments: Reformed theology and ecumenism. He was Reformed. The son of a Presbyterian elder, pastor of Reformed churches in the United Kingdom and the United States, first director of the Presbyterian Joint Office of Worship and Music, staff support for and expert on *The Worshipbook* (1970), Presbyterian representative from 1975 to 1997 to the Consultation on Common Texts (hereafter CCT), and ever wearing a dog-collar: Horace Allen was Reformed. He was also ecumenical. That vision of the Church, which came to him in 1954 as a youth steward at the World Council of Churches Assembly in Evanston, Illinois, led him to become the first ministerial Warden of the Iona Abbey in Scotland, to serve on CCT for 27 years, to represent it on the English Language Liturgical Consultation (hereafter: ELLC), and to advocate in Rome for

---

[1] This essay draws on a book I am writing in conversation with the Consultation on Common Texts, *Why That Text?*, a commentary on the Revised Common Lectionary's system of selection.

RCL. Though experiencing deep disappointment in his hopes for ecumenical cooperation along the way, in 2012 Horace Allen felt vindicated upon receiving from the Massachusetts Council of Churches the Forrest L. Knapp Award, created to honor those who have "contributed significantly to the advancement of ecumenism in Massachusetts,"[2] joining the ranks of other Reformed ecumenists: Eugene Carson Blake (1906-1985), George MacLeod (1895-1991), Aruna Gnanadason (1949–), and Najla Kassab (1962-).

Undoubtedly Horace's work on RCL stands as his most significant contribution to the *oikouménē*. David Gambrell, worship executive for the Presbyterian Church (U.S.A.), writes, "Among many other contributions, Allen's critical role in shaping RCL will stand as a tremendous gift, remarkable achievement, and enduring legacy."[3] He was instrumental in introducing it. When Lewis A. Briner (1917-2003) and Scott Francis Brenner (1903-1991), both active in ecumenical circles, brought the forthcoming Roman Catholic three-year lectionary to the attention of the Joint Committee on Worship,[4] "Horace deftly snuck into [the] *Worshipbook* …the few pages in the back that proposed a systematic way of reading the Bible in worship through the year."[5] Other church bodies quickly followed suit: the American Episcopal Church (proposed in 1970, adopted in 1977), the Christian Church (Disciples of Christ) (1971), the North American Lutherans (proposed in 1973, adopted in 1978), the United Church of Christ (1974), the Consultation on Church Union

---

[2] Rev. Laura Everett, "Rev. Dr. Horace Allen & Ecumenical Innovation" (April 28, 2012). See https://reveverett.com/2012/05/02/horace-allen/, accessed February 2, 2020. This paragraph draws upon Everett, "Rev. Dr. Horace Allen," op. cit.; Laura Everett, "Remembrance of Rev. Dr. Horace Allen," (March 3, 2019). See: https://reveverett.com/2019/03/05/horaceallen/, accessed June 2, 2020; Richard Floyd, "Remembering Horace T. Allen (1933-2019)," *When I Survey*. See: https://richardlfloyd.com/2019/02/12/remembering-horace-t-allen-1933-2019, accessed June 2, 2020; Gail Strange, "A 'fierce advocate for ecumenical liturgical reform,'" *Presbyterian News Service* (February 27, 2019). See: https://www.presbyterianmission.org/story/rev-dr-horace-t-allen-jr-dies/, Accessed June 2, 2020.

[3] Gail Strange, "A 'fierce advocate," op. cit.

[4] Horace Thaddeus Allen, Jr., "A Companion to the Worshipbook: A Theological Introduction to the Worship in the Reform Tradition" (PhD. Dissertation, Union Theological Seminary in the City of New York, 1980), 32-4.

[5] Everett, "Rev. Horace Allen," op. cit.

(1974), and the United Methodist Church (1976).[6] Over the 1970's the advantage of one lectionary all could use became apparent. Aside from small differences between the various denominational versions, its First Testament readings were of particular concern. Rather than giving those texts an independent voice, the three-year lectionaries of the 1970's used them to complement the gospel for the day. In 1978 ELLC, the organizing body initially of CCT, asked it to shape a common lectionary for ecumenical use. The first draft, the Common Lectionary, was published in 1983; RCL, in 1992. Serving on CCT throughout this time, Horace Allen was instrumental in its shaping. And then he worked at promotion. As well as writing extensively on the topic over thirty years,[7] he co-led a delegation in 1994 from ELLC to Rome, asking the Sacred Congregation for Divine Worship and Sacraments to consider approving RCL for experimental use. A reply has not yet been received.[8]

---

[6] See Allen, *Companion*, 261-9. Outside the US, the Anglican Church of Australia adopted a version of the three-year lectionary in 1977. The website of the Consultation of Common Texts lists 62 church denominations world-wide that currently report using RCL. See http://www.commontexts.org/rcl/usage, accessed January 22, 2021. That number is surely low.

[7] Horace T. Allen. Jr., "Is There an Emerging Ecumenical Consensus Concerning the Liturgy?" *Union Seminary Quarterly Review* 31(1976): 155-168; Idem and the Joint Office of Worship (U.S.), *A Handbook for the Lectionary* (Philadelphia: Geneva Press, 1980); Idem., "Introduction" in *Common Lectionary: The Lectionary Proposed by the Consultation of Common Texts* (New York: Church Hymnal Corporation, 1983), 7-27; Idem., "Using the Consensus Lectionary: A Response" in *Social Themes of the Christian Year: A Commentary on the Lectionary,* ed. Dieter T. Hessel (Philadelphia: Geneva Press, 1983), 264-8; Idem., "Preaching in a Christian Context, The Lyman Beecher Lectures on Preaching," an audiobook on cassette available from Yale Divinity School (New Haven: Paul Vieth Christian Education Service, 1987); Idem., "Emerging Ecumenical Issues in Worship," *Word & World* 9 (1989): 16-22; Idem., "The Ecumenical Import of Lectionary Reform" in *Shaping Liturgy: Studies in Honor of Archbishop Denis Hurley,* ed. Peter C. Finn and James M. Schellman (Washington DC: Pastoral Press, 1990), 361-384; Idem., "Common Lectionary: Origins, Assumptions, and Issues," *Studia Liturgica* 21 (1991): 14-30; Idem., "Lectionaries—Principles and Problems: A Comparative Analysis," *Studia Liturgica* 22 (1992): 68-83; Idem., "The Psalter in Common Lectionary Revised (1992)," *Reformed Liturgy and Music* 26 (1992): 85-6; Idem. and Joseph P. Russel, *On Common Ground: The Story of RCL* (Norwich, England: Canterbury Press, 1998); Idem., "Common Lectionary and Protestant Hymnody: Unity at the Table of the Word. Liturgical and Ecumenical Bookends," in *Liturgical Renewal as a Way to Christian Unity,* ed. J. F Puglisi (Collegeville: Liturgical Press, 2005), 61-70.

[8] Past statements had given Allen cause of hope. Allen, *Companion*, 261.

Two Forms of Scripture

Work on the lectionary led Horace Allen to balance two ways of selecting the scripture to be proclaimed in worship: those of the historic Reformed tradition and of the lectionary/calendar form. Historically the Reformed tradition has treasured the whole Bible for bearing the word of God—and "whole" in more than one sense. In the first instance it tells the whole history of salvation from Genesis to Revelation, from salvation history's creative beginning to its apocalyptic end. The Bible is also "whole" in the sense of comprehensive: all one need know for salvation is to be found in the Bible. The hymn "O Word of God Incarnate," from the pen of Bishop William Walsham How (1823-1897), interprets the word of God through the verse "I am the light of the world. Whoever follows me will never walk in darkness but will have the light of life" (John 8:12b). Its second stanza hymns,

> The Church from her dear Master
> Received the gift divine,
> And still that light she lifteth
> O'er all the earth to shine:
> It is the golden treasure
> Where gems of truth are stored;
> It is the heaven-drawn picture
> Of Christ, the living Word.

This understanding, that the believer encounters Jesus Christ in the whole word of God, led the Westminster Assembly (1645) to prescribe all books of the First and Second Testaments be read in worship over the course of a year in canonical order, ordinarily one chapter from each Testament at every gathering, "that the people may be better acquainted with the whole body of the scriptures."[9] In the first decade of the twentieth century a Presbyterian minister, the Rev. W. Taylor of

---

[9] "Of Publick Reading of the Holy Scriptures," in *The Directory for the Publick Worship of God* in the Westminster Directory (1648). See http://graceandtruthrpc.org/wp-content/uploads/2013/07/DirectoryPublickWorship.pdf, accessed July 12, 2019.

the Melville Parish Church in Montrose, Scotland, sparked an extensive symposium on how to read the Bible in Reformed worship with these sentences published in the pages of the *Expository Times*: "It is perfectly obvious that if we jump about from one part of scripture to another we will utterly fail to grasp the full import of the Divine Revelation. In this, as much as in any former age, it is necessary that the word of God should be read in an orderly, complete, and impressive fashion."[10]

Constructing a lectionary entails a different approach. It breaks scripture into fragments—pericopes—for use in liturgical structures and distribution across the church year. In "Break Thou the Bread of Life" Mary Artemisia Lathbury (1841-1913), the "Poet Laureate of Chautauqua," interprets the saying "I am the bread of life. Whoever comes to me will never be hungry" (John 6:35a) in light of Jesus' parry of Satan's taunt to "command these stones to become loaves of bread" (Matt 4:3b): "'One does not live by bread alone, but by every word that comes from the mouth of God'" (Mat. 4:4; Deut. 8:3). Finding Christ's presence in the Bible as in the Lord's Supper, the hymn's first verse sings,

> Break now the bread of life, dear Lord, to me,
> as once you broke the loaves beside the sea.
> Beyond the sacred page I seek you, Lord;
> my spirit waits for you, O living Word.

As one encounters Jesus in the breaking of the bread, so does one also in the breaking of the Word, the Bible. Significantly the lectionary form of scripture is associated historically with settled eucharistic traditions.

A typology for the ritual use of scripture gives insight into these two approaches. Using quotation marks to indicate double meaning, Kendall W. Folkert (1948-1985), a scholar of comparative religion, distinguishes two ritual "canons" using two forms of "scripture." He writes, "Canon I denotes normative texts, oral or written, that are present in a tradition principally by the force of a vector or vectors. Canon II refers to normative texts that are more independently and distinctively present within a tradition, that is, as pieces of literature more or less as such are

---

[10] W. Taylor, "The Reading of Holy Scripture," *Expository Times* 17 (October 1905-September 1906): 34. See also *The Montrose Year-book and Directory for 1907* (Montrose: Alex. Dunn & Co., Ltd, at "Review Office," n.d.), 53.

currently thought of, and which themselves often function as vectors."[11] The term "vector" here refers to the means a particular religious activity employs for carrying "scripture" and thereby serving as an interpretative context. Canon I is usually carried by ritual, Canon II typically by an integral sacred text, a scroll or a book. Furthermore, a given religion may use both "canons." In Judaism, for example, one finds Canon I in the practice of praying with phylacteries containing scripture, Canon II in Torah study.

In liturgical traditions of the West, Folkert finds Canon I in those churches with a lectionary tradition, Canon II with those who read "the contents of the Bible in a more random fashion."[12] In the former case scripture is carried as passages by the "ritual pattern of the Christian year, and are even more specifically vectored by the internal rhythm of the service itself."[13] This service is typically eucharistic; he observes, "the greater prominence of ritual communion is linked to a structured 'carrying' of the Bible."[14] Finally he notes that "the presence of a ritual vector implies the absence of the Bible."[15] Although scripture is present when Canon I is used, the Bible in book form is typically not. Rather scripture takes the form of pericopes. They are published only to serve the liturgy, to provide scripture to be read aloud or sung out in worship— in a gospel book, epistolary, psalter, lectionary book, missal, or missalette. With Canon II, on the other hand, historically found in "non-liturgical" churches using a word service, the Bible is typically present in worship. Folkert observes, "[the Bible's] physical presence as an 'icon' of sorts in churches is a clear index of those churches' near veneration of it as a 'sacred book'."[16] Its book form vectors scripture: presenting the whole of scripture and scripture as a whole as the word of God, bestowing holiness and authority upon scripture so understood, and carrying it through the ritual process. As an indication of its capacity to vector sacrality and authority, clergy in these churches typically stay in close

---

[11] Kendall Folkert, "The 'Canons' of 'Scripture'" in *Rethinking Scripture: Essays from a Comparative Perspective*, ed. Miriam Levering (Albany: State University of New York Press, 1989), 173.

[12] Op. cit., 177.

[13] Op. cit.

[14] Op. cit.

[15] Op. cit.

[16] Op. cit.

proximity to the Bible, carrying it in procession, reading from it on the pulpit or lectern, holding it when preaching, or displaying it open on the altar-table, pulpit, or lectern. [17] Thus the axiom "the less bishops, the more Bible."[18]

For an image to capture Canon I and Canon II, picture a collection of sacred writings in the first century CE. Think of the Dead Sea Scrolls stored in clay jars—no categories, no canon—or perhaps scrolls stacked in piles, scrolls upon scrolls. This is the scriptural raw material a Judeo-Christian community of faith draws upon to understand their humanity, history, morality, and identity, what God has revealed to them and what they might expect with God. Jews and Christian use primarily two forms to organize this raw material, the holy book and the lectionary. In Judaism scriptures take book form in the Tanakh, a lectionary form is the annual semi-continuous reading of the Torah coupled with the Haftarah readings found in synagogue prayer. In Christianity, one has the Bible as the book form of scripture and various lectionaries in Western, Orthodox, and Oriental churches. These forms of scriptural organization use *different units of scripture* to tell *different stories.* In the Christian Church, for example, a lectionary serves Canon I by selecting *passages from scripture (pericopes)* to tell *the story of Christ's coming (the liturgical year).* The Bible, used in Canon II, organizes *books of scripture* to tell *the story from creation to the end of time.* .

Folkert's observation that this Canon reads "the contents of the Bible *in a more random fashion* [emphasis mine]" calls for clarification. At first the two patterns used to select scripture for word services appear to contrast. On the one hand, the historic Reformed pattern of proclaiming the word of God through the systematic reading of the Bible does not appear random. On the other hand, the topical preaching common through much of the twentieth century in American Protestant worship does not seem systematic. Paradoxically these two, depending on one's perspective (and correcting Folkert's), can be seen either way. As compared to the lectionary, their selection is subjective and random.

---

[17] The use of RCL differs from Canon I in that its readings are often read from the Bible in book form. In Anglican/Episcopal and Lutheran settings one does find use of a gospel or lectionary book, but those churches typically using a word service have stayed with their historic pattern in reading scripture from the Bible.

[18] Op. cit.

Whereas with the lectionary form the Church—in the case of RCL, an ecumenical body representing denominations—prescribes pericopes to a set system, the preacher chooses Canon II. Canon I is institutional and set; Canon II is occasional and pastoral. From this perspective, Canon II is indeed "more random" than Canon I. At the same time, however, this "random" choice is exercised within a coherent conceptual framework, the Bible regarded as the whole word of God. Historic Reformed worship, referred to above, read the Bible systematically, typically semi-continuously through integral biblical units, books or segments thereof. A similar sense of the unity and completeness of the Bible pertains to texts preached topically. Northrop Frye writes, "The concept of 'text' in this sense implies that the Bible is a collection of authoritative sentences and that the center of the entire Biblical structure is whatever sentence one happens to be looking at. For the preacher's purpose the immediate context of the sentence is as likely to be three hundred pages off as to be the next or the preceding sentences."[19]

RCL developed along a path the Roman Lectionary (hereafter RL) first blazed. First RL and then RCL, working within the traditional lectionary form, increased both the amount of scripture used and the respect shown for the books and Testaments of the Bible. Here one finds Canon II influencing the lectionary form of Canon I. To be sure Canon I provides the fundamental shape for RL and RCL. They both use scriptural fragments (pericopes) to proclaim the Good News of God in the liturgy and tell the story of Christ's coming over the liturgical year; their pericopes are vectored by the "ritual pattern of the Christian year, and are even more specifically ... by the internal rhythm of the service itself."[20] At the same time, within that framework, RL initiated patterns to show respect for the integrity of biblical books: synoptic gospels mark each of the three years, both the gospel and epistle readings are appointed semi-continuously in Ordinary Time, and the Season of Easter takes series of readings from specific books: the Acts of the Apostles, the First Epistles of Peter and John, and the Book of Revelation. RCL built on this foundation in acknowledging the integrity of the two covenants. Rather than follow RL in using the psalm to support the gospel, RCL

---

[19] Northrop Frye, *The Great Code: The Bible and Literature* (New York: Harcourt Brace Jovanovich, 1982), 167. For Allen's thoughts on topical preaching, see Allen, *Companion*, 253-6, 262, and 265.

[20] Op. cit.

throws that support to the First Testament reading. In the two options RCL offers in the Season After Pentecost for the First Testament reading and the supporting psalm, one finds a further recognition of the covenant of God with Israel. While one option continues the complementary pattern found in the Season of Epiphany, with the First Testament reading supporting the gospel, the other uses three parallel semi-continuous series. Alongside the semi-continuous series from the gospels and epistles, RCL appoints another from the First Testament. Here one finds represented consecutive epochs in the history of Israel: Year A: the formation of the people of Israel with a concentration on Moses (pre-history to 1100 B.C.), Year B: the founding of the nation of Israel with a focus on David (1100-900 B.C.), and Year C: Israel's prophetic tradition with an emphasis on Jeremiah (900-450 B.C.).

Over the decades that the CCT pursued the path the Roman Lectionary had initiated, shaping the Christian use of Canon I under the influence of Canon II, Horace Allen served as its chair. In addition to the features of this development enumerated above, Allen understood the church year as a whole in light of this amalgam. Writing about the continuities and discontinuities between the lectionary pattern the Roman Catholic Church developed (1969) and those CCT proposed in the *Common Lectionary* (1983), he notes,

> This analysis uncovers an important aspect of the Christian calendar, namely, that the structure and duration of the church year is actually limited to the approximately six months between the 1st Sunday in Advent and the Day of Pentecost. The Sundays after Pentecost are not integrally part of that year, hence their distinction in the Roman calendar as "Sundays of the Year," or Sundays in Ordinary Time". Those Sundays (well over twenty) are the occasion for the freeing of the canon from the calendar and for the sequential reading of the gospel, epistles, and (in the proposed revised table) Old Testament. Thus thematic integration is limited to

the Sundays of Advent, Christmas, Lent, and Easter as well as the days of Epiphany, Pentecost, and Trinity.[21]

Horace Allen pursued his work on the three-year lectionary fully aware of the two commitments he brought to bear upon it as a Reformed theologian and an ecumenist.

The Ritual of Reading

The hermeneutical implications of the approach to the lectionary that RL and RCL took can be seen in an aspect of "the internal rhythm of the service,"[22] the one immediately proximate to the proclamation of scripture: the ritual of reading. In the last third of the twentieth century the ecumenical liturgical consensus reclaimed this traditional ritual structure to organize the scripture proclaimed in a service, the pericopes read and the psalm sung. In both the Roman Catholic Mass and Protestant services of Word and Sacrament it provides a ceremonial and interpretative context for the proclamation of scripture. As a resource for the ecumenical liturgical consensus, the RCL serves this structure. True, RCL is utterly bereft of ceremonial. It does not even provide antiphons or responses for the psalms it appoints. As an ecumenical lectionary it leaves the choice of ceremonial (if any be used) up to denominations and their congregations. However, it does supply the scripture for the ritual of reading, listing the passages in the order that structure employs: first reading (from the First Testament save in the Season of Easter), psalm, epistle, and gospel. Reflecting the traditional pattern which regards the psalm as a hymn, RCL appoints three readings and a psalm.

The ritual of reading of the Roman Catholic liturgy offers a full-throated version of this liturgical structure. Being assumed by the Roman Lectionary, it constitutes a backdrop to the development of all subsequent versions of the three-year lectionary, including RCL. The table below, read from the bottom up, lays out how the Roman Liturgy

---

[21] Allen, "A Response," 267.

[22] Folkert, 177.

uses this ritual to project a hierarchy of revelation. Making no mention of Christ, the first reading from the First Testament can only reveal Christ under a veil; the Roman Lectionary relates to the gospel as prophecy to fulfillment. The versicles said in response, "The Word of God/Thanks be to God," indicate the Christological import of the First Testament reading. It is to be read in light of the Prologue to the Gospel According to John (John 1:1-14), as the capitalization of the term "Word" makes clear. The Word is the theological context for proclaiming the word of God spoken to the prophets. With the psalm the ritual turns definitively toward Christ. Given the traditional Christological interpretation of the psalter, the antiphon chosen is always Christological, often referring to some aspect of the gospel for the day. The response heard after the epistle repeats the one following the First Testament. As epistle readings refer directly to Jesus Christ, the Christological import of the phrase "The Word" becomes explicit. At the apex of this ritual, crowning its hierarchy, is the Gospel, in which the *vox Christi*— the very voice of Christ—is heard. The gospel acclamation, like the Alleluias greeting Jesus riding into Jerusalem, joyfully announce the coming of Christ.[23] Words spoken before and after the gospel, addressed directly to Christ in the second person singular, acknowledge his presence: "A reading from the holy Gospel According to _____."/"Glory to you, O Lord" and "The Gospel of the Lord"/"Praise to you, Lord Jesus Christ." The ritual climaxes in a *parousia* of the Lord.[24]

---

[23] The word "alleluia," a contraction of the Hebrew word for praise (Hallel) and Lord (Yahweh), evolved linguistically from "Hallel Yahweh" through "Hallel-u-Ya" to "Alleluia." See Lucien Deiss, "L'Alleluia ou le processional de l'Évangile," *Lectionnaire dominical*, Assemblées du Seigneur, 2ᵈ séries, no. 3 (Paris: Cerf, 1969), 75. ET: "The Alleluia or the Processional for the Gospel," in *The New Liturgy*, ed. Lancelot Sheppard (London: Darton, Longman, and Todd, 1970), 94.

[24] Ildefons Herwegen, "L'Ecriture sainte dans la liturgie," *La Maison-Dieu* 5 (1946): 15.

Revelation	Scripture	Explanation
How directly the scripture proclaims the revelation of Christ	Gospel	In the gospel Jesus Christ reveals himself directly to the assembly.
	New Testament Writing	More direct are the New Testament writings, composed by persons who knew Jesus Christ, either in person or the Spirit.
	Psalm	Traditionally the Psalter was thought to reveal Christ more directly than other books of the First Testament.
	First Testament	Though not mentioned in the First Testament, Jesus Christ is indirectly revealed through prophecies and images.

Traditional Understandings of Scripture in the Ritual of Reading
(to be read from the bottom up)

The ecumenical lectionary hermeneutic develops to full stature in Ordinary Time and thus will provide our example. A comparative look at the ritual of reading during this time provides a window into how first RL and then RCL moved to work with both Canon I and Canon II. This is not an apples to apples comparison, however. Whereas our example of the Roman Catholic ritual of reading included ceremonial, RCL—as noted above—does not, providing only the scripture for this ritual. Given this bare-bones approach of RCL, our comparison is necessarily limited to scripture alone. Even when reduced to this bare minimum the comparison is instructive, however. The table below compares the pattern RL uses in this half of the church year and the two found in RCL. It is to be read from left to right and bottom to top. The gospel is placed at the top, as it always holds the status of *primus inter pares*—first among equals. The vertical arrows aiming toward the gospel and indicating revelatory vectors, become dotted over readings offering it no support. The gray arrows pointing downward indicate the support of the psalm for the First Testament reading.

Going across the table from left to right the revelatory vector, found in fulsome form in the Roman Catholic version of this ritual, becomes increasingly attenuated, weakening at first and then disappearing. That vector has considerable strength in the seasonal cycles of both RL and RCL, weakened only by RCL directing the psalm toward the First Testament. In Ordinary Time an innovation of RL weakens it further: the epistle reading, drawn from independent semi-continuous series, is not related intentionally to the other two readings. The Roman Catholic ritual of reading still packs a punch, of course. With the short, focused First Testament readings RL appoints to support the gospel, with the Christological interpretation of the psalm, the revelatory vector moves the assembly confidently towards the voice of Christ heard in the gospel. But with a deflection. While the epistle like the gospel is focused on Christ, it delivers its own message. The other scriptures have some independence as well. The support the First Testament and psalm offer the gospel does not exhaust their meaning; they have proclamatory power in their own right.

RCL (complementary series) maintains the revelatory vector toward the gospel while reducing its thrust. Here two readings take their eyes off the gospel. The epistle does so by offering its own message; the psalm is turned toward the First Testament. Yet they weaken the vector in different ways. Though the epistle is not focused on the gospel of the day, it is focused on the gospel of Jesus Christ. The psalm is not. Its attention is on the covenant of God with Israel. Whatever reference it may make to Christ, it does so at one step removed. But what is the Second Covenant's loss is the First Covenant's gain. While the psalm's turn to the First Testament supports the covenant of the Lord Jesus Christ only indirectly, it gives the covenant of God with Israel its full attention.

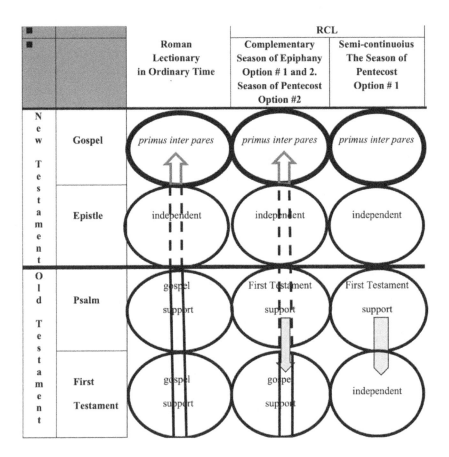

| | | Roman Lectionary in Ordinary Time | RCL | |
			Complementary Season of Epiphany Option # 1 and 2. Season of Pentecost Option #2	Semi-continuoius The Season of Pentecost Option # 1
N e w T e s t a m e n t	**Gospel**	*primus inter pares*	*primus inter pares*	*primus inter pares*
	Epistle	independent	independent	independent
O l d T e s t a m e n t	**Psalm**	gospel support	First Testament support	First Testament support
	First Testament	gospel support	gospel support	independent

Relationships of Scripture within Ritual of Reading In Ordinary Time Comparative Charts, RL and RCL
(to be read from bottom to top)

RCL's semi-continuous series pattern poses an even stronger challenge to the revelatory vector. While in this pattern the gospel of the day remains *primus inter pares*, no "upward" vector thrusts toward it. The last vestige of that vector, the complementary use of the First Testament, is gone. Accordingly, the three readings independently set forth a progression of witnesses drawn from three distinct moments in the history of salvation: the time of Israel, the time of the Church, the time of Christ. The result is bifocal. One lens brings the covenant of God with

Israel into focus. The proclamation of a reading from a series selected from the First Testament enjoys the full and undivided support of the psalm. Without a vector toward the gospel, these two scripture texts join to offer an independent witness to the covenant of God with Israel. The other lens focuses upon the covenant God made through Jesus Christ. While the witness of these passages is not coupled like those from the First Testament, they both have their sights on Jesus Christ: the gospel record of Jesus' ministry and saving work, the epistle's reflection upon some aspect of it.

In the semi-continuous series pattern the relationship of the gospel to the First Testament also rests on a covenantal foundation. These two semi-continuous readings—from the synoptic gospels and portions of the First Testament—are coupled series by series, not Sunday by Sunday. Specifically, RCL chooses each First Testament series to reflect how the synoptic evangelist for the year understands Jesus to fulfill the promises God made with Israel. Matthew, who holds Jesus to be the new Moses, is supported by his covenant; Mark, who sees Jesus fulfilling the Davidic covenant, is coupled with stories of that covenant; Luke, who regards Jesus as fulfilling the prophetic tradition, is coupled with readings from the prophetic corpus. This connection is abstract, however. From the perspective of the person in the pew, one has in the readings three independent series. Practically speaking the First Testament reading for each week is hermeneutically independent from the gospel of the day.

RCL's development of the ecumenical lectionary hermeneutic, bringing Canon II to bear on the Canon I, has theological implications. Whereas the complementary pattern offers a Christological orientation, the semi-continuous pattern offers a theocentric one. Whereas the complementary pattern stresses the particularity of the revelation of God in Jesus Christ, the semi-continuous pattern places it in a covenantal context: God reveals redeeming intentions, constant throughout the history of salvation, though with particularity in Jesus Christ. With segments of scripture used within the framework of the church year, RCL shows respect for how God reveals Godself in the whole book of the Bible. By taking into account the books and Testaments of the whole biblical word of God, the lectionary invites a dialogue between the lectionary hermeneutic and the Bible hermeneutic. On the strength of this ecumenical lectionary hermeneutic Horace Allen was able to maintain his dual commitments as a Reformed theologian and an ecumenist.

Apologia

Given Horace Allen's deep involvement with the three-year lectionary system, ultimately RCL, it was incumbent upon him to provide a rationale for its use. As an ecumenist he unflaggingly, unfailingly, and enthusiastically promoted the lectionary. Our interest here is narrower: How did he reconcile this support with the Reformed tradition? Two of his writings address this issue, notably his dissertation *A Companion to The Worshipbook: A Theological Introduction to Worship in the Reformed Tradition* (1980) and "Using the Consensus Lectionary: A Response," occasioned by James A. Sanders' critique of the Common Lectionary (1983).

In his dissertation Horace Allen sets forth a theological rationale for scripture and preaching. The necessary context for a Reformed theology of worship he found in the Nicene Creed, "I believe… in the one, catholic, apostolic church,"[25] where "apostolic" refers to those patterns of worship the apostles passed on. Specifically, it refers to

> St. Paul's *paradosis* or transmission to the church in Corinth of the Lord's own command to 'do this' (the Supper) 'to remember him.' … Before the church had produced creeds or even designated certain writings to 'scripture' there were a certain few events seen which by their faithful, obedient doing became signs of the presence of the one, holy church of God. These events included public preaching, prayer, praise, baptism and

---

[25] English Language Liturgical Consultation, *Prayers we have in common: agreed liturgical texts prepared by the International Consultation on English Texts.* (Philadelphia: Fortress Press, 1975), 6. (n.b. In his dissertation, Allen cites the author of this book as Consultation on Common Texts, p. 128, fn 19).

breaking bread, sharing of material goods and even miracles.[26]

Worship is a sign or mark of the church, "the activity by which the visible church of Christ may be discerned on earth,"[27] rendering visible what is invisible. In the triad "faith, hope and love" (1 Cor 13.13 et al), "summary definitions of the work of the Holy Spirit in the life of the church and the Christian,"[28] Christ becomes visible to the assembly. The preaching office gathers the Church in faith, the gospel sacraments of Baptism and the Lord's Supper build it up in love, and the pastoral offices (such as marriage, burial, ordination, care for the sick and other such rites) send its members out in hope.

That the reading of scripture is a constituent component of Reformed worship is an assertion—in Reformed terminology—of order, not form. Though that reading must be included in the *order* of a worship service, it may take various *forms*. Enjoying "freedom" within the limits of "law,"[29] however, the preacher's freedom in regard to form has its limits. When choosing scripture for preaching, the preacher has both latitude and limits. She is both free to choose scripture for preaching[30] and accountable to the Presbytery and the Word of God. Allen quotes the Presbyterian *Directory for Worship* (1961): "It is appropriate also that the readings (from both Old and New Testaments) follow, with such latitude as may be proper in varying situations, a set order or lectionary designed to assure that the fullness of God's Word be declared."[31] In 1970 Presbyterians understood they had the latitude to adapt and adopt the three-year lectionary as long as it assured "that the fulness of God's Word be declared."

This decision did not occur in a vacuum. The sixteenth century reformers had firmly rejected the lectionary form in favor of in-course reading.

---

[26] Allen, *Companion*, 120-1.

[27] Op. cit., 119.

[28] Op. cit., 132.

[29] Op. cit., 19-21, 58, 204-6.

[30] Op. cit., 206.

[31] Op. cit., 207.

Calvin regarded the lectionary of the Christian year as cutting up the Bible into unrelated scraps. It imposed an arbitrary arrangement on Scripture. As Calvin saw it, the pericopes of the lectionary often separate a text from its natural context. The texts of Scripture should be heard within the total message of a particular biblical author. A lectionary could not help but encourage over the years a stereotyped interpretation. [32]

In its stead these reformers affirmed the practice of *lectio continua* found in the early Church: "preaching through a book of the Bible or a major section of a book of the Bible starting at the beginning and continuing through, chapter by chapter or even verse by verse, in such a way that the whole message of the sacred writing is presented in an orderly fashion over a series of weeks or months. This involved preaching through a book of the Bible or a major section of a book of the Bible starting at the beginning."[33] To allow for such preaching they reduced the church year to a minimum, typically to the biblical festivals of Christmas, Easter, and Pentecost. In this manner, the selection of scripture showed respect for the story, structure, authors, covenants, and books of the Bible. As noted earlier, this approach was affirmed by the Westminster Directory (1645) and sparked a lively discussion in print at the turn of the twentieth century. Some honor this tradition yet today.[34]

As latitude is only granted within limits, Allen had to explain how the decision to adopt the three-year lectionary system was consonant with the Reformation tradition of scriptural selection. Describing that tradition in brief, he wrote, "Thus, in Reformation practice a right ordering of public reading of the scripture involved a measure of the

---

[32] Hughes Oliphant Old, *Worship. Reformed according to Scripture,* rev. and expanded (Louisville, London: Westminster John Knox Press, 2002), 74-5, here 75.

[33] Idem, *The Patristic Roots of Reformed Worship* (Zürich: Theologischer Verlag Zürich, 1975), 194-5.

[34] See Jean-Jacques von Allmen, *Preaching and the Congregation,* trans. B. L. Nicholas (Richmond: John Knox Press, 1962), 47-48; See Hughes Oliphant Old, *The Prophecies of Micah and The Gospel at Christmas, A Series of Sermons* (Danville, Illinois: Interstate Printers and Publishers, Inc., 1985), 1-7; ibid., *Worship That Is Reformed According to Scripture* (Atlanta: John Knox Press, 1984), 59-90; Bruno Bürki, "Ordannance des lecture bibliques chez le réformés francophones" in *Présence et rôle de la Bible dans la liturgie,* ed. Bruno Bürki, et al. (Fribourg: Academic Press, 2006), 266-7.

pastor's freedom and discretion, attention to certain central Christian festivals and celebrations, and the structure of the scripture themselves. It clearly did not preclude a fixed or 'set' system, as though that in itself would improperly compromise the freedom of the ministry of the Word."[35] Essential was that "over a period of time the people shall hear the full message of scripture."[36] Not only did the three-year lectionary do that, it did so aligned at several points with Reformed tradition: use of the church year, Sunday readings from the three major scriptural units of the Christian Bible (First Testament, gospel, and New Testament writings), psalmody, and a recognition of the books and testaments of the Bible. The one regret mentioned in his dissertation was the "typological" use of the First Testament readings in Ordinary Time, but even this—he noted—was being addressed in talks about revision at the time of writing. Horace Allen is here fighting on two fronts.[37] Against those clergy who were protesting the "limits" the lectionary placed on their "freedom" as preachers, he made clear the limits of that freedom. Against those who would hold to the Reformation pattern, he asserted that the latitude used to choose a lectionary fell within the limits of that tradition.

In promoting the three-year lectionary Allen had multiple aims. First and foremost was his concern that "the Bible has been almost lost to public worship."[38] Topical preaching, the plethora of secular "holy days" along with the neglect of systematic preaching had resulted in the Bible being reduced to perhaps one reading, perhaps one verse, chosen by the pastor alone. In light of this he could trumpet, "The usefulness of this particular lectionary, however can better be measured against the prevailing biblical poverty of both Protestant and Catholic worship of late, than against the standard of an ideal but as yet non-existent lectionary."[39] Secondly, he rejoiced in the ecumenical witness and cooperation it engendered. As multiple denominations adopted versions of the RCL, the same scripture could be heard in Roman Catholic and Protestant churches alike, and study groups sprang up across

---

[35] Allen, *Companion*, 210.

[36] Op. cit., 207.

[37] Op. cit., 264.

[38] Op. cit., 255.

[39] Op. cit., 264-5.

denominational lines to consider it. Finally, he hoped that this resource for preaching, so central in Protestant churches, might be a subversive vehicle for liturgical renewal. "[In the three-year lectionary] Horace and others saw an opening, an 'ecumenical wedge' as he called it, to graft the free churches onto [the] growing liturgical consensus."[40]

In 1983, in a response to James A. Sanders' critique of the lectionary, Horace Allen directly addressed the hermeneutical issues raised by the shift in scripture selection from the continuous reading of the Bible to lectionary/calendar. Much had changed in the three years since Allen had submitted his dissertation. CCT had produced a draft of an ecumenical lectionary, entitled the Common Lectionary, showing the First Testament increased respect. Not only had the support of the psalm been shifted toward the First Testament, but also independent semi-continuous series had been appointed from the First Testament in the Season After Pentecost. These innovations notwithstanding, Sanders—using the historic Protestant hermeneutic as his measure—identified five deficiencies in the Common Lectionary (1983).

1. The "tyrannical" dominance of calendar over canon.
2. The dominance of New Testament over Old Testament.
3. The dominance of a Christocentric over a theocentric approach.
4. The dominance of early first-century salvation history over versions found before and after, thus losing sight of God's saving action throughout history.
5. The dominance of selected over continuous readings.

This First Testament scholar advocated a thoroughly canonical lectionary, finding warrant for it in the Jewish practice of reading the Torah *lectio continua* in synagogue prayer.[41] For him continuous reading shows greater respect for the whole canon of God's story than a lectionary using pericopes.[42]

---

[40] Everett, "Rev. Dr. Horace Allen & Ecumenical Innovation," op. cit.

[41] James A. Sanders, "Canon and Calendar: An Alternative Lectionary," 257-263.

[42] John Goldingay (1942-), another First Testament scholar, wrote, "In my view the lectionary for the principal service each Sunday should seek to reflect scripture as a whole. RCL does not attempt to do so." See John Goldingay, "Canon and Lection" in

Addressing some of Sanders' concerns, Allen dismisses others. He acknowledges Sanders' concerns for "more canonical coverage"[43] and noted that the original three-year lectionary system included systematic reading from the Second Testament and its recent revision, the Common Lectionary (1983), from the First. He notes that the latter half of the church year, absent the strong themes of the seasonal cycles, "are the occasion for the freeing of the canon from the calendar."[44] Allen's main point, however, is that the hermeneutical context for scripture read in worship is liturgical, not biblical, that the context the lectionary assumes is "the un-Protestant (though not un-Reformed) weekly union of Word and Sacrament."[45] Behind the curious term "un-Protestant" lies his ultimate dismissal of Sanders' suggestions for being rooted in "the preaching tradition of the left-wing Protestant Reformation."[46] Allen here uses the term "Protestant" to contrast (and disparage) churches with a purely word tradition and no weekly Eucharist with the desires of the reformers—notably Calvin in Geneva—to celebrate the Lord's Supper weekly. But did not the reformers also ascribe hermeneutical significance to the whole Bible and practice *lectio continua*, per Sanders' suggestion? Were they not Protestant? Here Allen discounts one aspect of the tradition to emphasize another. His approach is more nuanced and less polemical in his dissertation. Whatever its past practice, the Reformed tradition is compatible with the use of the ecumenical lectionary, which meets the standard "that the fulness of God's Word be declared." And so does the Revised Common Lectionary, the jewel in Horace Allen's ecumenical crown, faithfully continue the tradition of Reformed worship.

For the life and ministry of Dr. Horace Thaddeus Allen, Jr., let all the people say: *Deo gratias.*

To Glorify God, eds. Bryan D. Spinks and Iain R. Torrance (Edinburgh: T&T Clark, 1999), 97.

[43] Allen, "A Response," 267.

[44] Op. cit., 266.

[45] Op. cit., 267.

[46] Op. cit.

4. LECTIONARIES AND HYMNS:

21ST CENTURY INTERSECTIONS

by Fred Graham

In the year 2012, many faith communities joined with Roman Catholic brothers and sisters in observing the fiftieth anniversary of the fruits of the Second Vatican Council, and the reforms deriving from it in the late twentieth century. The central document of the Council was the Constitution on the Sacred Liturgy (CSL) and from it, the *Ordo Lectionum Missae / Lectionary for the Mass and Feast Days* emerged. Its impact was felt in varied forms on worshipping communities throughout the world. One of the derivative offspring is seen in the *Revised Common Lectionary* (RCL) published by the Consultation on Common Texts (CCT) with the enthusiastic participation of Horace Allen, Jr.

It is instructive to examine the connections between the Roman Catholic *Ordo*, (OLM) and two of its close cousins adopted widely in the Protestant and Reformed world, the *Common Lectionary* (CL, 1983) and the *Revised Common Lectionary* (RCL, 1992). This essay intends to touch on the principles behind the organization of the RCL, and to observe one particular side effect, namely, the composition of new hymn texts to complement the expanded catalog of readings. Definitions related to the acronyms used here will be found below.

The following observations are linked to the latest articulation of the RCL and its background as found in "RCL – 20ᵗʰ Anniversary Annotated Edition" with a forward by the Lutheran scholar, Gordon Lathrop. [1]

In December 1963, the CSL document proclaimed that the Roman Catholic Church would provide "more abundant, varied, and appropriate reading of the Sacred Scriptures." [2] The choice of this objective has had a lasting impact on the entire spectrum of Christian worship.

Lists to support oral proclamation in Christian praxis have been a part of religious culture for centuries. As examples, we could list Roman, Gallican, Mozarabic, Byzantine, Jerusalem [Armenian and Georgian], Coptic, and also East and West Syrian documents. Preoccupation with a fixed lectionary seemed less important until a liturgical calendar was created, and even then, the process was uneven. Many traditions favoured three readings; one tradition mentions use of five readings. By the seventh century, the liturgical year was widely recognized,[3] and the existence of lists of appropriate readings point to the fact that "the lists of the Mass readings [predated] the first sacramentaries."[4] The first organized lectionary for the Tridentine Roman Mass in the West appeared in 1570 and was used in the Roman Catholic domain until 1971. The lists of prescribed readings contained an epistle reading and a gospel reading for each of the fifty-two Sundays in a year. This twelve-month cycle was widely imitated throughout Europe in both Protestant and Catholic contexts. The whole year had only three Old Testament readings. Year after year, the cycle was repeated. We note that the scope was extremely narrow. In stark contrast, CSL advocated "a more abundant, more varied" scriptural diet at the Mass.

As early as 1920, a resurgence of interest in biblical scholarship and in enriching the liturgical year occurred among church leaders leading up to

---

[1] *The Revised Common Lectionary, Twentieth Anniversary Edition.* © 1992, 2012 Consultation on Common Texts. All rights reserved. Published by Fortress Press, (Minneapolis, MN) an imprint of Augsburg Fortress. 161 pp. and 8 Appendices.

[2] CSL, Art. 35.56:109

[3] See Thomas J. Talley, *The Origins of the Liturgical Year* (New York, 1986; 2ⁿᵈ Ed., Collegeville, 1991) passim.

[4] Antoine Chavasse, "Évangéliaire, épistolier, antiphonaire, et sacramentaire: Les Livres romains de la messe, au VII et VIII siècle." *Ecclesia Orans* 6 (1989): 177--89 and 249--55.

Vatican II, and as a result the need for readings better suited to each season became apparent. Hence, CSL advocated for "more appropriate" selections. Catechists from multiple cultures also called for a richer scriptural base for baptismal candidates and their preparation during Lent; their wish was honored, especially in what we know as Year A. The period leading to Baptism at Easter now commences with the temptation of Jesus in the wilderness, and proceeds to the story of Nicodemus (one must be born of water); the revelation of the Messiah to the Samaritan woman at the well; the miracle of healing of the blind man; and the death of Lazarus, as context for the saying of Jesus: "I am the resurrection and the life."

In Rome, a research group was set up in 1964. They reviewed intensely all the Latin lectionaries from the 6th to the 12th centuries, fifteen Oriental lectionaries, and all the existing Protestant lectionaries. After consultation and critique, the new Ordo came into use in all Roman Catholic parishes on the first Sunday of Advent, 1971, Year A.

Organized on a three-year rotation of Gospel readings, each year focussed on a synoptic gospel: Matthew in year A, Mark in year B, and Luke in year C. Selections from the gospel of John were interspersed in each cycle, especially for important feast days. Each Sunday and each feast-day listed three readings and a psalm: an Old Testament passage and a thematically related psalm; an Epistle; and a Gospel pericope. As mentioned above, the three-year format had historical antecedents, but also allowed people to revisit the whole scope of biblical narratives within a time frame of thirty-six months. The Gospel reading was the guiding energy, acting as a filter for the passages chosen from the Old Testament. Regarding Epistles, they complemented the Gospel in the Festal Seasons, but were permitted to unfold in sequence *(lectio continua)* in Ordinary Time. More recently, many have argued for a year highlighting John's gospel, however, the OLM (and later the RCL) opted to use passages from John to highlight certain major festivals such as Christmas and Easter. Since the lectionary readings were planned for use within a Eucharistic context, the overall length of readings was a consideration. Such a limitation may have provided a challenge when dealing with the Johannine discourses for even the most capable scholars!

Ecumenical circles observed these changes with lively interest, and the Joint Liturgical Group in Britain became very active in designing a new 2-year scheme of readings, while communicating their activity to Roman leaders. In North America, meanwhile, many spontaneous efforts at emulating the Roman Catholic model erupted. In fact, it could be said that the unity desired by having readings in common almost derailed into a display of dis-unity.

Eventually, a round-table discussion amongst 13 denominations took place in Washington, DC in 1978, and five years later, the members of the Consultation on Common Texts (CCT) produced the *Common Lectionary* (CL). The compilers had decided to follow the same three-year pattern, with notable changes in approach. First, they opted to revise the first readings to be fully "representative of the Hebrew bible and not simply prophetic or typological."[5]

The word typological underpins the understanding that the gospel is regarded as pre-eminent, and influences the choice of all other readings. For example, as seen in the OLM, the gospel for Proper 9 (year C) is Luke 10: 1-11; that pericope is matched with Isa. 66: 10 - 14 to complement the content of the Gospel pericope. In contrast, the compilers of RCL chose a different method for the post-Pentecost season. Although they had followed typological or parallel readings in the first half of the calendar, they opted to observe *lectio continua* in the post-Pentecost period. On the same Sunday in RCL, the Gospel is identical, but the Old Testament reading, 2 Kings 5: 1-14 with Ps. 30, opens a sequence of Sundays featuring Old Testament prophets and Wisdom literature. It is clear that the two lectionary schemes are very similar from Advent through Pentecost, and virtually identical in the case of the Gospel pericopes throughout the cycle. Provisions for Old Testament and Epistle selections differ frequently for the post-Pentecost period.

Under the rubric of *lectio continua,* initiated by OLM, and visible in all three years of the CL/RCL, the narrative within a book of the Bible, or of one of the apostolic letters, is allowed to unfold sequentially.

Upon its publication in 1983, CL immediately underwent a multi-year review, week by week, assisted by hundreds of practitioners and scholars. Their observations were treated carefully by the CCT members during plenary meetings, and conclusions were applied in the refinement and

---

[5] Minutes of the CCT, March, 1978.

revision of the CL, a process undertaken by a subcommittee that met in Manhattan 10 days a year for four years, 1988-92. At that table were representatives from the Church of England (UK) and the Anglican Church of Canada, The Episcopal Church (USA), the Evangelical Lutheran Church in America, the Presbyterian Church (U.S.A.), the Roman Catholic Church (UK), the United Methodist Church (USA) and The United Church of Canada. The convener of the working group informed the full Consultation twice a year of progress made and challenges identified. Some of the aims of revising the CL were as follows:

- To meet needs of several episcopal denominations (e.g. The Episcopal Church, USA, and the Evangelical Lutheran Church in America) there was a desire to ensure more extensive use of typologically oriented readings by providing a parallel but not competing scheme of readings called Complementary. By way of illustration, we look at the two tracks for Proper 10, Year C:

> Semi-continuous track
> Amos 7: 7-17; Psalm 82; Col. 1: 1-14; Luke 10: 25-37
>
> Complementary track
> Deut. 30: 9-14; Ps. 25: 1-14; Col.1: 1-14; Luke 10: 25-37

- To expand the canon of Old Testament readings, as seen in the addition of the stories of Noah, and of Joseph and his family during Year A; the expansion of readings from Job, and Hannah's prayer and her song during Year B; and a stronger profile for Elijah in Year C.
- To bring to the attention of congregations the biblical stories showing women to be leaders, e.g., the stories of Sarah, Hagar and Rebekah, and Leah.
- To expose congregations to feminine images for God. Examples may be found in Wisdom 7.22ff (Proper 19, Year B); in Sirach 24.12-27 in Years A, B and C; in Luke 13.34 (Lent 2, Year C) or Matt. 13.33 (Advent 1, Year B).

- To avoid intended or unintended mistreatment of ethnic minorities, Jewish persons, or others. Special sensitivity was exercised in relation to the Passion narrative, and the related roles of Jewish persons.
- To promote inclusivity, as seen in the story of David and Jonathan (1 Sam. 17) and their close relationship as males in that society.

Publication of the RCL immediately sparked a multitude of preaching and Christian education resources, and influenced to some extent every mainstream religious organization in Canada and the USA, among others. In subsequent years, its use has spread around the world under the monitoring of the English Language Liturgical Consultation (ELLC)[6] with the support of CCT [7] whose website reports that the RCL is used in part or in whole in at least 50 denominations world-wide.

As stated above, an annotated version of the RCL was published in 2012 by the Consultation on Common Texts, twenty years after the initial publication of 1992. The anniversary edition presents the historical development of lectionaries, and in particular the lectionaries in frequent use leading up to the Second Vatican Council. In the meantime, other entities have published the African American lectionary;[8] the Year D lectionary;[9] the Narrative Lectionary,[10] and others.

As we consider the whole gesture of public worship, a related question is this: what if any effect did the receipt of the refreshed lectionaries have on hymn output? How were writers such as Mary Louise Bringle, Dan Damon, Ruth Duck, Fred Pratt Green, Fred Kaan, Michael Joncas, Shirley Erena Murray, and Herman Stuempfle influenced by the expanded pool of pericopes?

To begin answering this question, we take note of an addition to the lectionary in Exodus 1.8 – 2.10, detailing the birth of Moses and the role

---

[6] English Language Liturgical Consultation, www.englishtexts.org

[7] Further information is available at www.comontexts.org

[8] www.theafricanamericanlectionary.org.

[9] www.theyeardproject.blogspot.com. See also the essay by Heather Josselyn-Cranson in this volume.

[10] www.narrativelectionary.org and www.workingpreacher.org.

of the midwives Shiphrah and Puah (Proper 16, Year A.) Hymn writer Mary Louise Bringle revised one of her existing texts in 2003 to reflect this narrative, and to add to the repertoire describing the role of women in Hebrew and Christian life.

In boldness, lean on God for strength
to take a righteous stand,
like midwives from our Hebrew past,
enslaved in Egypt's land,
with skill and cunning, saving lives
from Pharaoh's harsh command.

In boldness, look to God for help
like womenfolk who dared—
to ask that Jesus cure a child,
that crumbs of grace be shared,
that outcast ones be welcomed to
the feast God has prepared.

In boldness, lean on God for strength
And healing from disease—
of mind and body, heart and will,
whose bondage Jesus frees.
Reach out and touch the hem of Christ
and gather spirit's ease.

In boldness, learn from God the truth
of Mary's "better part":
by fear and censure undeterred,
determined in her heart
to kneel at Jesus' feet and hear
the wisdom he imparts.

In boldness, love, nor count the cost.
Confront the world's harsh stare—
like one who washed the feet of Christ,
and wiped them with her hair;
poured perfume to anoint her Lord,
and left love's fragrance there.[11]

The enumeration of biblical incidents involving women flows throughout this piece. In addition to the reference to the midwives' role from Exodus in stanza one, stanza two directs our attention to the Canaanite woman mentioned in Matthew 15: 27 or alternatively the Syrophoenician woman in Mark 7:28 who begged on behalf of a child for the healing power of Jesus. There is also a cross-reference to Luke 14:23 where all are invited to the banquet. Stanza three reminds us of the woman with the hemorrhage mentioned in Mark 5 (Year B). Stanza four reminds us of Jesus' visit to Mary and Martha, and the phrase "Mary has chosen what is better." Stanza 5 engages Luke 7. 36-50 (Year C) where we are told of the woman who washed the feet of Jesus with her hair, and anointed him with perfume.

Looking at a passage later in the First Testament, we note the inclusion in the RCL of the Prayer of Hannah and the Song of Hannah (1 Sam.1:4ff; and 1 Sam. 2.1ff) towards the conclusion of Year B, Proper 28. The Song has been paraphrased by Emily Brink as follows:

My soul is filled with joy in my Redeemer,
for God has lifted me and set me high.
There is no Holy One, no Rock like our God,
who answered my request, who heard my cry.

---

[11] "In Boldness, Look to God" by Mary Louise Bringle, 2000, alt. 2003
Copyright © 2002 GIA Publications, Inc. All rights reserved. Used by permission.
Suggested Tune: MORNING SONG 86.86.86 from Wyeth's *Repository of Sacred Music, Part Second*, 1813.

My soul is filled with joy in my Re-deem-er, for God has lift-ed me and set me high. There is no Ho-ly One, no Rock like our God, who an-swered my re-quest, who heard my cry.

All those who talk with pride now see who God is,
who weighs our deeds and knows our every move.
Proud ones are humbled, but the poor are lifted,
all might and power are yours, O God of love.

The strong have fallen, but the weak are strengthened;
those who were hungry have enough to spare.
She who was barren sees her children's children;
all things are ever in your loving care.

O God, you set the earth on sure foundations;
help for your saints is found in you alone.
Those who oppose your truth will fall in judgment,
but you will strengthen your anointed one.[12]

Readers familiar with the nativity story in the Second Testament will immediately recognize the similarities with the Song of Mary (Magnificat) in this Song of Hannah. Nearly every phrase echoes the scriptural base in 1 Samuel, and the location of this reading just days before the Advent readings for Year C provides a suitable anticipation of the Christ-event to come.

From the scriptures of the Second Testament as described for use in Year C, we turn to Proper 7 to find Luke 8.26-39, the healing of the Gerasene demoniac. Although this story appears in Year B at Proper 19, the Lukan version is an addition to the Lectionary. Author Richard Leach has provided the following paraphrase and reflection. [13]

Disturbed and wild and desperate
a man to be restrained –
yet when the people bound him,
he broke their every chain.
Perhaps with stronger shackles
the wild man could be held.
But how could chains bring healing,
or binding make him well?

"Do not torment me, Jesus,"
a shouted cry of dread—
yet Jesus was not daunted,
"What is your name?" he said.
Not shackles, but the naming
of powers that hurt and held
was what began the healing
to make the wild man well.

When we confront the wildness
around us and within,
and shackles give no healing,
however strong the chain,
then listen to the story

---

[13] Richard Leach, 1993, © 1996 Selah Publishing Co., Inc. All rights reserved. (Used with permission of Selah, October, 2020.) Suggested tune: LLANGLOFFAN 76 76 D; or FAIRFIELD 76 76 D.

in which our hope is held,
and seek the word of Jesus,
to name and to make well.

In this hymn, the author takes biblical references to "chains" in both literal and metaphorical senses, sponsoring personal reflection on "the Legions" of "powers that hurt and [hold]" in our own circumstances. The poem culminates in our hope for being clothed in our "right mind" (Luke 8.35) to enable a cure for all our ills.

A parable found in three synoptic gospels, and in each year of the lectionary relates to "The Prodigal." (Matthew 18.15ff: Year A; Mark 2.17ff: Year B; Luke 15.1ff: Year C). Jaroslav Vajda, Lutheran scholar and pastor, altered the biblical sequence of this and two preceding parables, to effect a dramatic catalog of God's love in his writing of "A Woman and a Coin."

A woman and a coin, the coin is lost!
How much it means to her, what time and toil,
what part it was to play in her bright dreams!
Am I that treasured coin worth searching for?
I'm found, and you rejoice! What love! What love!

trea-sured coin   worth search-ing for?   I'm

found, and you re - joice! What love! What   love!

A Shepherd and a sheep, the sheep is lost!
Far from the flock, the one in hundred cries,
then, risking life, the shepherd's voice and staff!
Am I that treasured sheep worth dying for?
I live, and you rejoice! What love! What love!

A parent and a child, the child is lost!
The parent feeds on memories and hope,
the prodigal on husks and one last chance.
Am I that treasured child worth waiting for?
I'm home, and you rejoice! What love! What love!

Dear God, you sought us when the world was lost,
you gave your only son at what a cost;
your spirit welcomes home the tempest-tossed;
now we can be all you were dreaming of.
We're safe, and you rejoice! What love! What love! [14]

The poetic structure followed by Vajda is both accessible and personal. The scriptural base is stated at the top of each stanza, the inherent challenge is contextualized, and its meaning transferred to the life of the reader with promise of restoration, resolution, and redemption.

These are but a few illustrations of the rich cornucopia of hymn texts that poured forth in the two decades following the revision of the *Common Lectionary* (1983) and the *Revised Common Lectionary* (1992). Worship planners today have easy access to resources in the area of complementary hymn texts and tune suggestions that reinforce the messages of traditional and innovative readings, so that the Word proclaimed and the Word sung find resonance, each with the other.

The CSL, birthed by the Second Vatican Council, the resulting mandate – adopted in many judicatories – to broaden the scope of scriptural diet for Sunday worship, the dedication of thousands of persons to facilitate the quest for "more abundant and varied reading of the sacred scriptures" all betoken the presence of the energy of the Holy Spirit in building the Body of Christ, bonding worshippers in whose music God is glorified, and giving witness to the whole of Creation as it sings "Hallelujah!"

Section 2

Presbyterian Worship History

5. A BRIEF HISTORY OF BLACK WORSHIPPING COMMUNITIES AND LEADERS IN THE PRESBYTERIAN CHURCH

by Lisa M. Weaver

Introduction

A history of Black Presbyterian worship in the United States is a complex endeavor to record. The overarching complexity of the task is that this topic is situated at the intersection among three emerging narratives: (1) the narrative of European immigrants who voluntarily fled their native countries, took up residence in what would become a new nation, and began to build that new nation where indigenous people were already living, (2) the narrative of African people who were involuntarily brought to this new land and then enslaved by some European immigrants, and (3) the narrative of the establishment of the Presbyterian Church and its subsequent ministry to and incorporation of Africans and African Americans into the life and structure of that church. Each of those narratives grows and becomes more complex as more immigrants arrive, as more Africans are brought, as each of these communities begins to have the first "American" descendants of their respective groups, and as their lives become economically bound, though socially and juridically separate.

A history of Black Presbyterian worship in the United States is also an intricate endeavor to record by virtue of the legal status of Africans and African Americans during the country's nascent period as well as the particularities of their worship practices. Minimally, there are three reasons why this is so. First, Africans brought their culture with them, and that culture included their language and their worship practices. Thus, a history of Black Presbyterian worship practices would have to include a discussion of the presence, absence, or influence of African practices on Black Presbyterian worship in the U.S.

Second, as men of European descent began to design and build the economic, political, and juridical infrastructures of America, Africans and African Americans were progressively marginalized and disenfranchised until they were completely enslaved. This point is made more complex when one takes into account the chronologies of (a) the establishment of the original colonies (eleven of the thirteen original colonies were established in different years, and two were established in the same year) and (b) the enactment of different laws ("slave codes") restricting Africans and African Americans from fully and freely participating in the activities of ordinary life. Different colonies enacted slave codes at different times. In fact, some colonies enacted slave codes before other colonies were formally established.[1] The laws became increasingly prohibitive until Africans and African Americans became enslaved human beings in America. One of the many negative effects of their enslaved status was that the act of teaching them to read or write was criminalized. The immediate challenge this introduces is the dearth of primary source (i.e., eyewitness) testimony from these early years *from the perspective of the enslaved person*. From the "slave"[2] narratives that do exist, we know that religious life was part of the fabric of the narrators' lives. However, it should be noted that the "slave" narrative is a literary genre that does not emerge in the American context until the first half of the

---

[1] For example, in 1710, the Virginia Public Office Law made it illegal for anyone of African descent to hold or assume public office. Yet, Georgia was not formally established as a colony until 1732.

[2] I use the term "enslaved" rather than "slave" because I do not subscribe to the notion that any human being or category of human beings *are* slaves but rather have been "*enslaved*." The word "slave" will appear in quotation marks to acknowledge the nomenclature of the literary genre *vis-à-vis* my position regarding the use of this word to describe human beings.

nineteenth century, and its primary goal was not to preserve and describe the ritual details of worship practices but to support antislavery efforts.[3] Subsequently, one's quest for information and insight into the earliest African and African American worship practices generally, and ritual acts (i.e., Baptism, Eucharist, etc.) specifically, requires a multifaceted approach and sources different from the "slave" narrative.

Third, an examination of African and African American worship practices would have to be conducted regionally and then compared. The work of accounting for similarities and differences in practice poses one immediate problem. If a practice exists in two different regions, it cannot immediately be assumed that the practice migrated from one region to another. In the early years of the enslavement of African people, Africans from the same tribe were often separated (not only to break down kinship ties but as a measure against the possibility of enslaved blacks planning revenge, revolt, and/or escape). So, analyses of lines, direction, and degrees of influence on practices among regions must be held with due caution. And this is before 1698, the year the first Presbyterian church emerges in America in Philadelphia.[4] When one then introduces the chronology of the establishment and expansion of the Presbyterian Church with its prescribed liturgy (that allows for the exercise of some options within the liturgy), as well as presbyteries and synods, in this new context, the complexity and scope of data and analyses far exceed the limits of this essay.

Therefore, this is a *general* history of Black worshiping communities and their leadership in the Presbyterian Church in the United States. As

---

[3] "With the rise of the militant antislavery movement in the United States in the 1830s came a demand for slave narratives that would explicitly highlight the harsh realities of slavery, thereby supporting the movement's call for immediate and unconditional emancipation. Radical 'immediatist' abolitionists such as William Lloyd Garrison were convinced that the eyewitness testimony of former slaves against slavery would touch the hearts and change the minds of many in the northern population of the United States who were either ignorant of or indifferent to the plight of African Americans in the South." William L. Andrews, "Introduction" in *The Civitas Anthology of African American Slave Narratives*, William L. Andrews and Henry Louis Gates Jr., eds. (Washington, DC: Civitas/Counterpoint, 1999), 2.

[4] Leonard L. Haynes, Jr. *The Negro Community Within American Protestantism: 1619-1844* (Boston, MA: The Christopher Publishing House, 1953), 44; Robinson, *Testimony and Practice of the Presbyterian Church in Reference to American Slavery*, (Cincinnati, OH: John D. Thorpe, 1852), 10.

such, this essay examines the integration of Africans and African Americans into the worship life and clerical leadership of the Presbyterian Church and the subsequent development of independent African and African American Presbyterian worshiping communities with black leadership. This choice does not serve to disregard churches that comprised predominantly or exclusively Africans and African Americans but that were led by European American ministers. These churches are part of the three-strand narrative of Black Presbyterian worship communities in the United States. Rather, the choice is intended to center Black Presbyterian worshiping communities in the United States around Black people.

Free European and African Immigrants, African Slavery, and Presbyterianism

Each of the three narratives that merge to constitute the historical underpinnings of the narrative of Black Presbyterian worshiping communities in the United States fits within larger respective narratives. Europeans had been immigrating to different points on the eastern seaboard of the New World for centuries before the formal establishment of the first British colony of Jamestown, Virginia, in 1607. Africans were present and free in the New World before the first ship carrying enslaved blacks arrived in Jamestown, Virginia, in 1621. The earliest record of the first known African in America dates back to the early 1500s.[5] In the time between the early 1500s and 1621, African and European immigrants enjoyed freedom in the New World, and there were some among both groups who served periods of indentured

---

[5] Exact dates vary. Mary Frances Berry and John W. Blassingame offer a date of 1502. Henry Louis Gates, Jr., states, "In 1513… [Juan] Garrido rejoined Ponce de Léon as he explored and claimed the island of Bimini and all of Florida for Spain, thereby becoming the first known African to set food on what was to become the United States." See Mary Frances Berry and John W. Blassingame, *Long Memory: The Black Experience in America* (New York and Oxford: Oxford University Press, 1982), 7. See also Henry Louis Gates, Jr. and Donald Yacovone, *The African Americans: Many Rivers to Cross* (United States: Smiley Books, 2013), 3-4.

servitude. Equity between the two groups begins to shift in the 1660s. Statutes emerge that begin to socially separate blacks from whites, with more and more statutes and ordinances enacted until slavery become a permanent status for black people.[6] By the time the first Presbyterian church is established in the New World in Philadelphia in 1698, the roots of these cultural and juridical separations and shifts are entrenched in the New World ethos. This cruel ethos would become more severe and systemically entrenched over the next century and a half.

Early Presbyterians and the Issue of Slavery

While the topic of slavery was raised at meetings as early as 1744, an actual discussion of the topic at the national level did not take place until 16 May 1787 at the Synod of New York and Philadelphia.[7] The Synod was asked to consider an overture regarding the issue of slavery. The Synod responds that while they approve the "general principles in favor of universal liberty" in America, they thought that extending that same liberty to enslaved Blacks would be "in many respects dangerous" because enslaved persons lacked the "proper education" and "habits of industry" necessary to function in "civil society."[8] In theory, they agreed

---

[6] Lerone Bennett, Jr. *Before the Mayflower: A History of Black America, fifth edition.* (Harrisburg, VA: Johnson Publishing Company, Inc., 1982), 45. A 1662 Virginia enacted what is known as a Hereditary Slave law where the status of the child is determined by the status of the mother. Thus, if the mother is an enslaved person, the child "inherits" the mother's enslaved status (contra England where a child's status is determined by the father's status). The 1664 Maryland Marriage Law prohibited black men from marrying white women.

[7] Presbyterian Church in the U.S.A. General Assembly. *The Slavery Question: Action of the General Assembly from 1774 to 1850,* 1.

[8] "The Synod of New-York and Philadelphia do highly approve of the general principles, in favor of universal liberty, that prevail in America; and the interest which many of the states have taken in promoting the abolition of slavery. Yet, inasmuch as men introduced from a servile state, to a participation of all the privileges of civil society, without a proper education, and without previous habits of industry, may be, in many respects dangerous to the community. *Therefore*, they earnestly recommend it to all the members belonging to their communion, to give those persons, who are at

with the principle of liberty for all. However, as a practical matter, they presumed that granting enslaved Black persons freedom would disrupt "civil" society and, therefore, recommended providing them with a "good education" to prepare them to enjoy freedom and sufficient time to earn a "moderate" amount of money to secure their freedom. However, that same year would begin to usher in legislation that would make the task of abolishing slavery a more difficult one. The United States Constitution was approved in September of that same year. In it, Article 1, section 9 prohibited Congress from abolishing slavery until 1808.[9] The following year, exactly one month after the last meeting of the Synod of New York and Philadelphia, on 21 June 1788, ratification of the United States Constitution was complete. Thus, by the time of the first General Assembly of the Presbyterian Church, slavery was legislatively codified at the national level of American government. While it evident how this legislation would be an impediment for abolitionists and a victory for enslavers, what the Presbyterian Church (and other churches as well) did not anticipate was the theo-political machinations that they would soon be engaged in, trying to justify participation in a system that, while legislatively codified and economically profitable, was morally untenable and theologically indefensible.

The next time slavery was discussed on the national level would be at a General Assembly, and perhaps the way in which the Synod of New York and Philadelphia was divided after the 1788 meeting foreshadowed the differences that the northern and southern Presbyterians would

---

present held in servitude, such good education as may prepare them for the better enjoyment of freedom.—And they, moreover, recommend, that masters, wherever they find servants disposed to make a proper improvement of the privilege, would give them some share of property to begin with; or grant them sufficient time, and sufficient means, of procuring, by industry, their own liberty, at a moderate rate: that they may thereby be brought into society, with those habits of industry, that may render them useful citizens.—And, finally, they recommend it to all the people under their care, to use the most prudent measures, consistent with the interest and the state of civil society, in parts where they live, to procure, eventually, *the final abolition of slavery in America.*" *Acts and Proceedings of the Synod of New-York and Philadelphia: A.D. 1787, & 1788* (Philadelphia, PA: Jane Aitken, 1803), 3-4.

[9] "The Migration or Importation of such Persons as any of the States now existing shall think proper to admit, shall not be prohibited by the Congress prior to the Year one thousand eight hundred and eight, but a tax or duty may be imposed on such Importation, not exceeding ten dollars for each Person."

undergo in the future regarding the matter of slavery. The new synods were the Synod of New York and New Jersey, the Synod of Philadelphia, the Synod of Virginia, and the Synod of the Carolinas. During the intervening period between the Presbyterian discussions on slavery, the enactment of the 1790 Naturalization Act[10] by Congress more deeply embedded slavery into the law and ethos of American life. The deepening of the cultural entrenchment of slavery made the work of abolition and equity, in the Church and society, more difficult to achieve and seemingly discuss.

At the 1795 General Assembly, the slavery issue shifted from the 1787 focus on the emancipation of the enslaved to the eucharistic fellowship among white Presbyterians, in which the view of the morality of slavery is the potential dividing factor. The question was this: If a member of a Presbyterian congregation believes slavery is "a moral evil, highly offensive to God and injurious to the interests of the Gospel," should that member receive Eucharist with other Presbyterians who agree in principle that slavery is a moral evil yet still enslave black people and tolerate the practice of slaveholding in others? The resolution stated the following: (1) slavery is one among many issues on which all Presbyterians do not agree, (2) other Presbyterians in the Church hold these disagreements yet still live in "charity and peace" with one another, therefore, (3) those who think slavery is a moral evil, "*especially to those whom it immediately respects*" [emphasis added] should do the same (i.e., live in "charity and peace" with those who do not), and (4) refer to the past General Assembly minutes on the matter, especially from "the late Synod of New-York and Philadelphia, published in 1787...."[11] There are two noteworthy points about the General Assembly's response to this question. First, those for whom this matter (eucharistic fellowship with those who supported slavery) was a concern (and especially the person who raised the question), were basically admonished to get over it. Second, the General Assembly expression of their "deepest concern"

---

[10] "*Be it enacted by the Senate and the House of Representatives of the United States of America in Congress assembled,* That any alien, being a free white person, who shall have resided within the limits and under the jurisdiction of the United States for a term of two years, may be admitted to become a citizen thereof...." Act of 26 March 1790, 1 *Stat.* 2, ch. 3, sec. 1.

[11] *Acts and Proceedings of the General Assembly of the Presbyterian Church; in the United States of America, A.D. 1795 & 1796* (Philadelphia, PA: Samuel H. Smith, 1796), 5.

about any "vestiges" of slavery was to dismissively minimize the brutality and injustice of the system of slavery that, in 1795, showed no evidence of relenting. Third, the General Assembly points back to previous records of historical expressions of their "deepest concern" for the eradication of slavery. Parsing the 1787 resolution is beyond the scope of this article, but it is enough to note that the language recommends a process that will lead to the *final* abolition of slavery in America, not its immediate end.

Whereas the 1795 minutes describe the person who raised the question of Eucharist with enslavers as "a serious and conscientious person," the 1815 General Assembly minutes record that some elders raised the issue of "holding" enslaved persons, and the Synod of Ohio raised the issue of buying and selling enslaved persons. With respect to the first question, the General Assembly first declared that they repeatedly applauded the principles of civil liberty as recognized by the federal and state governments, expressed their regret that slavery still existed "even among those within the pale of the church," recommended the religious education of enslaved persons as preparation for their liberty, and referred the petitioners back to the 1787, 1793, and 1795 meeting minutes regarding this matter. Two things are noteworthy about this response. First, the response of the Synod at the 1787 meeting was to make an "overture"[12] on slavery, and the response does not specifically address the issue of "holding" enslaved persons. They reiterate their praise of civil liberty as recognized by the federal and state governments, regret for the enslavement of Africans, and urged Presbyterians to commit to religiously educating enslaved persons. Second, the substance of the 1795 matter was *not* about slavery as a moral evil but rather whether two Presbyterians who hold opposite views on slavery (one viewing slavery as a moral evil, the other not) should share in the Eucharist. Rather than outrightly dismissing the question, the General Assembly gives a response that fails to address the substance of the question.[13]

---

[12] The process of making an overture is part of Presbyterian parliamentary procedure, and it involves bringing a matter or a proposal in a meeting to the body (in this case, a synod) for deliberation and vote.

[13] *Extracts from the Minutes of the General Assembly of the Presbyterian Church, in the United States of America, A.D. 1815* (Philadelphia, PA: Jane Aitken, 1815), 259-60.

With respect to the second question, the General Assembly begins by stating that "in some sections of our country, under certain circumstances, the transfer of slaves *may* [emphasis added] be unavoidable." They responded to the matter as non-specifically as it was presented ("concerning the buying and selling"), thereby allowing them to circumvent rendering a judgment on the matter of slavery. They continue by extending the response beyond the substance of the question to include the *treatment* of enslaved persons ("...and all undue severity in the management of them, as inconsistent with the spirit of the Gospel"). Thus, the recommendation to do everything prudently possible to "prevent such shameful and unrighteous conduct" can be read as referring to the *treatment* of enslaved persons and not the matter of enslavement itself.[14]

The queries, and to some extent the responses of the General Assembly, raised at subsequent meetings indicate that there was an increasing dissonance among Presbyterian Church members between participation in the slavery system and the ethical demands of the Gospel. At the 1818 General Assembly, a report was presented to the General Assembly "on the subject of selling a slave." However, the committee assigned to the task was instructed to write a report *in general* on the subject of slavery. In response to the *general* report on the subject of slavery, the General Assembly rendered five positions on the matter, stated that it was the duty of all Christians to earnestly work to abolish slavery, expressed their gratitude that the Presbyterian Church began the work of abolition "as early as any other [church]" in the country and their "sympathy" over the places in church and the country where slavery was still operating but "where the number of slaves, their ignorance, and their vicious habits generally, rendered an immediate and universal emancipation inconsistent alike with the safety and happiness of the master and the slave." The General Assembly recommended the church (1) to engage the services of a society established for "colonizing in Africa, (2) to allow and make arrangements for the religious instruction of enslaved persons (which echoes, in part, the 1787 recommendation to educate enslaved persons "in preparation for freedom"), and (3) to discourage and prevent, as much as possible, cruel treatment of enslaved persons, especially by (a) separating spouses or family units, (b) selling

---

[14] *General Assembly 1815*, 260.

enslaved people where they won't hear the Gospel or where the Gospel will not be proclaimed, and (c) selling a *Christian* enslaved person against her/his will.[15] It is here, at the end of probably the most sustained treatment of slavery until this point, that we see the General Assembly address the question with which the committee was originally tasked, the selling of an enslaved person who is a member of the church. The General Assembly's clear failure to respond substantively to the overtures brought forth indicates a lack of commitment to the practice of "universal liberty" but only the theory. The immediate future did not bode well either. As Forrest G. Woods remarks of the 1818 General Assembly,

> ...the Presbyterian General Assembly condemned slavery only to find its position undermined by the insistence of subsequent assemblies that the church should be concerned only with the "moral" aspects of bondage, not its "civil" aspects. The legality of the institution of slavery was a civil matter for which, conservative "Old School" Presbyterians declared, the church has no responsibility.[16]

The matter of slavery would eventually cause a split in the Presbyterian Church. However, this was not to happen before they would split along conservative-liberal lines. In the eighteenth century, the Presbyterian Church experienced a schism along conservative-liberal lines in which the sides were identified as the "Old Side" and the "New Side." In the nineteenth century, it was the 1837 General Assembly meeting that led to the split in the Presbyterian Church in the U.S.A. into the "Old School" and the "New School." However, within each of these

---

[15] Slavery (1) was "a gross violation of the most precious and sacred rights of human nature," (2) was "inconsistent with the law of God," (3) was "irreconcilable with the spirit and principles of the gospel of Christ," (4) "created a paradox in the moral system," and (5) deprives the enslaved person of her/his natural right. *Minutes of the General Assembly in the United States of America from Its Organization A.D. 1789 to A.D. 1820 Inclusive* (Philadelphia, PA: Presbyterian Board of Publication, 1890), 691-694; Leonard L. Haynes, Jr., *The Negro Community Within American Protestantism: 1619-1844* (Boston, MA: The Christopher Publishing House 1953), 111.

[16] Forrest G. Wood. *The Arrogance of Faith: Christianity and Race in America from the Colonial Era to the Twentieth Century* (New York, NY: Alfred A. Knopf, Inc., 1990), 74-75.

"schools," the constituencies were still divided on the issue of slavery. Both the Old School and the New School divided on party lines, which changed the conservative/liberal divide to a slavery/anti-slavery divide. Geographically, it split the Presbyterian Church into a northern faction and a southern faction.[17]

Early Presbyterians and the System of Slavery

Baptism was not part of the American initiation plan that many early English settlers had for enslaved blacks. Early settlers thought that enslaved blacks would interpret their freedom in Christ to include freedom from enslavement. It was easier not to baptize them. It eliminated enslaved blacks from expecting societal equality as a result of Baptism, while simultaneously relieving early English settlers of the work of having to theologically and ethically think about the practice of slavery. However, the challenge in the early years of the republic was that both blacks and whites were indentured servants and slaves. In addition, many early settlers did not even consider that some enslaved blacks were already Christians whose practices may or may not have been shaped by the cultural practices that formed them. Christianity was present in Africa before Africans were forcibly brought to American shores. In some places where Christianity was introduced, people converted to Christianity. In some other places where Christianity was introduced, it did not supplant existing religious beliefs and practices. Rather, the Christian God was incorporated into their current belief systems and practices. Thus, when Africans forcibly arrived on American shores, many of them were already Christians.[18] The presumption and labeling of African people as not Christian or without a God construct coupled with pejorative interpretations and subsequent dismissal and stripping of African culture and language prevented colonizers from actually knowing that Africans *en masse* did not need to be "Christianized." Abolitionists

---

[17] Sydney E. Ahlstrom. *A Religious History of the American People* (New Haven and London: Yale University Press, 1972), 265-279, 462-468, 659-661; also Dwight N. Hopkins. *Down, Up, and Over: Slave Religion and Black Theology* (Minneapolis, MN: Fortress Press, 2000), 36; Gayraud S. Wilmore. *Black and Presbyterian: The Heritage and the Hope, revised and enlarged* (Louisville, KY: Witherspoon Press, 1983), 39.

[18] Ira Berlin. "From Creole to African: Atlantic Creoles and the Origins of African-American Society in Mainland North America" in *The William and Mary Quarterly*, Apr., 1996, vol. 53, no. 2 (Apr. 1996), 251-288; Wilmore. *Black and Presbyterian*, 5.

presented challenges to the early Christian settlers regarding the enslavement of Africans who were made in God's image. What was needed was an ideology to justify the exclusive enslavement of African people.[19]

At first, the rationalization was based on a false notion that Africans were heathens, and as such, were good candidates for religious education. The problem with this was that it did not provide a permanent solution. The question then arose as to whether it was a sin to baptize enslaved people? After impassioned, scripture-filled debates, it was determined that it was the duty of the Christian to baptize "heathens." The irony of this is clear: the inherent dignity and humanity of Africans had to first be diminished in order for them to be worthy recipients of Baptism. And in a move to make both the enslaved status of Africans as well as the profit stream of the enslavers exist in perpetuity, in 1667 Virginia enacted a law that states, in part, "…that the conferring of baptisme doth not alter the condition of the person as to his bondage or freedome…."[20]

Most enslaved people learned about Christianity in an informal fashion through the various quotidian interactions of life. Enslavers varied in their feelings regarding the spiritual needs of enslaved blacks. Some were indifferent to the enterprise, only insisting on "strict control over any religious activities on their plantations." Others were conscientious about religious formation, not often out of any primary or genuine concern about the souls of enslaved blacks, but rather that they be inculcated in a belief system that engrained the practices of hard work and obedience as spiritual virtues. Camp meetings were another mode of religious formation for enslaved blacks, particularly from 1790

---

[19] Lerone Bennett, Jr. *Before the Mayflower: A History of Black America, fifth edition.* (Harrisburg, VA: Johnson Publishing Company, Inc., 1982), 45.

[20] "An act declaring that baptisme of slaves doth not exempt them from bondage." "WHEREAS some doubts have risen whether children that are slaves by birth, and by the charity and piety of their owners made partakers of the blessed sacrament of baptisme, should by virtue of their baptisme be made free; *It is enacted and declared by this grand assembly, and the authority thereof,* that the conferring of baptisme doth not alter the condition of the person as to his bondage or freedome; that diverse masters, freed from this doubt, may more carefully endeavour the propagation of christianity by permitting children, though slaves, or those of greater growth if capable to be admitted to that sacrament." Grand Assemblie, 23 September 1667, Act III. See also Bennett, *Before the Mayflower,* 46.

through 1830. For enslaved blacks who became Presbyterians, their introduction to religious life commonly occurred in the homes of their Presbyterian enslavers. Enslaved blacks "were taught to read and memorize passages from the Shorter Catechism and the Bible." According to Gayraud S. Wilmore, the Reverend Samuel Davies was responsible for the first organized Presbyterian outreach to enslaved blacks, begun in 1747. Davies would later become president of Princeton University.[21]

Worship and Ministry Challenges for Black Presbyterians

Outside of church, life was already difficult for enslaved people. Every aspect of their lives was codified, legislated, and scrutinized. The one place where enslaved people *should* have felt fully affirmed in their humanity and free to inhabit the space was the Church. However, the practices of civil society and the theoretical commitment to "universal liberty" as expressed at General Assemblies converged in the local Presbyterian church in ways that reminded enslaved people of their subjugated status. As was noted earlier, some enslaved people were religiously educated through the Shorter Catechism and the Bible, if their enslavers were Presbyterian. Thus, enslaved Presbyterians became as committed to their Presbyterian identity as their enslaver counterparts. The difficulty of integration and service lie not with the enslaved people but with the church, for while some of the challenges that faced enslaved Presbyterians faced enslaved people of other denominations, the enslaved Presbyterian had additional challenges that made serving God in a ministerial capacity even more difficult.

In the same way that enslaved people were black and American in society, they were black and Presbyterian inside the church. In other words, within the church, enslaved people were black first and

---

[21] W. H. Franklin. The Early History of the Presbyterian Church, in the U.S.A., Among the Negroes (Pittsburgh, PA: The Board of Missions for Freedmen, 1920), 4; Andrew E. Murray. *Presbyterians and the Negro—A History* (Philadelphia, PA: Presbyterian Historical Society, 1966), 49-51; Albert J. Raboteau. *A Fire in the Bones: Reflections on African-American Religious History* (Boston, MA: Beacon Press, 1995), 26-27; Wilmore, *Black and Presbyterian*, 31-32.

Presbyterian second.   At times echoing Ernest Trice Thompson, Andrew E. Murray outlines five challenges that the enslaved Presbyterians faced. The first challenge was that enslaved black people's ecclesial status as baptized Presbyterians had no bearing on how they were treated within church.   They were treated based on their subordinated civil status as enslaved people and not as equals in the family of God. Enslaved black parishioners were seated in the gallery, while white parishioners were seated on the floor. Enslaved black parishioners received Communion only after white parishioners had received Communion. One example Murray offers of this kind of inequitable treatment relates to the use of communion tokens. Whereas the white communicants had silver communion tokens, enslaved black people had communion tokens that were made of some kind of base (i.e., lesser quality) metal. While not a barrier to communion, it was a visible, tangible symbol that reinforced the inequality of individuals who theologically should have been understood to be and treated as equals. Second, worship services for enslaved black people (a) were held after the services for white people were concluded and (b) had to be held under the supervision of a white person in order to prevent "nervous excitements" (translation: to ensure that the expressive and dynamic worship expressions that are characteristic of black worship did *not* occur). The third and fourth points are related and have implications for the ministry pathway for enslaved black ministers. The third challenge for enslaved black people was that they were not permitted to hold church office, and fourth, it was quite difficult for enslaved blacks to receive the requisite education required for ministry within the Presbyterian Church. It should be noted that seminary education was not the norm for white men during this time. Often men were prepared for ordained ministry under the tutelage of an older ordained man in ministry. Both Thompson and Murray are critical of the Presbyterian Church on this point.   Thompson contends that the Presbyterian Church's failure to attract enslaved blacks to the church compared to the Baptists and Methodists was because (1) the educational standard for ministry for the Baptists and Methodists was lower than it was for Presbyterian ministers, (2) the Baptists and Methodists were more affective in their ministry (contra the Presbyterian's appeal to the intellect), (3) enslaved black Presbyterian clergy were not as well-resourced as their free white counterparts,[22] (4) the congregational polity of the Baptists and the itinerant system of the Methodists were both superior to Presbyterian polity, and (5) the Presbyterians were apathetic towards enslaved black people in general. Murray characterizes the Presbyterians as being unwilling to adapt methods to the particular needs of enslaved black people, particularly their failure to use enslaved black people to minister to their fellow enslaved people. This was true in the south as late as the mid 1800s.[23] With respect to church, enslaved black Presbyterians fared slightly better in the north and earlier. Murray captures a significant difference between enslaved black Presbyterians in the north versus the south. Of the north he writes

> … independent Negro churches developed when Negro Christians were frustrated in their efforts to achieve full equality in white churches. …. This pattern of separate Negro congregations also became the pattern of Negro Presbyterian churches. Though Negro Presbyterian churches might be linked formally to the denomination through the presbytery, this did not bring them full acceptance, socially or ecclesiastically. The separate Negro Presbyterian congregation was a means by which white Presbyterians could discharge their missionary responsibilities for Negroes without having to admit them to their churches. It was also a way by which Negro

---

[22] While the Presbyterian Church held to the principle of ministry parity, the reality for enslaved black men was that their congregations did not have the resources to support him. At the same time, unlike the Baptist and Methodist denominations, the Presbyterian Church did not look favorably on we now term bi-vocational ministry. Missionary agencies did provide some financial support to enslaved black clergy, as well as individuals and churches who were sympathetic about ministry to enslaved black people. The enslaved black clergy themselves often supplemented their meager salaries by writing or teaching, which was preferred by the Presbyterian Church. Andrew E. Murray. *Presbyterians and the Negro—A History* (Philadelphia, PA: Presbyterian Historical Society, 1966), 30-32, 39, 61-62.

[23] Andrew E. Murray. *Presbyterians and the Negro—A History* (Philadelphia, PA: Presbyterian Historical Society, 1966), 30.60-61; Ernest Trice Thompson. *Presbyterians in the South (vol. 1): 1607-1861* (Richmond, VA: John Knox Press, 1963), 64, 66, 71-72.

Presbyterians could secure the necessary resources with which to build their own institutions"[24]

Of the south he writes

No matter how pious he might be, the Negro Presbyterian in the South could not aspire to the office of ministry. .... The basic problem of the Presbyterian in the South in relation to the Negro was this: He would not allow him to organize a separate Negro church, neither could he permit him to participate fully in the white Presbyterian church. In spite of their sincerity and dedication, the white Presbyterian missionaries to the Negroes in the South were restricted in their efforts by necessity of subordinating the Christian message of the parity of believers to the social controls of the slave system. After emancipation, when the slave was finally given a choice, he preferred a church which he could make his own, rather than the Presbyterian church which offered him only second-class membership."[25]

Black Presbyterians in America

Separate worship spaces for enslaved black people were initially discouraged, in part because enslavers created the narrative that enslaved blacks were untrustworthy so that they had to be watched, and in part because enslavers were afraid of the potential for insurrection and rebellion. So, the denomination was making efforts to evangelize and incorporate enslaved black people into their respective churches, and the challenges looked different in the north versus the south. The Presbyterian Church was no different in this regard. The Presbyterian Church in the south had three challenges. First, the largest population of enslaved black populations was located in the "back country" in the

---

[24] Andrew E. Murray. *Presbyterians and the Negro—A History* (Philadelphia, PA: Presbyterian Historical Society, 1966), 31-32.

[25] Murray, 61-62.

south. According to Murray, Presbyterians did not have as much contact with the southern lowlands as they did in other southern regions. Second, the Presbyterians did not demonstrate any willingness to adapt their approach to these efforts. Murray notes that the Baptists and Methodists were more adaptable in their methods, and as a result, had far greater influence and impact than the Presbyterians. Interestingly, he correlates that phenomenon to the differences in training of the Methodists and Baptists clergy vis-à-vis the Presbyterians clergy; Methodists and Baptists did not require their clergy to be as highly trained as the Presbyterians did. He also noted, again, the affective difference between the Presbyterians and the other two denominations. The third reason Presbyterians did not have as much success as their denominational counterparts is their failure to make enslaved black people one of their evangelization goals; ministry to enslaved black people was incidental to the Presbyterian efforts towards white people. However, while southern Presbyterians as a body were not as successful as their denominational counterparts in incorporating enslaved blacks into the denomination, white Presbyterian churches at the local level made the incorporation of enslaved black people their evangelistic goal.[26]

By the time the Civil War had begun, many Presbyterian churches had been established in the north where blacks were free. This was in part the result of white Presbyterians feeling that segregated churches would be best for both blacks and whites. This was also due, in part, to blacks desiring more agency, participation, decision-making, and leadership in their own institutions. This made the north a more desirable place for enslaved black people to be Presbyterians, but that was not without its challenges as well. Congregations and clergy of black Presbyterian churches faced challenges in the north. Congregations often could not support and sustain a clergy person because they lacked the financial resources to do so. On the other hand, the clergy person, because he was one of the few people in the congregation who had the benefit of education and training, was often compelled to devote much of his time to the struggle for social and political rights.[27]

Directly after the Civil War, the southern Presbyterian Church ("PC(US)") was still wrangling over the issue of slavery. One example is

[26] Murray, 52.
[27] Murray, 45-46.

the 1865 meeting of the General Assembly in Macon, Georgia. There was a proposal for the northern and southern churches to reunite. The southern delegates refused it, arguing (erroneously) that the northern church was advocating social equality for blacks and "while the institution of human bondage *may* have been wrong... the respective position of master and servant were correct." In the years to follow, the PC(US) vacillated in their inclusion and incorporation of blacks in the church. This lasted until the 1874 General Assembly meeting in Columbus, Mississippi when the call for the establishment of a separate black worshiping body was set forth.[28]

Before emancipation, Baptism made enslaved blacks members of the Presbyterian Church and eligible to receive Communion, though they were unable to fully participate in the life of the church. Emancipation did not change that. While free according to the law, blacks still encountered barriers to full participation in the church as well as society. They were prohibited from fully participating in society and government, and they continued to be prohibited from participating in the leadership of the church. Black agency in the Presbyterian Church came through the establishment of separate worshiping bodies for Black people. According to Appendix VI of *All Black Governing Bodies: The History and Contributions of All-Black Governing Bodies*, among the three reunited bodies that comprise the PC(USA), there were six all black synods (Snedecor Memorial, Atlantic, Catawba, East Tennessee, Blue Ridge, Canadian) and

---

[28] "Overture No. 8 is a paper adopted by the Synod of South Carolina in November, 1872.... It declares that, 'in the judgment of said Synod, the way is clear (the General Assembly concurring) for our ministers to assist the coloured people to organize themselves into Presbyterian churches, separate from our Presbyteries.... Overture No. 9 is a memorial from the Presbytery of East Hanover, asking the Assembly 'to take order...for organizing the coloured members into a separate ecclesiastical organization.... Overture No. 10 represents that, in the judgment of the Synod of Memphis, our Church can most efficiently promote the spiritual interests of the coloured people by organizing them into a separate church.... Overture No. 11 is a memorial from the Synod of Mississippi... that a natural instinct leads the colored [sic] people to desire a separate organization...." Minutes of the [Southern] Presbyterian General Assembly 1874, vol. 3, 516-517; see also Forrest G. Wood. *The Arrogance of Faith: Christianity and Race in America from the Colonial Era to the Twentieth Century* (New York, NY: Alfred A. Knopf, Inc., 1990), 306.

forty all black presbyteries from 1866 to 1988.[29] The availability of historical resources, the intricately intertwined relationship of all-black Presbyterian churches with white Presbyterian churches, and the parameters of this article do not permit an equitable examination of each black Presbyterian church's liturgical life and practices. However, there are a few significant communities and individuals that merit attention. It is to these that we now turn.

Black Presbyterians in the South

Zion-Olivet Presbyterian Church.

Zion-Olivet (previously Zion Church) in Charleston, South Carolina, has the distinction of being "only one verifiable Black Presbyterian church in the South prior to the American Civil War."[30] This remarkably interesting history is well worth retelling.

In 1847, Rev. John B. Adger, who also taught at Columbia Theological Seminary, proposed establishing a separate congregation for enslaved black people. He had come to believe that the galley was not adequate for enslaved blacks to worship. He also believed that the sermons were geared for the white congregants with little consideration for the enslaved blacks who worshiped there. Adger's idea was vehemently opposed by some; his Columbia colleague who was also a missionary to enslaved blacks Charles Colcock Jones also advised against it. In spite of all the opposition, Adger's father and brothers continued to give him their support. Then the tide changed. Adger preached a sermon from Matthew 11:5: "the poor have the gospel preached unto

---

[29] Presbyterian Church (U.S.A.). *All Black Governing Bodies: The History and Contributions of All-Black Governing Bodies* (Louisville, KY: The Office of the General Assembly, 1993), 189-190.

[30] Special Committee to Document the History and Contributions of All-Black Governing Bodies of the Presbyterian Church (U.S.A.). *All-Black Governing Bodies: The History and Contributions of All-Black Governing Bodies in the Predecessor Denominations of the Presbyterian Church (U.S.A.)* (Louisville, NY : The Office of the General Assembly, 1996), 24.

them." After that, the Second Presbyterian Church and the Charleston presbytery gave their consent. He then received the consent of the citizens of Charleston, along with $7,700 from the white citizens of Charleston for the construction of an edifice. Zion Church ended up being the largest church in the city. Adger was succeeded by Rev. John Lafayette Giradeau. Described by one person as "a great white preacher whose life is consecrated to the salvation of Negroes," Giradeau's renown as a preacher grew and travelled. So great was his preaching that the question was raised, "Why did this man, the equal of any in America, refuse calls to New York and Philadelphia ... where he could have been admired, renowned and influential...work among slaves, Negro slaves, and to the most inferior of them, even to the Gullah Negroes of the tidewater section of South Carolina?" and his worship there was characterized as "revival services," of which southern Presbyterians generally did *not* approve.[31]

This explains the growth that Zion experienced. Additionally, Zion church also had what, for that time, was an unusual seating arrangement: blacks sat on the floor and whites sat in the gallery. A white layman named Edward C. Jones from Second Presbyterian Church who assisted Giradeau was summoned by a white gentleman. This gentleman told Jones (1) that he felt it his duty to have his children sit under Giradeau's teaching and (2) that he himself wanted to join Giradeau's mission church, and (3) that there were five to six others who wanted to join him. A special dispensation was given by the Charleston Presbytery for white Presbyterians to join Zion, and if they did want to join, they were required to sign a covenant. It read:

> That we enter this church as white members of the same,
> with the fullest understanding that its primary design and
> chief purpose is to benefit the colored and especially the
> slave population of this city, and the white membership
> is a feature added to the original organization for the
> purpose of better securing the ends of that organization.
> We declare, further, that we have chosen to attach
> ourselves to this church, not only for the benefit of

---

[31] *All Black Governing Bodies*, 32-33; see also Alex. R. Batchelor. *Jacob's Ladder: Negro Work of the Presbyterian Church in the United States* (Atlanta, GA: Board of Church Extension, Presbyterian Church in the United States, 1953), 60-61.

ourselves and our families, which we believe will be secured by such a connection, but also that we may assist by our means and our personal efforts in the support and protection of this missionary work.[32]

Giradeau left the church to serve in the Civil War. He returned to the pastorate after the war, and the church increased by 450 people. After a time, Giradeau left Zion and became a professor at Columbia Theological Seminary. Zion recalled Jonathan Gibbs, a black missionary sent by the north who was at Zion while Giradeau was at war, to the pastorate and later merged with Olivet Church to become Zion-Olivet Presbyterian Church.[33]

Charlotte Church (Colored), the Biddle Institute, and Catawba Presbytery.

After having their segregated spaces consistently repurposed until there was no worship space for them left within the sanctuary, enslaved blacks stopped attending First Presbyterian Church of Charlotte (NC) (White) and attended hush harbor churches,[34] listening to African

---

[32] *All Black Governing Bodies*, 33; Batchelor, 57-60, 62-63.

[33] *All Black Governing Bodies*, 34-35; Batchelor, 63.

[34] A brush arbor is an open-air shelter constructed by driving vertical poles in the ground and putting poles across the top to hold cut branches creating a roof. Worship services and revivals were held under them. However, they hold particular historical significance for Blacks. Albert J. Raboteau writes that in "brush arbors (shelters of cut branches also called 'hush harbors') throughout the South, slaves held their own religious meetings where they interpreted Christianity according to their experience, applying the stories and symbols of the Bible to make sense out of their lives. They were even willing to risk severe punishment to attend forbidden prayer meetings so they could worship god without white supervision or control. Out of the presence of whites, the slaves were free to express openly their desire for freedom in this life as well as the next." Raboteau, *Canaan Land: A Religious History of African Americans* (New York, NY: Oxford University Press, 2001), 43.
Of hush harbors, Nicole Myers Turner writes, that "In the hush harbors where enslaved people worshipped clandestinely and independently, they developed a separate identity for themselves. .... The hush harbor independent and clandestine worship spaces were characterized by enslaved people's resistance to white domination through the act of 'stealing away'—secretly removing oneself from the plantation." Nicole Myers Turner, *Soul Liberty: The Evolution of Black Religious Politics in Postemancipation Virginia* (Chapel Hill, NC: University of North Carolina Press, 2020), ch. 1, Amazon Kindle e-book.

Methodist Episcopal and Baptist preachers. However, being fully committed to their Presbyterian identity, they petitioned the pastor and the session for their own service. The pastor and session consented, and enslaved blacks worshiped on Monday evenings in the basement of the church for six months. Sometime after these six months, these enslaved blacks Presbyterians secured and moved into their own worship space. They were able to sustain themselves through the end of slavery and the Civil War. In 1866 the church was formally organized, and in 1867 it was named the Charlotte Church (Colored).[35] This church "became a major focal point for Black Presbyterianism in the southeast."[36] In that same year, Charlotte Church (Colored) was itself the seedbed for an educational institution called the Biddle Institute. Over time, this institution would grow and join the ranks of what are known as historically black colleges and universities ("HBCUs") under its current name, Johnson C. Smith University.[37]

---

[35] There is another narrative of the beginnings of the First Presbyterian Church (Colored) that is found on the website of what is now First United Presbyterian Church. I say "another" and not "alternate" as not to privilege or diminish either narrative but rather (1) to cast light on often erased women's voices and (2) to offer that between the two narratives I believe we are given a more robust and detailed description of this community.

"The church became one of the paramount institutions to emerge. It was in 1866 when Kathleen Hayes, a former slave who worshipped at First Presbyterian Church in Charlotte, North Carolina, challenged about 30 other black members to "come down out of the gallery and worship God on the main floor." Her efforts coincided with a movement by the Northern Presbyterian Church to send missionaries down south to assist in the Christianization of recently emancipated slaves. Mrs. Hayes' dreams were realized when Reverend Samuel C. Alexander, a white missionary from Pittsburgh, Pennsylvania, came to Charlotte shortly after the war and purchased land on the corners of Davidson and Third Streets in his name. It was later transferred to blacks, where Mrs. Hayes' new church, The Colored Presbyterian Church of Charlotte, was established." From "Our History" on the website of First United Presbyterian Church (https://fupcc.org/about-us/our-history, accessed 6 August 2020); see also *All Black Governing Bodies*, 29.

[36] *All Black Governing Bodies*, 28.

[37] Murray, 177-78; see also *All-Black Governing Bodies*, 26-28.

Black Presbyterians in the North

According to Murray, the earliest northern churches comprised enslaved blacks who were formerly members of white southern Presbyterian churches.[38] The first church organized for enslaved blacks was established in 1807 and was located in Philadelphia. Although it was located in the north, First African Presbyterian Church's first members would be from Philadelphia and Tennessee.

Rev. Archibald Alexander pastored the Third Street Presbyterian Church in Philadelphia. In 1806 he had a conversation with a few of his colleagues about the idea of forming a Christian society in Philadelphia. The following year, 1807, the Evangelical Society of Philadelphia was formed, and one of its goals was to organize a Presbyterian church for enslaved blacks in Philadelphia. Meanwhile, in Tennessee, efforts at organizing a Presbyterian church for enslaved blacks did not go as well. At the General Assembly in Lexington, Kentucky, John Gloucester was recommended for licensure to be a missionary to enslaved blacks. Rev. Gideon Blackburn was the link that connected Alexander and Gloucester.

Rev. Gideon Blackburn was a member of the Presbytery of Union in the Tennessee synod as well as a minister to the Cherokee people. While Blackburn had enslaved blacks, over time his view on slavery shifted such that he manumitted several of them. In one man, John Gloucester, Blackburn recognized gifts for ministry to enslaved blacks. Blackburn began to supervise Gloucester's education and would later manumit Gloucester for this purpose. Sometime later, Blackburn took a trip to Philadelphia to see if there might be a place where Gloucester's gifts could be used.

At the 1807 General Assembly held in Lexington Kentucky, the Presbytery of Union (Synod of Tennessee) requested advice regarding the licensure of John Gloucester. While Gloucester had studied literature and theology for years, he had not completed all of the qualifications for licensure. However, the request was being made based on Gloucester's noteworthy gifting, anticipating that he would be valuable in ministry.

---

[38] Murray, 177-78.

The General Assembly recognized the report of the presbytery, affirmed all that was said in it, and authorized the Presbytery of *Philadelphia* (not Union) to consider Gloucester's case. On hearing the report, Alexander quickly approached Blackburn about the possibility of Gloucester serving under the Evangelical Society of Philadelphia. Blackburn immediately accepted Alexander's invitation, and as soon as possible brought Gloucester to Philadelphia.

On July 7, 1807, Gloucester's case came before the Philadelphia Presbytery. They decided that since Gloucester was educated under the Presbytery of Union, they were better situated to decide Gloucester's readiness for ministry than they, and the case was sent back to the Presbytery of Union. Gloucester returned to Tennessee; he understood the decision and yet was not dismayed by it. After almost three years, on April 30, 1810, upon satisfactorily answering all of the questions of the ordination committee, Gloucester preached his ordination sermon, was ordained "by prayer and the laying of hands of the Presbytery," charged to faithfully discharge the duties of ministry, and ordered to immediately report to Philadelphia and join the presbytery there. Gloucester did so and began his work for the Evangelical Society of Philadelphia. In the beginning of his work, he held prayer meetings in private homes and preached on the streets as a way of gathering members for the First African Presbyterian Church. The following year, in 1811, First African Presbyterian Church was officially received by the Presbytery. The church flourished under Gloucester. However, the church was not able to compensate him enough to fulfill one important goal: to accumulate enough money to purchase the freedom of his wife and four children. Subsequently, Gloucester had to do preaching tours to raise the money needed. Some speculated that his preaching tours were the reason First African Presbyterian Church experienced similar levels of growth as other black churches in Philadelphia. Gloucester conducted preaching tours for four years to earn enough money to purchase his family's freedom. However, during his absence, the church suffered. Eventually, he was able to secure his family's freedom, and they joined him in Philadelphia. However, the toll of all his preaching tours and travel on his body was great. Even though he was in compromised and then declining health, he returned to focus on the church. Gloucester's tenure as pastor resulted in the church growing both numerically and spiritually.[39]

Women Religious Leaders

Even though women could not be ordained in the Presbyterian Church until the middle of the twentieth century,[40] and the first African American woman not until 1974, women have always contributed significantly to the life and ministry of the black church, inside and out. In addition to the recognized but more often unrecognized great labor that black women expended in the church, it must also be remembered that black women contributed substantially in the area of education.

A black man who was given the title of exhorter had a daughter who became known as a superb educator in the Presbyterian Church in the north. Southern presbyteries were resistant and, in many cases, failed to grant equal access and standing to black Presbyterians after 1865. A few years prior to emancipation, the session of the Presbyterian church in Macon, Georgia, part of Hopewell Presbytery, developed ministry plans for black Presbyterians and created the role of "exhorter." In April 1866, the black members of the Macon church petitioned the presbytery to organize as a separate church. The presbytery consented. They appointed and ordained three black men: Robert Casters and Joseph Williams were ordained exhorters who would serve with David Laney, who was ordained to Word and Sacrament. Laney was married and had

---

[39] William T. Catto. *A Semi-Centenary Discourse, delivered in The First African Presbyterian Church, Philadelphia, on the Fourth Sabbath of May, 1857* (Philadelphia, PA: Joseph M. Wilson, 1857), 19-26, 35, 38-48; Carol. V.R. George. *Segregated Sabbaths: Richard Allen and the Rise of Independent Black Churches, 1760-1840* (New York, NY: Oxford University Press, 1973), 151; Andrew E. Murray. *Presbyterians and the Negro—A History* (Philadelphia, PA: Presbyterian Historical Society, 1966), 33; Wilmore, *Black and Presbyterian*, 26.

[40] Louisa Woosley is the exception to this. By November 1889, Woosley had satisfactorily demonstrated to the Nollin, Kentucky presbytery that she was called to ordained ministry, and she convinced them to ordain her. See Rosemary Skinner Keller and Rosemary Radford Ruether, eds., *In Our Own Voices: Four Centuries of American Women's Religious Writing* (New York, NY: Harper San Francisco, 1995), 296-97.

a ten-year old daughter named Lucy. These men were among the first free black men to be ordained in the Presbyterian Church after the Civil War. However, Hopewell Presbytery added a condition to their ordination. Laney et al. were invested with the faculty to preach, administer the sacraments, and perform the other rites of the church, with the stipulation

> 1. That these men shall be regarded as ordained ministers in the Presbyterian Church only in connection with their own people; and 2. That Presbytery will not set them apart to work above designated, unless they shall obtain, from them, previously, a public expression of their adhesion to the doctrines and discipline of the Presbyterian Church, and are fully persuaded of their personal piety, and their competency to instruct colored congregations in religious matters. [41]

Lucy was born during the last years of slavery in Macon, Georgia, in 1855. Her mother worked in the home of the Campbell family, the family who enslaved the Laneys. They allowed the Laney family to live together in their own home. Lucy learned to read and studied Latin, taught by members of the Campbell family. She graduated from Atlanta University in 1873 and afterwards worked as a teacher in Georgia and South Carolina. Due to health reasons, Lucy had to return to Augusta (presumably where she taught while in Georgia). Ever a teacher, Lucy opened a school in the basement of Christ Presbyterian Church in Augusta so that black children had a school to attend since they were prohibited from attending the public schools. Her work caught the attention of a minister who encouraged her to "present her work at the General Assembly." Her work was endorsed at the General Assembly. Additionally, although the endorsement did not come with financial support, Lucy became friends with Mrs. F.E.H. Haines, who was a member of the Women's Executive Committee of the Home Mission Board. So generative was Lucy's friendship with this woman that she named her school after her: Haines Institute. Lucy became the first black woman to be appointed by the Presbyterian Freedmen's Board to

---

[41] Murray, 146-47. While Murray writes that her work was endorsed by the 1886 General Assembly that met in Minneapolis, Minnesota, there is no mention of Lucy Laney in the minutes. Only her father's name appears, and it appears only once.

lead one of its major branches. One of Lucy's most famous students was Mary McCloud Bethune. She began her teaching career under Lucy Laney's tutelage, integrated many of Laney's teaching philosophies into her own, and went on to become a national leader in the civil rights movement.[42]

The Reverend Dr. Katie Geneva Cannon made history on April 24, 1974 by becoming the first African American woman to be ordained in the Presbyterian Church. Her groundbreaking accomplishments continued after that. Dr. Cannon was a professor of Christian ethics at Union Presbyterian Seminary though she taught at other institutions during her career. She is celebrated for her pioneering work in 1988 book *Black Womanist Ethics,*[43] using African American women's literary tradition as a methodological tool. With seven books, over 20 chapters in edited collections, over 30 articles, along with innumerable lectures, speeches, and presentations, Rev. Dr. Cannon's contributions to womanist scholarship, church and society are so vast and so deep that The Katie Geneva Cannon Center for Womanist Leadership was established in her honor at Union Presbyterian Seminary.

African American Presbyterians: In Worship and In the World

There is a significant treasure of scholarship on worship by African American Presbyterians. The work of Dr. Melva Wilson Costen and the Reverend Dr. Gayraud S. Wilmore centered on both worship and music practices. Dr. Costen was both a church musician and a scholar; as such, the two strands of her scholarship are worship and music. Among all that she has written, her two published books bear clearest witness to this truth. Dr. Costen wrote *African American Christian Worship* and *In Spirit and In Truth: The Music of African American Worship.*[44] The dedicatory

---

[42] Murray, 186-87.

[43] Katie Geneva Cannon. *Black Womanist Ethics* (Eugene, OR: Wipf and Stock Publishers, 1988).

[44] Melva Wilson Costen. *African American Christian Worship* (Nashville, TN: Abingdon Press, 1993); *In Spirit and In Truth: The Music of African American Worship* (Louisville, TN: Westminster John Knox Press, 2004).

of the second book was exclusively in honor of her late husband, Rev. Dr. James H. Costen, a minister and educator who served as dean of Johnson C. Smith Theological Seminary and later served as president of the Interdenominational Theological Seminary ("ITC"). As a church musician, she had a deep knowledge of and appreciation for liturgy. She wrote about worship as an enterprise but also about its discrete constitutive components of music and prayer, always holding them in the balance.

Rev. Dr. Wilmore provided critical theological frameworks through which to examine and understand African history and culture, make connections among belief, praxis, and mission, and maintain the liberative aspect of worship, while constantly maintaining a critical and evaluative eye on the entire liturgical enterprise. Wilmore's scholarship invites an intense cultural parsing of the norms of current theology and worship practices for evidence of importation, influence, and confluence of those practices. The African community and the African American church are well resourced because of the work of these two scholars.

Conclusion

The goal of this essay is to present an overview of the emergence and presence of Black Presbyterian worshiping communities in the United States, how they emerged as a distinct constituency in a new country and within a new ecclesiastical context. Neither government nor church were new. Rather, theological, political, and ideological tenets and governance structures were reimagined, re-envisioned, and re-engineered for this new world by European settlers who were once themselves oppressed. While Great Britain and Scotland provided templates of political and ecclesiastical structures, the oppressive rule from which the early European settlers were fleeing was regrettably duplicated by their own hand in the new world. The formerly oppressed became the new oppressor as legislative systems in this new nation gradually and systematically enacted laws eroding civil rights for Africans and African Americans. Racial constructs were created to separate "blacks" from "whites." Indentured servitude intensified and shifted, causing black people to go from being indentured servants for a prescribed period of time to being enslaved people in perpetuity. The weeds of slavery grew so deep that the new European enslavers developed two systems, two sets of rules for life in the New World, one for "blacks" and one for "whites" in order to preserve a way of life that served their economic interests. This created a theo-political quagmire for enslavers, most of whom identified as Christians, because they now had to reconcile the implications of theological positions they were espousing for the sake of their economic and political gain. In order to present the illusion of a new world that functioned with integrity in both church and society, early settlers enacted laws to legislatively protect the theologically indefensible yet economically profitable system that they created for themselves. In this system, enslaved black people were segregated and treated inequitably in both church and society.

Enslaved blacks worshiped with whites in Presbyterian churches and some eventually became Presbyterian themselves. In spite of the marginalization and unequal treatment they experienced by enslavers in church, enslaved black Presbyterians were committed to being black (about which they had no choice) and being Presbyterian (about which they had a choice only after emancipation). Over time, enslaved black Presbyterians requested their own services where they could fully participate in the worship. There was support from some whites who were sympathetic to the cause of enslaved blacks and who may or may not have also been committed to abolition. In some cases, worship spaces were made for enslaved blacks that were overseen by white ministers. In other cases, blacks were allowed to have their own worship services under the watchful eye of an overseer. Eventually, in some presbyteries, some enslaved blacks were authorized to preach but only to enslaved communities. After a while the Emancipation Proclamation was signed. Though blacks were now legally free, the same barriers to full participation in society and the church still existed. However, after emancipation, black Presbyterian communities and synods began to emerge. So even as society was slow to grow into the "more perfect union" of which it spoke, where blacks were allowed to fully participate in all aspects of society, the black Presbyterian church became the sacred space where free blacks could fully participate in all aspects of the life of the church. The strength of both identities prevailed. Black Presbyterians served in church and over time in all aspects of society, and they continue to do so today. For the black Presbyterian heritage, legacy, and contributions to the academy, the church and the world, the entire church is both beneficiary and herald.

6. ROOTS OF THE 1993/2018 BOOK OF COMMON WORSHIP:

FROM 1789 TO 1970

by Peter C. Bower

Nearly three decades ago, four cornerstone documents undergirding the Church's worship were published within only a few years:

- a translation of the Bible: New Revised Standard Version (NRSV): an English translation of the Bible published by the National Council of Churches (1989)
- Directory for Worship (published by the Presbyterian Church (U.S.A.), 1989)
- *The Presbyterian Hymnal: Hymns, Psalms, and Spiritual Songs* (1990)
- a service book: *Book of Common Worship* (published by the Presbyterian Church (U.S.A.), 1993)

All four of the above bedrock mainstays are equally valuable but the Bible is more equal. Reformed worship is rooted in the words and world of the Bible which engenders our human words that form the basic texts of liturgy.

In addition, three complementary resources augmented these four foundational documents:

- Supplemental Liturgical Resource on Daily Prayer (published by the Presbyterian Church (U.S.A.), 1987)
- Revised Common Lectionary (published by the Consultation on Common Texts (CCT), 1992)
- *The Psalter: Songs and Canticles for Singing* (published by Westminster/John Knox Press, 1993)

Notably, all seven of these essential building blocks for the Church's worship appeared in print within a half dozen years, an unprecedented period in the worship life of American Presbyterians for such a cluster of primary liturgical resources to be produced.

Some might say the publication of all these liturgical resources within this brief time frame could be characterized as the Presbyterian Church's "Vatican II moment". For others, however, that might be too unnerving if not too frightening a phrase to employ, so let's recast it as a *kairos* moment of opportunity for growth in the Church's faith and life à la *lex orandi, lex credendi*.

Since that flurry of publications, the Presbyterian Church (U.S.A.) has witnessed a new hymnal, *Glory to God: The Presbyterian Hymnal* (2013), and a revised edition of the *Book of Common Worship* (2018) which refined some sections, sanded some rough edges, and buffed other elements of the 1993 edition. What initiated the ferment resulting in this constellation of liturgical volumes? What were starting points and what were turning points? In the words of T. S. Eliot:

> "What we call the beginning is often the end
> And to make an end is to make a beginning.
> The end is where we start from . . . " ("Little Gidding," V:1-3)

Our end is the beginning of remembering that what always was at stake for Reformed congregations was not a service book but the authority to choose their own forms free *from* outside intervention (especially a monarch or a state church), and the freedom *to* establish forms grounded in scripture (as opposed to human-created texts, as evidenced in the 19th century brouhaha regarding hymn texts).[1] One could say that our Reformed ancestors were, in effect, the "inventors" of

---

[1] The following history might be augmented by reading chapter 8, especially p. 157ff.

placing a service book in the hands of the people. That is precisely what psalm books were: a prayer book for the people.

But one example with which to reckon is that for decades, the prescribed forms of the Lord's Prayer and Ten Commandments were woven into the fabric of corporate worship in the Reformed tradition. And, for evidence that Reformed congregations were originally sustained by set prayers, one need look no farther than the title of Calvin's Genevan service book: *The Forme of Prayers.* When Calvin served as pastor to the French exiles in Strasbourg, he used (with some alterations) a French translation of Martin Bucer's German service book (including its printed prayers!), which Calvin brought with him when he returned to Geneva. Subsequently, Calvin's version, *La Forme des Prières* ("*The Form of Prayers*") became the standard for most Reformed churches on the continent and beyond.

Bear in mind that such liturgical consistency was made possible only by the printing press' breakthrough ability to mass produce books which, ironically, meant that the people's prayer book, to the astonishment of many people nowadays, was an innovation of the Reformation, because prior to the printing press, service books were in the hands of only the clergy.

After 1560, John Knox introduced in Scotland *The Form of Prayers* or *Book of Common Order* as it was sometimes called. Regarding this service book, William D. Maxwell wrote

> We must also remember that this 'service book' was not a fixed and absolute formulary, but rather a standard of worship which left much to the minister's discretion. At the same time, it is a mistake to imagine either that it was a mere directory or that it was never in wide use. It continued to be the standard of worship in Scotland for over eighty years after the establishment of the Reformation.[2]

---

[2] William D. Maxwell, *An Outline of Christian Worship: Its Development and Forms* (London: Oxford University Press, 1960), 127.

The sixteenth century repeatedly testifies to the necessity for order and form, as evidenced by its kid-glove treatment of the Roman Canon or prayer of consecration, now commonly called a eucharistic prayer. One could characterize sixteenth century worship in the Reformed churches as a series of reworked structured forms and fixed prayers. So the antipathy which some Presbyterians of the nineteenth and twentieth centuries brandish toward printed prayers and fixed structures does not categorically reflect concerns of the sixteenth century reformers.

The seventeenth century, however, witnessed the decline of service books when in 1644 the Westminster Assembly, unable to agree on the composition of a new service book, agreed to a compromise between those who desired to maintain service books and those who preferred to discard such. The unanticipated consequence was the birth of the Westminster Directory of Worship, characterized by James Hastings Nichols as:

> not a liturgy or service book at all, after the fashion of Calvin, Cranmer, or Knox. . . It is not a service book to be placed in the hands of all literate worshippers, but a manual for the discretionary use of ministers . . . Such deep distrust of forms of prayer . . . would have astonished the Reformers of the sixteenth century.[3]

The more Puritan than Presbyterian Westminster Directory, in effect, marked the end of service book use within English-speaking areas of the Reformed tradition.

In 1786, American Presbyterians appointed a committee to revise the 1644 Westminster Directory for Worship. The committee commenced the task with some lofty aims of shaping worship which gave worthy homage to God, but also services that impress the worshiper and evoke sincere devotion as well as unify the worship of American Presbyterians around some acceptable norms. The end product, however, seems far short of such intentions.

---

[3] James Hastings Nichols, *Corporate Worship in the Reformed Tradition* (Philadelphia: Westminster Press, 1965) 99-100.

The mood from the outset opposed even a suggested liturgy as well as "pattern prayers" (i.e., examples) and explicit instructions regarding how worship should proceed, or even models for ministers to study or to use. Not only were the revision committee's proposed pattern prayers proscribed, but the topics of prayer listed in the 1644 Directory were excluded, opening the door to increased ministerial freedom regarding public prayer, particularly the typical twelve-to-twenty-minute pastoral prayer. The extent to which prepared, much less set, prayers were frowned upon is exemplified by the fact that despite the revision committee's advocacy, like the Westminster Directory, of including the Lord's Prayer in public worship, even that element was deleted in the final version.

Though the eventual Directory, adopted in 1789, duplicated the Westminster Directory's call for frequent celebration of the Lord's Supper, it left the frequency decision in congregational hands ("local option") which, in effect, supported infrequency, certainly less than quarterly. And it maintained the words which extolled the values of "sacramental seasons": rural churches' prevalent custom for a series of services surrounding the Sacrament which attracted crowds of worshipers from the countryside, which seemed to some to turn the sanctity of the Sacrament into a spectacle to see.

Unsurprisingly, in striving to shy away from prescriptive directions and to shun texts, the adopted Directory of 1789 simply left many matters indefinite, though the Directory did call for more attention to music while discouraging the practice of "lining out." In short, as Julius Melton wrote, "the denomination produced what could almost be described as a non-directive Directory." Two centuries later, Charles Briggs of Union Seminary in New York City took the [1789] Directory for Worship to task for "the extremely permissive character of the American Directory, which he felt allowed dangerous individualism in worship."[4] A minimal minimum set of standards seemed to be the acceptable order of the day.

Until the late nineteenth century, little attention or even interest was given to the Directory though the church had experienced the eighteenth

---

[4] Julius Melton, *Presbyterian Worship in America: Changing Patterns Since 1787* (Richmond, Virginia: John Knox Press, 1967), 27, 118.

century psalmody-hymnody controversy, and the nineteenth century muddled through a dispute regarding instrumental music. But then the materializing of underlying discontent and maverick publications ended the "out of sight, out of mind" attitude toward prayer books.

Many credit Old School minister Charles W. Baird's (1828-1877) *Eutaxia* ("Orderliness") or *Presbyterian Liturgies: Historical Sketches* (1855) with sparking renewed interest in worship. And Baird soon followed with another work: *A Book of Public Prayer Compiled from the Authorized Formularies of Worship of the Presbyterian Church as Prepared by the Reformers Calvin, Knox. Bucer, and Others* (1857). This compilation of a book of prayers and forms (though no reference to the Christian year, or even Christmas or Easter, but still an advance upon all predecessors) spurred responses from both sides of the aisle: some supporting uniform forms of worship (including publication of a manuals for public worship) while others vehemently opposed.

Critics, even within the church, unsurprisingly declared that compared to most Christian worship, Presbyterian worship was a gallimaufry of disordered, colorless, drab, pedantic patchwork lacking in devotion, and far too dominated by clergy. Such a hodgepodge, however, also provided a *kairos* moment, a teachable moment for sweeping liturgical reform in the Presbyterian Church. Opportunity thus knocked for revitalizing worship life in Presbyterian churches. And, those answering the call included a cluster of ministers who came together in common purpose in 1897 as the first Church Service Society in America, a branch of the Scottish Church Service Society founded in 1865. This had been

> formed by three young ministers of the Church of Scotland in 1865 – a time when Presbyterian worship had lost some of its classic expressions and had become rambling and verbose. Their object was 'the study of the liturgies – ancient and modern – of the Christian church, with a view to the preparation and publication of forms of prayer for Public Worship and services for the

administration of the Sacraments, the celebration of marriage, the burial of the dead etc.' [5]

Scottish worship renewal provided not only the model for the Church Service Society in America, but also some of its sources. In 1898, Presbyterian elder and Philadelphia banker Benjamin Bartis Comegys (1819-1900) prepared and published the inaugural American edition of the Scottish Church Service Society's manual entitled *Euchologion. A Book of Common Order* for the study and discussion of worship. Publication of this edition coincided with the organization of the Church Service Society in America (in which Comegys was actively involved) whose intended goal was to build on the constitutional document of the Directory for Worship to establish some "forms of service in an orderly worship."

The first meeting of the Church Service Society in America found among its members not only Comegys but also John DeWitt of Princeton Seminary, T. Ralston Smith, co-author of the 1861 worship manual *Presbyterian's Handbook,* and social justice activist Robert Ellis Thompson. The two foremost and effective advocates of worship reform were the president, Louis Benson (1855-1930), a Philadelphia pastor, and Henry van Dyke (1852-1933), a New York poet-pastor. Julius Melton compactly documents the Society's work, and shows how the Society blended with other efforts to produce the 1906 *Book of Common Worship.*[6]

In delineating the origins of the Church Service Society, and its brief three-year tenure, 1897-1900, Sidney Finch unearthed the rhizomes of the twentieth century liturgical renewal. The initial seed was planted during the Society's founding meeting on March 2, 1897 at the Brick Presbyterian Church in New York City where the Society adopted a "Statement of Principles," of which Article IX aimed to prepare "forms of service in an orderly worship." Prior to embarking on this task, however, the Society undertook "an inquiry into the present conduct of public worship in the Presbyterian Church to find out how far a

---

[5] "History and Purpose," the Church Service Society, last modified November 15, 2007, http://churchservicesociety.org/history.

[6] Melton, *Presbyterian Worship in America*, 118-124.

"common and distinctive" service existed, and the "degree of uniformity" in conduct of worship.

Though the Church Service Society faded into the pages of history within a couple of years, its enduring influence was manifested by the 1903 General Assembly which appointed a special committee to prepare a "book of simple forms and services." Moreover, the Society's import extended into the work of the General Assembly's eleven-member special committee in which six of the eleven had been active in the Society, especially the two most influential members of the special committee, Henry van Dyke (named chairman) and Louis Benson (principal organizer of the first Church Service Society).[7]

The 1903 special committee encountered a formidable task from the outset because the Directory for Worship had been last revised at its adoption in 1789, and provided only vague guidance (as noted above) or – in the case of ordination – no guidance at all. Nevertheless, over the next three years, the special committee persevered in preparing a "book of simple forms and services" to set before the 1906 General Assembly meeting in Des Moines, Iowa. Henry van Dyke presented the final report of the Special Committee on Forms and Services, including *The Book of Common Worship* which, as directed by the 1905 General Assembly, declared on the title page, "For Voluntary Use" – a sign of the still problematic issues for Presbyterians in developing a service book.

And, indeed, the proposed service book was hardly popular. Prior to the General Assembly, the book was attacked in the church press and triggered twenty presbytery overtures asking that either public release of the book be suppressed or the project terminated. The animated floor debate stretched across two sessions over two days, punctuated by applause and cheers, boos and hisses, and a copy of the book flung through the air [a redux of the "Jenny Geddes incident"? In 1637, she allegedly tossed a stool at the head of the minister in St Giles' Cathedral in objection to the first public use of the Scottish Episcopal Book of Common Prayer in Scotland]. Van Dyke, the press reported, maintained

---

[7] R. Sidney Finch, "The First Church Society," *Reformed Liturgics* 1, no. 2, (1964), 23-33.

his composure through it all, and made his final appeal in terms of "useful forms" and "personal freedoms".

When it became apparent that opponents had sufficient votes to defeat any language that might suggest the book was "authorized" or even "recommended" by the Assembly, van Dyke promptly agreed to the most neutral language possible, and with that, debate ended and *The Book of Common Worship* was printed with the title page reading: "Prepared by the Committee of the General Assembly of the Presbyterian Church in the U.S.A. For Voluntary Use."[8]

On one hand, the saga of Presbyterians' long and problematic history with prayer books and liturgical forms continued. And, indeed, the 1906 BCW functioned as more of a manual for ministers who exercised considerable freedom regarding its use.

On the other hand, the pioneering *Book of Common Worship* (1906), influenced by the work of the Church Service Society, established a new norm in that since then, Presbyterians have had a denominationally-related service book. The publication of the *The Book of Common Worship* (1906) was, therefore, a momentous milestone in the reshaping of modern Presbyterian worship. In 1932, the text was revised – the last edition in which van Dyke had a personal hand, and the copyright lodged with the Board of Publications. Concurrently, the General Assembly of the Presbyterian Church in the United States (the "southern" Presbyterians) adopted the 1932 *Book of Common Worship*, approving it only for optional use.

In 1941, however, the *Book of Common Worship* attained status as an "official publication" of the PC(USA), an historic feat engineered by highly influential Stated Clerk William Barrow Pugh (1889-1950). By pressing for inclusion of the ordinal – forms for ordaining ministers, official services requiring adherence with no variation, the 1941 General Assembly added the *Book of Common Worship* to publications classified as "official" though when some people objected, Pugh straddled a high wire

---

[8] Kenneth J. Ross. "Form and Freedom: Henry van Dyke and the 1906 Book of Common Worship." Presbyterian Historical Society Blog. June 14, 2016. https://www.history.pcusa.org/blog/2016/06/form-and-freedom-henry-van-dyke-and-1906-book-common-worship.

in clarifying that forms other than the ordinal were for voluntary use (so only part of the book was "official"?). The phrase "For Voluntary Use" on the title page was replaced by the telling words "Approved by the General Assembly of the PC(USA)."

Accompanying the action to recognize the BCW as "official" was the shifting of supervision of the BCW to the Office of the General Assembly. The 1941 General Assembly also established a committee, working with the Stated Clerk, to bring to the Assembly at stated intervals any suggested changes in the 1932 BCW for approval. This unwittingly set in motion what eventually became known as the 1946 *Book of Common Worship.*[9]

Suggested changes in the 1932 BCW turned out to be far more substantive than even the committee imagined. For starters, "The Psalter" and "Ancient Hymns and Canticles" were omitted because both were included in *The Hymnal.* In contrast, to express the present needs in society, the "Treasury of Prayers" were substantially enlarged with "Prayers for the Christian Year," "Prayers for the Year," and others. It also broke new ground regarding wider church relationships in explicitly seeking balance in adhering to "the Standards of our own Church" and recognizing our part in the "Holy Catholic or Universal Church."

More importantly, the *Book of Common Worship* (1946) was heavily influenced by the Church of Scotland's *Book of Church Order* (1940) both in its liturgical forms and liturgical language, notably in recovery of "Prayers for the Christian Year" and adoption of the Scots' two-year lectionary so that "more careful consideration [could] be given to the reading of Holy Scripture in public worship."

Most importantly, the 1946 BCW drew mightily from the Scottish 1940 BCO for the "Lord's Supper or Holy Communion." Though why the curious decision to truncate Calvin's hoped for regular Lord's Day service of Word and Sacrament by curtailing the Word aspect and naming the service "Lord's Day or Holy Communion"? Also, the service is entombed in the middle of the book following five "Orders of Public

---

[9] Office of the General Assembly, Presbyterian Church of the United States of America, *Minutes of General Assembly*, Volume 1 (Philadelphia: Office of General Assembly, 1941), 196-197.

Worship," so it is hardly surprising that the "Lord's Supper or Holy Communion" received less than frequent use.

Likewise, buried in the Preface is a matter-of-fact note about this most significant change for the first time in an American Book of Common Worship: Word and Sacrament were structurally united in the same service. The Preface references this most extraordinary inclusion in a low-keyed reference that

> Another order [of worship] is given which conforms closely to that used by the Reformers, giving a complete and unified Communion Service. [an understated understatement?][10]

An indication of the now radically evolving liturgical situation in the church are some of the striking contrasts between the Westminster Directory of 1644 and the *Book of Common Worship* of 1946, which included:

- Westminster is strictly a directory; the BCW is a full service book, replete with responses, rubrics, forms, and orders (against which Westminster specifically inveighs).
- Westminster breathes a Puritan spirit; the BCW a Presbyterian spirit.
- Westminster assigns choice of scripture to preachers, though counseling sequential or "in course" reading week-by-week; the BCW provides a complete two-year lectionary, according to the seasons of the Christian Year (not even mentioned by Westminster)[11]

Though the *Book of Common Worship* had gained approval as an "official publication" in 1941, it had not yet attained wide acceptance, and the 1946 BCW did not appreciably increase its endorsement or use.

---

[10] *The Book of Common Worship* (Philadelphia: Publication Division of the Board of Christian Education of the Presbyterian Church in the United States of America, 1946), viii.

[11] Horace Thaddeus Allen, Jr., "A Companion to *The Worshipbook*: A Theological Introduction to Worship in the Reformed Tradition," (Ph.D. dissertation, Union Theological Seminary, New York, 1980), 8.

Like the 1906 service book, the 1946 service book found its way to the hands of ministers for whom the book served as more of a manual for ministers and, therefore, it never became the people's pew book.

Several silent years passed, but in 1955, as a means to revise the *Book of Common Worship* (1946), the General Assembly reactivated the Committee on the Book of Common Worship which met that fall. The Committee quickly concluded that the 1946 BCW necessitated a prior revision of the constitutional standards for worship codified in the Puritan-based "Directory for Worship" which had lain substantially unchanged since 1789. In addition, the Directory and the 1946 BCW were out of alignment in a number of places. So, the Committee asked and received authorization from the 1956 General Assembly to study and probably revise the *Book of Common Worship* (1946): "the time had come for a complete reexamination of the Book of Common Worship, the practices of our churches in worship, together with the historical and theological bases"[12]

Meanwhile, the three major American Presbyterian branches – United Presbyterian Church of North America, Presbyterian Church U.S.A. ("northern stream"), and the Presbyterian Church U.S. ("southern stream") who shared a common heritage had been engaged in years of conversation about reuniting. Prudently, the 1957 PC(USA) General Assembly approved the formation of a Joint Committee on Worship (JCW) composed of representatives of all three communions.

In 1958, the United Presbyterian Church of North America and the Presbyterian Church U.S.A. ("northern stream") reunited to form the United Presbyterian Church in the United States of America (UPCUSA, 1958-1983). Though negotiations continued with the Presbyterian Church U.S. (PCUS) ("southern stream") who were not yet part of the UPCUSA, all three communions agreed on standards for a "transitional directory" until the new directory was approved. In essence, the "temporary" directory was a patchwork of the directories of all three church bodies, intended to break no new ground, so nothing original was

---

[12] Office of the General Assembly, Presbyterian Church of the United States of America, *Minutes of General Assembly,* Volume 1 (Philadelphia: Office of General Assembly, 1956), 219.

composed, but it did include a complete set of liturgies, thus a book of services.

Also in 1957, the Church Service Society in America was reborn (1957-1962). Though an autonomous group, the Society considered itself a daughter organization of the Church Service Society of Scotland, founded in 1865, and a sibling of the former Church Service Society in America (1897-1900) which had provided much behind-the-scenes inspiration and bulwark of the *Book of Common Worship* (1906). The reborn Society brought together pastors, teachers, musicians, and others from varied backgrounds.

The guiding light of this rebirth was the Dean of the Chapel at Princeton University, Ernest Gordon (1916-2002). His "Suggested Constitution" of the Society that accompanied his letter of invitation (14 December 1956) to prospective members stated that the Society intended "to study the liturgies – ancient and modern – of the Christian Church, and the principles of public worship, to encourage order, reverence, beauty, and reality in worship."

During this period of the regenerated Society, it issued the first of their occasional newsletters in November of 1958, followed by a newsletter in March of 1959, including a seven-page paper by Horace T. Allen, Jr. on the "Service of Ordination." In February of 1960, the newsletter was officially labeled "Sanctus." This lasted until 1963, when it morphed into "Reformed Liturgics," edited by Carl D. Reimers. Throughout the 1960s, "Sanctus" and annual meetings of the Society helped to deepen and spread the insights of the group. Some members of the Joint Committee on Worship (JCW) were officers of the Church Service Society (e.g., both Scott Brenner and Lewis Briner (1917-2003) were governing council members, and Dwight Moody Chalmers (1899-1974) was a member of the Society). Contact between the JCW and the Society involved bi-lateral discussions and counsel on various matters liturgical.

The revived Church Service Society also influenced Reformed worship renewal by highlighting the work of its members such as Donald R. Kocher (1926-) "Towards a Revision of the Directory of Worship" (1957) as well as ecclesiologists such as Geddes MacGregor whose major work on worship, *The Coming Reformation* (Philadelphia: Westminster,

1960), advocated celebrating the Lord's Supper ("the heart of the Christian liturgy") every Sunday. The Society also indirectly advanced its liturgical influence on the Joint Committee on Worship and the Presbyterian Church by engendering dialogue about worship in the popular "Monday Morning: The Magazine for Presbyterian Leaders," and by highlighting the multi-volume series "Ecumenical Studies in Worship." These included Oscar Cullman and Franz Leenhardt's *Essays on the Lord's Supper,* in which they asserted that the New Testament provides overwhelming evidence that Christian gatherings normatively included the breaking of the bread.[13] As with the *Book of Common Worship* (1906), the Church Service Society and its members' insights were welcomed, valued, and influential in the work of the Joint Committee on Worship.

As the Committee's work proceeded on drafting the new Directory for Worship (whose principal writer was Robert McAfee Brown (1920-2001)), they also included appraisals, counsel, and recommendations from more than 100 theologians, professors of theology and worship, and professors of church history (a polar opposite approach from that employed for the 1946 *Book of Common Worship*).

As a constitutional document that shapes the church's worship, a directory for worship provides the theological framework that guides and, perhaps, prescribes orders of worship, congregational song, biblical readings, music, liturgical texts, worship environment, and so forth. Theoretically, a directory for worship furnishes a foundation for preparing a (revised) service book but, operatively, a good deal of the service book's drafting occurred prior to the 1961 General Assembly's adoption of the revised Directory. That matter, however, is addressed in other works (e.g., Harry Winter and Stanley Hall)[14] but it is fair to state that the drafting of a service book influenced the writing of the 1961

---

[13] Oscar Cullmann and Franz J. Leenhardt, *Essays on the Lord's Supper.* Ecumenical Studies in Worship, No. 1 (Richmond: John Knox Press, 1958).
[14] See Harry E. Winter "Presbyterians Pioneer the Vatican II Sunday Lectionary: There Worship Models Converge," *Journal of Ecumenical Studies*, 2001 and Stanley R. Hall, "The American Presbyterian Directory for Worship: History of a Liturgical Strategy," Ph.D. Diss., University of Notre Dame, 1990.

Directory, exemplifying the proverbial "placing the cart before the horse."[15]

The 1961 Directory for Worship emphasized worship as an act of the church, that worship was the congregation's response, that the fundamental structure of worship consisted of God's action and the Church's response (i.e., participation by the people). Moreover, the 1961 Directory underscored public worship as communal or corporate, and the Lord's Day (Sunday) service as the primary template or model for other occasions of worship:

The core issue addressed though was worship on the Lord's Day, particularly the normative model of Word and Sacrament, of preaching the Word of God and celebrating the Lord's Supper. This is the most significant "innovation" in the 1961 Directory. In part, drawing on the spirit of the Reformation manifested by Calvin's desire (and Knox to some extent) for weekly celebration of the Lord's Supper, for the first time, an explicit statement in a directory for worship advocated weekly celebration of the Lord's Supper – thus, linking Lord Day with Lord's Supper – though, admittedly, still equivocally phrased to allow some "either-or" wiggle room:

> The session shall [*i.e., must*] determine how often the opportunity to partake of [the Lord's Supper] may be provided in each church. It is fitting that it be observed as frequently as on each Lord's Day, and it ought to be observed frequently and regularly enough that it is seen as a proper part of, and not, an addition to, the worship of God by his people. (1961 Directory, 6.1)

The Directory's chapter 6, "The Sacrament of the Lord's Supper" contrasts the "once for all" character of Baptism with "the continual spiritual nourishment" of the Supper, by which God "sustains" his followers "in the fellowship of the body of Christ" (1961 Directory

---

[15] This same sequence was repeated with the 1993 BCW and 1990 Directory. The lengthy process that led to the 1993 BCW was well underway at the time of the writing of the 1990 directory, and so as in the previous generations of these documents, it was primarily the service book that influenced the directory, not the other way around.

21.01). Indeed, as in Calvin's paraphrase of the Didache, the Lord's Supper is "an enactment of the gospel." It also voices an eschatological note ("until Christ comes again") in a communal context of "the people of God" participating, in the service "as members of a corporate fellowship," including "the communion of saints" (1961 Directory 21.03). Both the corporate sense and active participation by the community of faith in the Lord's Supper contrast starkly with the individual tone of the 1789 Directory (chapter 9). Moreover, the sustenance theme in the 1961 Directory serves as the base for the frequency of celebrating the Lord's Supper "as frequently as each Lord's Day" (1961 Directory 21.01), so that "it is seen as a proper part of [*i.e., not an isolated action*], and not an addition to, the worship of God by his people." This contrasts with the 1789 Directory's simple call for "frequent" celebration.

In 1961, the revised Directory for Worship of the UPCUSA was approved, providing the theological foundation for revising the Book of Common Worship which would manifest the Directory for Worship. And, in 1963, the Board of Christian Education (often engaged in a fractious relationship with the JCW) published a thirty-eight-page "Study Guide for the Directory for Worship" authored by Norman Langford.[16]

Meanwhile, although the Presbyterian Church of the United States (PCUS) worked with the JCW for several years, agreement on a joint Directory for Worship could not be reached. So, in 1963, the (PCUS) (a.k.a. "the southern stream" of Presbyterians, 1861-1983) adopted a new "Book of Church Order" and a revision of "The Directory for the Worship and Work of the Church." The title alone suggests an expanded notion of worship which continued through succeeding decades.

Key differences that evidence the challenge of finding a middle ground with the UPCUSA stand out in several areas, such as the jurisdiction of sources:

> The northern directory supplied models and suggestions for ordered worship; the PCUS directory assigned responsibility for "sequence and proportion of the

---

[16] Norman Langford, "Study Guide for the Directory for Worship" (Philadelphia: Board of Christian Education, United Presbyterian Church in the U.S.A., 1963).

various parts of public worship" to the pastor, "in consultation with the Church Session (1963 PCUS Directory, 202-2)[17]

Unsurprisingly then, the only "forms" included within the PCUS Directory were "formulaic" questions and exhortations for Baptism or admission to the Lord's Supper in concert with preceding directories of the PCUS.

Of most importance is the noticeable lack of even a hint of a normative Word and Sacrament Lord's Day service. The PCUS Directory presents a minimalist definition of "frequency" in affirming that the Lord's Supper is to be celebrated "frequently, but at least quarterly" (1963 PCUS Directory, 202-3). "Both directories acknowledged the diversity of viewpoint and practice within their respective denominations: PCUS 1963 by reticence in its prescriptions, and UPCUSA 1961 by its careful modulations of requirements, permissions, and advice."[18]

Despite such divergences in their respective directories, the PCUS and the UPCUSA continued to work together in producing a common service book. And, in 1962, the Cumberland Presbyterian Church joined the two teams representing the denominations on the JCW in revising the Book of Common Worship, now named "*The Worshipbook*," whose principal writer was David G. Buttrick (1927-2017). This book would eventually come to publication in 1970.

In autumn 1961, the reinvigorated Church Service Society began to exercise its influence again in a multitude of ways. For example, in the spring of 1963, the Society's occasional newsletter "Sanctus" was succeeded by the journal "Reformed Liturgics" which published six volumes (from 1963 to 1969) that included, among other topics, detailed studies of the various Lord's Day Services produced by the Joint Committee on Worship.

---

[17] Stanley R. Hall, "The American Presbyterian Directory for Worship: History of a Liturgical Strategy," (Ph.D. dissertation, University of Notre Dame, 1990), 382.

[18] Hall, "The American Presbyterian Directory for Worship," 400.

In December of 1965, Society member Dwight M. Chalmers presented copies of JCW's provisional Service for the Lord's Day at a Society regional meeting at the First Presbyterian Church of Auburn, Alabama (PCUS). Scott F. Brenner served as a member of JCW. Horace T. Allen, Jr. edited The Church Service Society's journal *Reformed Liturgics* from 1969-1974 and then the renamed iteration of the same journal, *Reformed Liturgy and Music,* until 1975. By 1970, of the twenty-seven Presbyterians involved in the theological preparation of *The Worshipbook*, five were members of the Church Service Society. Shortly thereafter, the Society merged its life (and its journal *Reformed Liturgics*) with the official programmatic work of the United Presbyterian Church in the U.S.A. (and its journal *Reformed Liturgy and Music*). Through the Church Service Society's journal, and its members' presentations, seminars, workshops, and service on committees, the Society directly influenced the JCW and Presbyterian worship more than any other group.

As noted above, the Church Service Society also indirectly influenced the Joint Committee on Worship by highlighting Oscar Cullmann's essays, among others, regarding New Testament evidence that Christian gatherings normatively included the breaking of the bread. Also, Cullmann's claim that the New Testament provides overwhelming evidence that Christian gatherings normatively included the joyful breaking of the bread is embodied in *The Worshipbook*'s normative order of worship and the color of its eucharistic texts. But only one example of how the subtle influence of the Church Service Society was ultimately manifested in *The Worshipbook* is illustrated in the "Invitation to the Lord's Supper" which transmutes from present to future to present to past:

from present experience

> Leader: Friends, this is the joyful feast of the people of God

to an eschatological biblical verse about the *future* messianic banquet: (*Luke 13:29*)

> People: They will come from east and west, and from north and south, and sit at table in the kingdom God

to present experience of an invitation to the Lord's table: (Directory for Worship, 21.03)

> Leader: This is the Lord's table. Our Savior invites those who trust him to share the feast which he has prepared

to a remembered past about the risen Christ, a remembering (not the death of Christ but) in the new context of all that Christ's life has accomplished

> Leader: According to Luke, when our risen Lord was at table with his disciples, he took the bread, and blessed and broke it, and gave it to them. And their eyes were opened and they recognized him. (*The Worshipbook*, p. 34)

The mood is "joyful." The gathering of people is for a meal, specifically a "feast." And, the Lord's Supper is linked with the presence of the risen Christ (i.e., with resurrection appearances)

The prior *Book of Common Worship* (1946) opens the "Invitation" with biblical exhortations to find rest in the Lord as well as the Bread of Life (Matthew 11:28-29; John 6:35, 37b, Matthew 5:6, KJV) followed by the Pauline "words of institution" (I Corinthians 11:23-26, KJV) that invoke scriptural warrant for the Sacrament. A stark contrast to the "Invitation" encompassed in *The Worshipbook* which celebrates a meal in the joyful expectation of the return of Christ without any reference to his death — thus, a polar opposite mood.

In 1966, the JCW continued its mode of receptivity (contra the 1946 BCW's lack of transparent process) to critiques, comments, and suggestions by publishing *The Book of Common Worship: Provisional Services and Lectionary for the Christian Year*, which stated

> The present book . . . contains, in addition to a revision of the [booklet] "Service for the Lord's Day"[1964], other services for congregational use. This book is not the last step. The title includes the word 'provisional,' which is to say that the Joint Committee on Worship

> [JCW] again invites the guidance and the insights of the
> people of the churches. . . . Presbyterians value variety
> and *freedom* [emphasis added] in worship, but they
> emphasize equally the virtue of *orderliness* [emphasis
> added]. The services in this book provide a pattern for
> responsible planning of worship.[19]

Upon Horace Allen's return to the United States in April 1970 from serving as warden in Scotland's Iona Abbey, he accepted an appointment as the first Director of the Joint Office of Worship (JOW) of both the northern and southern streams of the Presbyterian Church (UPCUSA and PCUS), a position that he held until 1975. Allen's initial and formidable task as Director of JOW was to introduce the new service book (*The Worshipbook*, 1970), the likes of which had never been seen in the history of the Presbyterian Church,

In conducting churchwide seminars on the Joint Committee on Worship's final product, *The Worshipbook* (1970), congregations, presbyteries, seminaries, and summer conferees finally encountered the two resources of the Directory (1961) and *The Worshipbook* (1970) for the first time. The contents seemed to some as monumental changes that represented a shifting of liturgical tectonic plates that challenged the seven last words of the Church: "We've never done it this way before," at least not among English-speaking Presbyterians.

The earth-moving reformations embodied in *The Worshipbook* (1970) were presciently foreshadowed in 1967 by Julius Melton's concise comparison of the 1961 Directory with the 1789 Directory:

> Among the important differences between the new
> Directory and the old [1789] were these: The 1961
> Directory admitted the desirability of freedom in worship
> but stressed that a more responsible ordering of worship
> was needed. . . ., this Directory stated that worship should
> draw its order and content not only from Scripture but
> also from the historical experience and resources of
> Christianity. The service was now explicitly called the

---

[19] *The Book of Common Worship: Provisional Services and Lectionary for the Christian Year* (Philadelphia: The Westminster Press, 1966), 5.

people's service, thus ruling out the possibility of viewing it as a meeting at which they were silent spectators. Increased attention to the Christian year was defended, and readings from both Testaments were seen as the proper pattern. The Directory also now called for a unison confession of sin and for an assurance of pardon by the minister. . . . Ways were suggested for the people to respond following their hearing of the Word in the sermon and the sacrament – namely, their saying the Creed, making their offerings, and joining in intercessory prayers. This was in contrast to the earlier idea of a quick conclusion following the sermon. Indicative of how greatly Presbyterians had been influenced by research into liturgies and Reformed history was the new Directory's emphasis on the unity of Word and sacrament. *The sacraments*, it insisted, were integral to the full ordering of Christian worship and not occasional appendages. While they might not be celebrated each Sunday, they were to be viewed as the natural accompaniment of an act of worship and not as separate occasions.[20]

The chief cornerstone of *The Worshipbook*'s role in liturgical renewal, undoubtedly, is its reunification of the historic Word-Sacrament service (a structural component) with the Lord's Day in Reformed worship, succinctly elucidated by Horace Allen:

> . . . it is not the case that 'Sunday is a little Easter,' but that 'that Easter is a big Sunday' . . .and the church's worship on that day must inevitably focus on the risen Lord who is 'invisibly present' (Barth) and, therefore, must include as its inevitable climax that repeated and commanded event by which the church has always and

---

[20] Julius Melton, *Presbyterian Worship in America* (Richmond: John Knox Press, 1967), 140-41.

everywhere celebrated that promised presence, the sacrament of the Lord's Supper.[21]

Unquestionably, the most enduring contribution of *The Worshipbook* is the recovery of the Lord's Day service of Word and Sacrament.

Additional principal foundational blocks on which *The Worshipbook* was constructed include:

- interrelated components of calendar (i.e., liturgical year) and a common lectionary (a 3-year cycle of readings in this case)
- increased and widespread participation by the people and lay leadership which engaged if not all then certainly many more of the people of God in worship.
- restoration of the vernacular language texts:

> The vernacular language had to be on the lips of all the people–the liturgical texts placed in their hands and turned into song. It generally comes as a sharp surprise to modern heirs of John Calvin that he attached such significance to the use of people's service books and singing the service.

> Clearly therefore it was necessary to translate the Bible and the liturgy. The next step was to print it and put it in the people's hands. It was also necessary to compose or arrange music and then to teach it.[22]

It would be remiss here to ignore a critical omission in *The Worshipbook*–no explicit Psalter–making it a most atypical Presbyterian book. Though context can offer multiple explanations regarding competing new translations at the time, no universally accepted musical system, and so forth, nevertheless, as Horace Allen laments, "to lose the

---

[21] Horace T. Allen, Jr., "Lord's Day–Lord's Supper," *Reformed Liturgy & Music* 18, no. 4 (Fall 1984), 164.

[22] Horace T. Allen, Jr., "Catching Up to Calvin: Liturgical Developments Among Presbyterians," *Worship* 48, no. 10 (December 1994), 581-582.

Psalter, either totally, or just as music, is to suffer what must be understood as a devotional, liturgical privation of the first order, for those 150 Psalms comprise, in Bonhoeffer's' powerful phrase, 'the Prayer Book of the Bible.' "[23]

Nevertheless, over the span of several centuries and liturgical movements, *The Worshipbook* emerged as a culmination of almost 200 years of liturgical developments which set the stage for the proliferation of the next stage of liturgical resources in the 1980s and 1990s, notably the BCW (1993) and, now, the Revised BCW (2018).

Over the past couple of centuries, liturgical developments among Presbyterians groped their way through lingering shadows of the past, meandered through valleys of apathy, and zig-zagged across roiling rivers of contention by balancing on stepping stones of directories and service books to find a way from the Directory in 1789 to *The Worshipbook* in 1970. Undoubtedly, the bookend documents of the Directory for Worship (1961) and *The Worshipbook* (1970) significantly contributed to the liturgical renascence of the church during the 1970s, which then became an unexpected accelerant to the production of a raft of primary liturgical resources within a half dozen years in the late 1980s and early 1990s. And so, we reach our ending which is the beginning of a new period of liturgical ferment in the name of Christ.

---

[23] Horace T. Allen, Jr., "Is There an Emerging Ecumenical Consensus Concerning the Liturgy?", *Union Seminary Quarterly Review* 31, no. 3 (Spring 1976), 167.

7. A SACRAMENTAL CONTINENTAL DIVIDE

INVITATION TO CHRIST AS A
WATERSHED DOCUMENT FOR THE PC(USA)

by Tom M. Trinidad

In 2006 the 217th General Assembly (GA) of the Presbyterian Church (U.S.A.) (PC(USA)) received and endorsed the dissemination of a report and a pastoral letter for study throughout the denomination. The report, to be published in the form of a sixty-seven-page booklet, was entitled *Invitation to Christ: Font and Table; A Guide to Sacramental Practices.*

Eight years earlier, the 210th GA (1998) had received an overture to amend the constitutional Directory for Worship. It sought to change the language inviting people to the Lord's Supper. The overture was referred to what was then called the Office of Theology and Worship. The 214th GA (2002) referred another overture to this same office, this time concerning the relationship between baptism and the Lord's Supper as it related to the catechumenate. This same GA authorized "a full and substantive study of the sacraments both within the Reformed tradition and in the ecumenical context, in order to help the church discern the history and theology of baptism and the Lord's Supper, as well as their appropriate relationship."[1]

The Sacraments Study Group (SSG) was formed in 2003 with a three-year tenure to conduct this study and respond to these overtures. During its work, in 2004 the 216th GA referred another overture to the SSG. This overture was essentially the same as the original 1998 overture, using slightly different language to achieve the same end.

The General Assembly understood that the questions posed to it were not merely pastoral or practical matters, but a theological inquiry requiring an answer drawn from biblical studies, soteriology, ecclesiology, history, eschatology, hermeneutics, ecumenism, social theory, anthropology, and ritual studies at least. The Sacraments Study Group consisted of pastors, professors, denominational theologians, independent scholars, and ecumenical partners. I was privileged to be among them.

In the language of the day, the question raised among Presbyterians had to do with "open table" practice. In earlier days, "open table" was a question about whether Christians of differing denominations could serve one another the Eucharist. "Open table" is still used this way. Later "open table" was a question about whether baptized children who were not confirmed could participate in the Lord's Supper. This usage has less currency today because Presbyterian (and much ecumenical) practice changed in the 1970s and 1980s to permit baptized children to come to the Lord's Supper. This change in practice then spawned the more recent question, which is: Shall unbaptized persons be invited and served Communion at the Lord's Supper? This was the question that had come before the General Assembly starting in 1998.

The Sacraments Study Group made an interesting observation early on. The overtures to the General Assembly came from both prominent tails of our denominational bell curve—the conservative evangelical and the progressive mainline. Both sides were interested in opening the table but for different reasons.

---

[1] Presbyterian Church (U.S.A.), Minutes of the 217th General Assembly, Part 1 (Louisville: Office of the General Assembly, 2006), 1102-1108.

Some conservative churches had adopted variants of the "seeker friendly" church service and delighted in having "unchurched" adults attending worship. In the occasional service of the Lord's Supper, the invitation "to the baptized" alienated those seekers who had "found Christ" but who were not baptized. The proposed condition or qualification for admittance to the Lord's Supper was instead suggested to be "acknowledging Jesus Christ as one's Lord and Savior."

On the progressive side, for some churches which followed the tradition but were also critical of it, it was a matter of justice. How could the church withhold "the grace of the Lord Jesus Christ, the love of God, and the communion of the Holy Spirit" on the basis of a ritual? Throughout the tradition there are examples of the church using ritual exclusion to marginalize minority groups. From this perspective, the practice excluded people and appeared elitist. The proposed condition or qualification for admittance to the Supper was being a "person of faith." This formulation would allow the church to issue an open and gracious invitation and trust an individual's sense of propriety to determine participation.[2]

The Study Group came to view these overtures coming from diverse ecclesial perspectives as sharing a common impulse, namely, the desire to make disciples. Evangelicals wanted new or on-the-way-to-becoming believers to feel included. Progressives hoped all people would feel unconditionally welcome in the church. Both were concerned that restricting participation in the Lord's Supper on the basis of Baptism was inhibiting the formation of disciples.

Issues of discipleship, whether arising out of the priorities of evangelism or justice, are indeed essential to the Gospel. The General Assembly wisely questioned whether such concern is enough to change the inherited practice, and the theology and tradition underpinning it, of ordering the sacraments with baptism preceding the Lord's Supper. This remains a vital question among liturgical leaders and ecumenical conversationalists, but from the perspective of the Sacraments Study Group, "the central invitation that both baptism and the Lord's Supper

---

[2] See the "Rationale" section of Item 13-04 for a description of the overtures addressed by *Invitation to Christ* in the aforementioned Minutes of the 217th General Assembly, Part 1.

extend, together with the Word proclaimed, is the invitation to know the Lord Jesus Christ and to live in the world as his disciples."[3]

Invitation to Christ did not offer an answer to the question per se, nor did it provide a "Presbyterian" sacramental theology. What *Invitation to Christ* did was testify to the power of increased sacramental visibility to evoke sacramental curiosity, to increase sacramental practice, and to deepen sacramental appreciation. It seemed to the Study Group that if the heart of the issue is discipleship, then what better way to initiate that conversation than to invite dialogue about supping with the Lord? If that sounds familiar, it is because it is the story Luke 24:13-35 tells of two of Jesus' followers walking with the hidden Resurrected Christ on the road to Emmaus.

During that walk on the night of his resurrection, the Resurrected Christ explores the thoughts, feelings, and experiences of Cleopas and his unnamed companion. Drawing from the Scriptures, he provides a new interpretation, beginning a new tradition, culminating with a meal during which he took bread, blessed it, broke it, and gave it to the two. At that moment, the text says, their eyes were opened and they recognized him as their Lord Jesus.

Drawing from this account, we determined at the beginning of our work that we would need to study the scriptures and the tradition, listen to our contemporary experiences, dialogue with the wider church, and practice sacramental worship together in order to fully understand disciple-making and faithfully respond to the General Assembly.

To these ends, through six meetings over three years, we read a number of texts in common,[4] assigned particular research topics and presented them to one another, and conducted interviews with people within and beyond our denomination. We focused these activities around four loci: Scripture, History, Theology, and Culture. This curriculum would have been incomplete, and our response to the General Assembly

---

[3] Presbyterian Church (U.S.A), *Invitation to Christ* (Louisville, KY: Office of Theology and Worship, 2006), 6.

[4] Many of these are included in the sections "Suggested for Further Reading" in both original and extended versions of *Invitation to Christ*.

deficient, had we not also practiced daily prayer, baptismal remembrance, and the Lord's Supper together each time we gathered for study.

Our answer to the presenting question about language requiring baptism for admission to the table, and to the larger question of the relationship between Baptism and the Lord's Supper—whether or not one must be baptized in order to partake of the Lord's Supper—as already mentioned, was a non-answer. Instead, we proposed a process. The process we proposed emulated our own process as the Sacraments Study Group. We equipped congregations to complement the experience we had and to discern the most faithful application to their own communities.

Thus the heart of *Invitation to Christ* is the identification of five simple congregational practices: (1) Set the font in full view of the congregation; (2) Open the font and fill it with water on every Lord's Day; (3) Set cup and plate on the Lord's Table on every Lord's Day; (4) Lead appropriate parts of weekly worship from the font and from the table; (5) Increase the number of Sundays on which the Lord's Supper is celebrated. We believed that if congregations would begin these five simple practices, their appetite for sacramental experience and knowledge, indeed for the Risen Christ, would grow. Evangelicals and progressives both would grow as disciples. The rest of the report basically consists of our testimony and the reports of our studies.

The five simple practices as a response to the overtures burst upon us like an angelic chorus toward the conclusion of our three-year study period. Specifically it was on Thursday, February 3, 2005, during our fifth meeting. Our meeting minutes declare: "KEY CHANGE OF COURSE!" in bold. This was a watershed moment in the work of the Sacraments Study Group.

We had already discerned that responding to the invitation to the Supper was just as much an act of faith as responding to the call to Baptism. That the church had failed to recognize this was evidence, not only of the poverty of our sacramental theology, but also of the denial that our culture had entered the liminal space of "post-Christian." People outside the church wanted the sacred encounter offered by the Lord's Supper. What many of them were largely ignorant of, and what many pastors did not routinely practice, was a call to baptismal faithfulness.

People from the post-Christian culture were simply responding to the only invitation they were given, that was to the Lord's Supper.

It also occurred to us that these questions about the relationship between Baptism and the Lord's Supper surfaced because of the increased attention to the Lord's Supper. Congregations seeking to satisfy the contemporary spiritual hunger with the traditional Lord's Supper and to extend a gracious invitation to alienated people rediscovered the baptismal requirement. As we studied this correlation, the Sacraments Study Group reversed the question: Instead of "lowering" the threshold of Communion, why not "elevate" the value of Baptism? Would doing so pique the interest of the uninitiated to explore the font just as the invitation to the Lord's Supper had done the table? We thought it might.

Further, we decided that in our contemporary context we needed to offer language that was affirming of a broader spiritual journey and welcoming of those who did not know how to articulate that journey, even though the weight of traditional theology and ecumenism landed heavily toward the sequence of Baptism before Supper. We felt the responsibility to identify God's always-prevenient grace, gift, and call, regardless of to which invitation an individual might respond. And we needed to affirm the role of the community of faith and the role Baptism has in engrafting one into that community.

A final factor that we deliberated was the politics of the General Assembly. The upcoming General Assembly was going to receive two heavily anticipated reports. One report was on the "peace, unity, and purity" (abbreviated PUP) of the church, the final report of a major task force whose name alluded to a quotation from the ordination vows minsters, elders, and deacons take. The other was a report on language to be used for the triune God. General Assembly "watchers" were eager to see if the "PUP" and Trinity reports would adequately address the concerns of some within the PC(USA) about homosexuality and heterodoxy respectively. *Invitation to Christ*, we feared, would get lost in General Assembly politics if it was not tied to one if not both of these reports, or if it failed to offer something unique.

In our conversations, we recognized that sacramental theology has much to offer relative to the "peace, unity, and purity" of the church, as well as how humanity relates to the triune God. In the end, we pursued the path of "something unique" to distinguish our report from the others. Our report could be unique if it were simple. It could be unique if there were a short and a long version of it—one actionable, the other academic. It could be unique if it were invitational rather than authoritarian.

Following the course of our communal studies and sacramental practice, we accepted that there could not be a single unassailable right answer for the denomination. Congregational culture, ecclesiastical context, and individual pastoral/parishioner relationships are all variables that must be factored into the discernment of how to invite people to the Lord's Supper and what to do when they respond, whether they are children or adults, whether baptized or not.

We also treasured the discovery of our own process of formation as disciples. Through our study, prayer, and practice of the sacraments, we grew as disciples and as a community. So we turned our attention to how to offer this process and this experience to churches within our denomination. The five simple practices became our focal point, our "key change of focus." So in our "pastoral letter" to the denomination we testified:

> While we prayed, studied Scripture, read history, talked theology, wrote papers, surveyed churches, interviewed congregational leaders, and visited with ecumenical partners—it was the power of God's presence in our worship together around pulpit, font, and table, that we came deeply to trust. Consequently, it is this same attention to sacramental life and immersion in rich sacramental practice that we are now eager to commend to the whole church.[5]

Historically speaking, any "official" liturgical direction assumes that the opposite behavior is a practice in need of correction. In other words, the five simple practices indirectly suggest that in the PC(USA) the baptismal font was rarely used, that the table was largely ignored on non-Communion Sundays, that liturgical leadership did not regularly relate to

---

[5] Presbyterian Church (U.S.A), *Invitation to Christ*, 5-6.

the sacraments, and that the Lord's Supper was celebrated too infrequently. We hoped the five simple practices, in addition to stimulating a deeper understanding of the sacraments, might also catalyze more disciplined sacramental practice throughout our denomination. Just as they became our watershed moment within the Sacraments Study Group, we hoped the five simple practices would provide watershed moments in our congregations. Looking back today, we can be encouraged.

In 2009 the Presbyterian Panel conducted a survey related to the celebration of the sacraments in PC(USA) churches. It found that, "Almost half of pastors (47%) and one-third of specialized clergy (36%)—but only about one in five members (16%) and elders (22%)— are *very familiar, familiar,* or *a little familiar* with the 2006 report *Invitation to Christ: A Guide to Sacramental Practices.*"[6] These may seem like modest numbers, but in a subsequent report the following observations were made with regards to hypothetical visitors to congregations familiar with *Invitation to Christ* during non-sacramental Sunday worship services:

> The odds of recognizing that one had dropped in on an *ITC* congregation would be greater on a Sunday when the Lord's Supper was *not* celebrated. Visitors would be twice as likely to see the bread and cup on the Lord's Table . . . twice as likely to see parts of the service led from the table. . . As with the Lord's Supper, the difference between an *ITC* congregation and another congregation would be likely more noticeable on a Sunday without a baptism. In more *ITC* congregations the font would be uncovered and filled with water and water would be poured into it at some point in the service. Also, more would have some part of the service led from the font.[7]

These observations are consistent with what the Sacrament Study Group envisioned.

-----

[6] Presbyterian Church (U.S.A.), The Sacraments: The Report of the February 2009 Presbyterian Panel Survey (Louisville, KY, Research Services, 2011), 7.

[7] Presbyterian Church (U.S.A.), Sacramental Practices of Congregations: Summer 2011 Survey (Louisville, KY, Research Services, 2012), 2-3.

In 2010 the 219th General Assembly approved a recommendation stating that, "The approach to the Lord's Table always be gracious and invitational, not scrutinizing membership credentials, but extending Christ's welcome to the people of God." Further, "the invitation to the Lord's Supper be gracious and hospitable," and that, "congregations renew the practice of the invitation to discipleship—a call to baptism and to the reaffirmation of baptismal commitment." Finally, "That not yet baptized persons who present themselves at the Lord's Table be warmly received and promptly invited into conversation on the significance of the sacraments, in order that their hunger for spiritual nourishment might be met by a gracious invitation to Christ and to Christian life through baptismal discipleship."[8]

The Assembly noted that, "In the three years that have passed since the publication of *Invitation to Christ*, it seems clear that a season of sacramental renewal has begun to flourish in this denomination." It cites that more than 500 congregations responded to the call to engage the five practices, 7,000 copies of *ITC* had been distributed, a website dedicated to providing additional resources received an average of 1,000 visits per month the previous year, that *ITC* had been translated into Korean and had been included in numerous conferences, and that in the past decade monthly celebrations of the Lord's Supper had increased from sixty percent to seventy-five percent.

In 2012 the Association for Reformed and Liturgical Worship "extended" *Invitation to Christ* to the broader audience of non-Presbyterian Reformed communions. Marney Ault Wasserman, the convener of the original Sacraments Study Group served as editor for the revised and updated *Invitation to Christ—Extended*.[9]

---

[8] Presbyterian Church (U.S.A.), Minutes of the 219th General Assembly, Part 1 (Louisville: Office of the General Assembly, 2010), 1198-1199. All further quotations from the General Assembly in this section come from the same document.

[9] *Invitation to Christ—Extended* was self-published by the Association for Reformed and Liturgical Worship and is available for download at http://uccfiles.com/pdf/Invitation-to-Christ.pdf.

A number of articles and books reflect the influence of *Invitation to Christ*, including some of the   chapters in this volume.[10] Both the moderator and vice-moderator of the 220th General Assembly in 2012 had been members of the Sacrament Study Group. It was the only time, at least in recent history, that each worship service during the assembly included a celebration of the Lord's Supper. In 2020 the journal *Call to Worship* republished the extended version with commentaries so a new generation of readers, leaders, and congregations could benefit from the five simple practices.[11]

In the years since the introduction of *Invitation to Christ* to the PC(USA), we have revised our Directory for Worship, published the hymnal *Glory to God*, and revised the *Book of Common Worship*, all three of which show their indebtedness to the sacramental renewal to which *Invitation to Christ* contributed. The indebtedness of the PC(USA) goes further back than *Invitation to Christ*, of course. Horace Allen commented about the 1993 *Book of Common Worship* that, "The principle achievement of this book in Reformed liturgical history in North America must be reckoned as the formal recovery of the normative Word-Sacrament rite for the Lord's Day."[12]

While the unity of Word and sacrament is not yet as normative in practice as we would want, the sacramental waters do appear to be flowing in a welcome direction. That watershed moment of recommending sacramental practices and equipping congregations to reflect upon them has not returned void. In fact, following a service of Holy Communion during one of our meetings in Louisville, the Sacraments Study Group walked down to the fountain at Waterfront Park by the Ohio River where, with full-bodied and fully-clothed abandon, we remembered our baptism. Later that week Marney Ault

---

[10] See, for example, Ronald P. Byars, *Come and See: Presbyterian Congregations Celebrating Weekly Communion* (Eugene, OR: Cascade Books, 2014).

[11] Presbyterian Church (U.S.A.), *Call to Worship: Liturgy, Music, Preaching, and the Arts* Volume 54.2 (Louisville: Office of the General Assembly, 2020).

[12] Horace Allen, "Book of Common Worship (1993): The Presbyterian Church (U.S.A.), 'Origins and anticipations,'" in *To Glorify God: Essays on Modern Reformed Liturgy*, eds. Bryan D. Spinks and Iain R. Torrance, (Grand Rapids, MI: William B. Eerdmans Publishing Company, 1999), 24.

Wasserman wrote this poem. I close with it as further testimony to the joyful work of God's Spirit through the waters of baptism.

"The Fountain"[13]

a fountain by the river
shoots up spurts of water
through a metal grate,
10 x 10 – a hundred streams
of rising and falling water

it is the water that healed Namaan
and quenched the thirst of the Samaritan woman
it's the floodgates of creation washing away wrong
it runs sparkling through the city of God
and this city where children play
to rinse off summer's thick heat
it's the water Israel crossed to freedom and to home
the water that flowed
from Mary's legs and John's hands bringing Jesus to birth
and from Jesus' side sealing his death

> *Remember your baptism and be thankful...*
> And we are. Profoundly.
> *Wade in the water, children of God...*
> And we do.

shoes come off
pant legs roll
hands reach out to touch this water
we join the children
weaving
dancing
playing wet
and let the water do its work…

---

[13] This poem is used with permission of the author and of Dos Madres Press which will include it in the forthcoming volume entitled *A Thousand Gratitudes* by Marney Wasserman.

walking home
thoroughly soaked skirts hang heavy
but the heart is light
loads left in the fountain

26 August
Ordinary Time 2005
Louisville, KY
at a meeting of the Sacraments Study Group,
Presbyterian Church (U.S.A.)

Section 3

Presbyterian Worship Renewal

8. COMPASS AND MAP:

CHARTING A COURSE
FOR THE RENEWAL
OF PRESBYTERIAN WORSHIP

by David Gambrell

In May of 1965 the British Invasion of American popular music was well underway. "Ticket to Ride" was the number one song on the *Billboard* Hot 100 chart and the Beatles were preparing for their third U.S. tour. But Horace T. Allen Jr. had a ticket to fly in the opposite direction.

As Allen recounted in "A Liturgical Travelogue" published in *Reformed Liturgics*, he had been invited to attend the May 21, 1965, service commemorating the centennial of the Church Service Society of Scotland, held at the Kirk of the Greyfriars in Edinburgh. He was participating as an officer and representative of the Church Service Society of the U.S.A., a body established in 1957 for the purpose of "advancing a concept of worship which is both Catholic and Reformed ... preserving both the ageless values of the liturgy of the Universal Church and the acute insights of the classical Reformers."[1] Musing on this mission in light of the Scottish society's hundredth anniversary, Allen noted the contrasting contexts of their work. While the parent

---

[1] *Reformed Liturgics* 2, no. 1 (1965), inside front cover.

organization in nineteenth-century Scotland had been founded to stoke "interest and understanding of the Reformed liturgical heritage" at a time when this tradition had all but burned out, its twentieth-century progeny in the U.S. felt called "to temper the sometimes extraordinary experimentation which is going on" by drawing on the insights and influence of the ecumenical liturgical movement.[2] Allen affirmed the value of the "scholarly understanding of our own liturgical heritage," exemplified by the Scottish society, and admired their "willingness to use it … with a due sense for dignity, order, propriety, and subservience of all liturgical form to the order of God's Word."[3] Yet he asserted that the contemporary concerns of North American churches would demand "more than a knowledge of presbyterian liturgical history," but "an ecumenical commitment" to honor and receive the gifts of the Spirit through churches in other communions—particularly in the flowering and fruition of liturgical renewal that followed the Second Vatican Council.[4]

In the course of his journey Allen also paid visits to St. James' Presbyterian Church in Bristol, England, and to the communities of Iona and Taizé. At St. James, Allen experienced a Sunday evening service with "modern music, short prayers, [and] direct language in sermon and scripture."[5] The service spilled over into a rock concert in the church hall, where the parish pastor, "clothed in cassock and bands," waded into the throng of teenage "mods" and "rockers," in pursuit of "whatever human, pastoral relationship can be established."[6] On the isle of Iona (to which he would return the following year as ministerial warden of Iona Abbey), Allen attended an evening communion service enlivened by popular folk songs, remarking that the thirteenth-century church of St. Mary "really rocked that night!"[7] He appreciated the "sensitivity to the value of quiet solitude" demonstrated in other services, such as the daily morning office, and commended the "extraordinary understanding of

---

[2] Ibid., 9 (unnumbered).

[3] Ibid., 10 (unnumbered).

[4] Ibid.

[5] Ibid.

[6] Ibid.

[7] Ibid., 10.

Celtic and mystical piety" exemplified by the Iona community.[8] At Taizé, Allen found yet another "very rich" expression of Christian worship, observing: "In its beauty, and order, and depth it easily surpasses anything else I know of in Protestantism."[9] He was excited to encounter a community so faithful to the gospel, with "good music and tasteful color and movement" and an "ever-present ecumenical imperative."[10]

Like a latter-day Egeria, Allen offered us a fascinating glimpse of a pivotal period in the twentieth-century ecumenical liturgical movement. With this firsthand account of his "European tour," he illuminated the early inceptions of, among other things, what we have come to call contemporary and contemplative worship. Allen's travelogue also traced the first steps in his own vocational path—a lifelong pilgrimage of liturgical and ecumenical leadership. "There is a job to be done," Allen declared. "The whole Church seems to be stirring these days; and the new forms of Church life that are springing up everywhere will demand new forms of worship."[11] How would Presbyterian churches negotiate these demands and navigate this new terrain? We have our own traveler's tools—a compass and a map.

The Compass and the Map

Presbyterian directories for worship and service books may be compared to a compass and a map, respectively. **Like a compass, a directory for worship—such as the one found in the *Book of Order* of the Presbyterian Church (U.S.A.)—points us to primary things in liturgical theology and practice.** It helps us orient ourselves to the biblical and confessional principles that have guided centuries of Reformed worship. Especially when we lose our way, a directory for worship redirects us to our "chief end"—the glory of God. **Like a map, a service book—such as the PC(USA) Book of Common Worship—reveals the contours and key attractions of the liturgical**

---

[8] Ibid., 11.

[9] Ibid.

[10] Ibid.

[11] Ibid., 11–12 (unnumbered).

landscape. It offers us a record of reliable paths—prayers and patterns of worship that have led our ancestors into an authentic encounter with the living God. For an adventurous congregation, a service book might inspire us to explore new summits or allow us to avoid old pitfalls. Used together—but not always at the same time—the compass and map have helped generations of Presbyterians chart a faithful (although sometimes circuitous) course through the reform and renewal of the Church. A brief sketch of their history will demonstrate the dynamic relationship between these traveler's tools.[12]

Sixteenth century Protestant reformers composed, compiled, and seemed to value service books. John Knox relied on Calvin's *La Forme des Prières Ecclésiastiques* (1543) as the basis for his own *Form of Prayers* (1556) and *Book of Common Order* (1562) in Scotland. In the context of the political and religious conflict that divided seventeenth-century Britain, an attempt to impose the use of the Anglican *Book of Common Prayer* in Edinburgh led to a riot in 1637. Out of this controversy, the Westminster Assembly (1643–1653) developed its *Directory for the Public Worship of God* (1644), which was adopted by the Church of Scotland in 1645. While it drew inspiration from the *Book of Common Order* and its precursors, the Westminster directory aimed to correct perceived abuses of the Anglican service book. Scottish and Puritan immigrants brought this directory for worship to North America, where, in 1788, it was approved for use by Presbyterians in the United States.

For more than a century, the Westminster directory was the primary document ordering the worship of U.S. Presbyterians; fittingly, in the frontier era, Presbyterian worshipers were guided by a compass, but not a map. In the early twentieth century, however, Presbyterians began to call for a service book to stand alongside the denomination's directory for worship. The first *Book of Common Worship* (1906) was published by the Presbyterian Church in the U.S.A. in response to this demand; a 1932 revision was accepted by its sibling denomination, the Presbyterian Church in the United States. A third edition (1946) incorporated insights from the emerging ecumenical liturgical movement, including a lectionary borrowed from the Church of Scotland. These significant developments began to put a strain on the Westminster directory, now three hundred years old. At the same time, a new spirit of collaboration

---

[12] One detailed account of this history can be found in chapter 6, especially p. 119ff.

and reconciliation among U.S. Presbyterians began to accelerate the interplay between service books and directories for worship.

In the very milieu that inspired the reforms of the Second Vatican Council (1962–1965), new directories for worship were drafted for the (recently formed) United Presbyterian Church in the U.S.A. (1961) and the Presbyterian Church in the United States (1963). A new service book for Presbyterians soon followed, the *Worshipbook* (1970), produced by a joint committee of three Presbyterian denominations, including the Cumberland Presbyterian Church. The merger of the UPC(USA) and the PCUS to form the Presbyterian Church (U.S.A.) in 1983 occasioned the composition of a new directory for worship (1989) for the new denomination. The process to generate another service book was already underway, and so another edition of the *Book of Common Worship* (1993) arrived just a decade after reunion, close on the heels of the latest directory.

The turn of the millennium brought important changes in Church and culture—including different models of ministry, a season of sacramental renewal, and movements for racial justice and marriage equality. These and other factors led to a thorough revision of the Directory for Worship (2017) and new, expanded edition of the *Book of Common Worship* (2018). A notable feature of the 2018 *Book of Common Worship* is that it makes room for extensive quotations from the denomination's 2017 Directory for Worship. Often at odds with one another in the history of Presbyterian worship, the denomination's current directory for worship and service book are, at least at present, "on the same page."[13]

As they have come to exist in the U.S. Presbyterian Church over the past century, directories for worship and service books have distinct roles in the liturgical life of the denomination. A directory for worship, as part of the church's constitution, has an authoritative voice; key words, carefully deployed, signal practices that are mandated ("shall"), recommended ("should"), or optional ("may"). It contains no prayers or other liturgical texts; rather, it conveys the theological rationale and essential elements of the church's worship. Like a compass, it seeks to be

---

[13] For a more complete history of service books in the Reformed tradition, see the Presbyterian Church (U.S.A.) *Book of Common Worship* (Louisville: Westminster John Knox Press, 2018), xxvii–xxxiv.

an objective reference, indicating the policies and practices of the denomination in a clear and concise way. A service book, by contrast, is offered for voluntary use by pastors and congregations; while a few may follow it verbatim, most think of it as a starting point for creative adaptation and some eschew it altogether. It is filled with prayers and other forms for worship; its primary concern is not denominational doctrine or policy, but the ritual enactment of the church's teaching and tradition. Like a map, it represents a selective rendering of particular (liturgical) landscapes, reflecting intentional decisions about what to include or omit, as well as a certain vantage point and orientation to the world.

Further exploration of the metaphor of the compass and map yields some critical implications and principles for reform. *First, it is often valuable—and at times necessary—to use a compass and map together.* With only a compass, you may know what direction to travel, but you will be unaware of convenient pathways and potential hazards. Similarly, if you attempted to design Lord's Day worship using only the compass—that is, based exclusively on the brief guidance found in a directory for worship—you would be choosing to deprive a congregation of the wisdom of two thousand years, prayers and patterns of worship carefully developed by generations of ancestors in the faith. With only a map, you may have a detailed plan for the journey, but you may never reach your intended destination because you started out in the wrong direction. Similarly, if you sought to lead Lord's Day worship using only the map— that is, divining a path through the expansive range of options available in a service book—you would be likely to "miss the forest for the trees," following a route by rote without really knowing where you're going or understanding why.

Second, like the compass and map, directories for worship and service books have certain strengths and weaknesses. If, on the one hand, you are seeking to resolve a dispute regarding the theology or polity of the church, it is very helpful to know how to find "true north." In such situations, a directory for worship will help you get your bearings, while a service book would not be of much assistance. If, on the other hand, you are hoping to launch a new service or needing to address an unusual pastoral situation, it is very helpful to have a set of step-by-step instructions. In these circumstances, a service book might illuminate a variety of potential paths, while a directory for worship would have much less to offer.

Accordingly, for example, Presbyterians are apt to consult the directory for worship when wondering who may preside at the sacrament of Baptism, but to refer to a service book when in search of a prayer of thanksgiving over the water.

Third, and finally, there is value in maintaining a measure of independence between the compass and the map. The technology and design of the compass remain relatively constant through time, but maps must be updated more frequently to account for new construction and changing topography. Different maps might be more useful for different journeys (by foot, by road, by rail), whereas the same compass would do. Something similar might be said of directories for worship and service books. A directory for worship is somewhat more stable in its expression of the central convictions of the church; indeed, major changes in the theology and practice of worship would be destabilizing for a denomination. This fact allowed the 1644 Westminster directory to remain relevant for three centuries. A service book has to be nimble in navigating new contexts; indeed, a service book that does not respond to recent concerns will be quickly deemed out of date. This fact led to the 1970 *Worshipbook*, with its generic masculine language for humanity, having a relatively short shelf-life, in spite of it being a groundbreaking document in other important respects. Furthermore, one might even argue that a degree of friction or tension between the directory for worship and service book is an important catalyst for the ongoing reform of the church's worship. The examples below will illustrate this principle, along with other instances of the vital and dynamic interplay between compass and map.

Charting a Course: Three Examples

How have directories for worship and service books been used like a compass and map to plot out pathways for recent reforms in Presbyterian worship? In the section that follows I will describe three examples: the order of worship, frequency of communion, and language and culture.

Order of Worship

The 1989 Directory for Worship of the Presbyterian Church (U.S.A.) outlined a five-fold order of worship in the Service for the Lord's Day, consisting of the following actions: (1) gathering around the Word, (2) proclaiming the Word, (3) responding to the Word, (4) the sealing of the Word, and (5) bearing and following the Word into the world.[14] Subsequent denominational publications, however—including the *Presbyterian Hymnal* (1990), the *Book of Common Worship* (1993), and *Glory to God: The Presbyterian Hymnal* (2013)—referred to a four-fold pattern. The 1990 hymnal enumerated these elements as follows: (1) Assemble in God's Name, (2) Proclaim God's Word, (3) Give Thanks to God, and (4) Go in God's Name.[15] The 1993 *Book of Common Worship* and 2013 *Glory to God* hymnal listed the four elements in this way: (1) Gathering, (2) [The] Word, (3) [The] Eucharist, and (4) Sending.[16]

The numbering and nomenclature of the movements in the Service for the Lord's Day had thus become the cause for some confusion and consternation among Presbyterian congregations. The 1989 Directory for Worship sought to emphasize the centrality of the Word in Presbyterian worship, an important principle of the Reformation. The hymnals and service book that followed in 1990, 1993, and 2013 were intent on juxtaposing Word and Sacrament as the center of Lord's Day worship, another Reformed value, while also reflecting an emerging ecumenical consensus on the shape of the *ordo*. The divergence became a source of difficulty in worship committees, presbytery meetings, seminary classrooms, and ordination exams.

Given the shift in recent sources to a four-fold order of worship, the 2017 Directory for Worship followed suit, using this outline: (1) Gathering, (2) Word, (3) Sacrament, and (4) Sending; the combination of

---

[14] Presbyterian Church (U.S.A.) *Book of Order* (Louisville: Office of the General Assembly, 2015), W-3.3302. The *Book of Order* is subject to modifications with every General Assembly. I will be citing the 1989 Directory for Worship as it existed just prior to a major revision in 2017.

[15] *The Presbyterian Hymnal: Hymns, Psalms, and Spiritual Songs* (Louisville: Westminster John Knox Press, 1990), 12.

[16] *Book of Common Worship* (Louisville: Westminster John Knox Press, 1993), 46; *Glory to God: The Presbyterian Hymnal* (Louisville: Westminster John Knox Press, 2013), 1–13.

Baptism and Eucharist under the heading "Sacrament" was an effort to demonstrate their close relationship and position, both as a response to the proclamation of the Word.[17] In making this change from the 1989 directory, however, it was important to reassert and confirm two points suggested by the five-fold pattern. First, the centrality of the Word in Reformed worship; the 2017 directory affirms: "The Scriptures bear witness to the Word of God, revealed most fully in Jesus Christ, the Word who 'became flesh and lived among us' (John 1:14). Where the Word is read and proclaimed, Jesus Christ the living Word is present by the power of the Holy Spirit. Therefore, reading, hearing, preaching, and affirming the Word are central to Christian worship and essential to the Service for the Lord's Day."[18] Second, the theme of response to God; the 2017 directory states: "God acts with grace; we respond with gratitude. God claims us as beloved children; we proclaim God's saving love. God redeems us from sin and death; we rejoice in the gift of new life. This rhythm of divine action and human response—found throughout scripture, human history, and everyday events—shapes all of Christian faith, life, and worship."[19] With these statements, the 2017 directory gave necessary theological grounding for a significant change in the description of the order of worship (see second principle above: strength of the compass).

Clear direction from the *Book of Order* (see first principle above: using compass and map together) enabled the 2018 *Book of Common Worship* to reaffirm the four-fold order of worship for the Lord's Day: (1) Gathering, (2) Word, (3) Eucharist, and (4) Sending. A brief comment at the start of the service highlights and underscores this pattern: "We gather to praise the triune God, confess our sin, and seek God's grace. We hear the good news of the gospel and celebrate the Lord's Supper. We are sent forth to glorify God through the service of daily living."[20] The 2018 *Book of Common Worship* sought to elucidate the four-fold *ordo* in a more subtle way as well: streamlining the Service for the Lord's Day

---

[17] Presbyterian Church (U.S.A.) *Book of Order* (Louisville: Office of the General Assembly, 2019), W-3. Again, the *Book of Order* is subject to modifications with every General Assembly. I will be citing the 2017 Directory for Worship as it appears at the time of this writing.

[18] Directory for Worship (2017), *Book of Order* (2019), W-3.0301.

[19] Ibid., W-1.0102.

[20] *Book of Common Worship* (2018), 18.

in its first appearance by moving multiple options and alternatives to a sourcebook section. With a twelve-page order of worship in the 2018 service book—in contrast to thirty-six pages in the 1993 book—it is easier to apprehend the structure of the liturgy and appreciate its simplicity.[21] Thus, the service book becomes a more effective resource for liturgical formation (see second principle: strength of the map).

Frequency of Communion

Following the example of the 1970 *Worshipbook*, the 1989 Directory for Worship presented the Lord's Supper as a normative part of Lord's Day worship. A section on the time, place, and frequency of the Sacrament affirms: "It is appropriate to celebrate the Lord's Supper as often as each Lord's Day. It is to be celebrated regularly and frequently enough to be recognized as integral to the Service for the Lord's Day."[22] A later passage expresses similar encouragement, even as it asserts the minimal requirement for eucharistic celebration: "The session is responsible for authorizing all observances of the Lord's Supper in the life of a particular church and shall ensure regular and frequent celebration of the Sacrament, in no case less than quarterly."[23] These provisions prompted Presbyterian congregations toward more frequent communion, with a small contingent beginning to celebrate weekly Eucharist.

The 1993 *Book of Common Worship* sought to stay the course. This service book included the eucharistic liturgy as an ordinary component of the Service for the Lord's Day; a rubric offers an "exit ramp" for those not celebrating weekly Eucharist (still the majority of Presbyterian congregations): "If the Lord's Supper is not to be celebrated, the service continues on page 79."[24] In addition to Great Thanksgiving A, found within the primary order of worship for the Lord's Day, nine other patterns for eucharistic prayer (Great Thanksgivings B through J) are provided, showcasing some variety in structure and style.[25] Beyond the

---

[21] Ibid., 19–30; *Book of Common Worship* (1993), 48–83.

[22] Directory for Worship (1989), *Book of Order* (2015), W-2.4009.

[23] Ibid., W-2.4012.

[24] *Book of Common Worship* (1993), 66.

[25] Ibid., 69–73, 126–156.

Sunday service, the 1993 service book included special eucharistic prayers for the seasons and festivals of the liturgical year, along with weddings, funerals, and ministry with the sick.[26] While these additional eucharistic liturgies adhered to a fairly consistent form, they supplied some variety for congregations desiring more occasions to celebrate the Sacrament.

The 2006 sacrament study of the Presbyterian Church (U.S.A.), titled *Invitation to Christ: Font and Table*, called on congregations to (among other things) "Set cup and plate on the Lord's Table on every Lord's Day" and "Increase the number of Sundays on which the Lord's Supper is celebrated."[27] For congregations that accepted these challenges, the next several years were to be a fruitful season of sacramental renewal, with deep theological reflection around simple liturgical practices. Even those who did not engage the sacrament study directly were influenced by its insights as they experienced more frequent (and joyful) celebrations of the Eucharist at regional meetings and national conferences.

The 2017 revision to the denomination's Directory for Worship sought to reinforce and build on these developments. Alluding to Jesus' resurrection appearance on the road to Emmaus, the directory declares: "The Service for the Lord's Day is a service of Word and Sacrament. We meet in the presence of the living Lord, who appeared to his disciples on the first day of the week—the day he rose from the dead—to interpret the scriptures and break bread. Following Jesus' example, the Church proclaims the fullness of the gospel in Word and Sacrament on the Lord's Day."[28] The latest version of the directory now puts the onus of decision on a congregation's session to opt for a pattern other than weekly Eucharist: "The Lord's Supper shall be celebrated as a regular part of the Service for the Lord's Day, preceded by the proclamation of the Word, in the gathering of the people of God. When local circumstances call for the Lord's Supper to be celebrated less frequently, the session may approve other schedules for celebration, in no case less than quarterly. If the Lord's Supper is celebrated less frequently than on each Lord's Day, public notice is to be given at least one week in advance

---

[26] Ibid., 165–400; 853–881; 911–946; 998–1001.

[27] Presbyterian Church (U.S.A.), *Invitation to Christ: Font and Table: A Guide to Sacramental Practices* (Louisville: Office of Theology and Worship, 2006), 11, 12. A detailed history of this document is found in chapter 7, p. 140ff.

[28] Directory for Worship (2017), *Book of Order* (2019), W-3.0102.

so that all may prepare to receive the Sacrament."[29] These are two good examples of how a directory for worship may assist in advancing liturgical reform: by articulating biblical and theological rationale for liturgical practices and by connecting those practices with the church's polity (see second principle: strength of the compass).

The 2018 *Book of Common Worship* echoes the 2017 Directory for Worship in its insistence that "The Service for the Lord's Day is a service of Word and Sacrament. Together, Word and Sacrament form a unified liturgy—proclaiming and celebrating the fullness of God's saving word and action in Jesus Christ."[30] Again, a rubric makes allowances for congregations to refrain from celebrating the Eucharist, but not without reflecting on this decision in light of the guidance of the directory for worship: "The norm of Christian worship is to celebrate the Lord's Supper on each Lords' Day. If the Lord's Supper is omitted, the service may include a prayer of thanksgiving (149–51), concluding with the Lord's Prayer (144). The service then continues at the closing hymn."[31] In an effort to support weekly Eucharist, the 2018 *Book of Common Worship* includes fifty-five different eucharistic prayers; these texts feature more variety in style and structure, intended to enliven sacramental celebration and introduce worshipers to new facets of the feast. Since our directories for worship do not contain texts of prayers, this is the kind of contribution only a service book can make (see second principle: strength of the map).

Language and Culture

Inclusive language was a prominent issue for those who prepared the 1989 Directory for Worship, particularly in light of the changes in theological and liturgical discourse that had taken place since the 1970 *Worshipbook*. Accordingly, a section on "authentic and appropriate language" sought to anchor the church's proclamation and prayer in the witness of scripture, while simultaneously expanding their applicability to the whole community of faith.[32] The 1989 directory demonstrates a

---

[29] Ibid., W-3.0409.

[30] *Book of Common Worship* (2018), 18.

[31] Ibid., 25.

[32] Directory for Worship (1989), *Book of Order* (2015), W-1.2005.

concern about cultural context as well: "Since the Presbyterian Church (U.S.A.) is a family of peoples united in Jesus Christ, appropriate language for its worship should display the rich variety of these peoples. To the extent that forms, actions, languages, or settings of worship exclude the expression of diverse cultures represented in the church or deny emerging needs and identities of believers, that worship is not faithful to the life, death, and resurrection of Jesus Christ."[33]

The 1993 *Book of Common Worship* endeavored to put these principles into practice. As the preface to this service book indicates: "Care was taken in the development of the *Book of Common Worship* that its language be inclusive, not only in reference to the people of God but also in language about God and address to God. Guidelines for inclusive language adopted by the General Assembly in 1975, 1979, 1980, and 1985 were implicitly followed in the preparation of the texts. The result is that a richer biblical imagery is employed than was the case in prior service books."[34] Indeed, gendered pronouns for the first and third persons of the Trinity are avoided and generic masculine terms for humanity ("mankind") are absent. It is somewhat harder to discern how the 1993 *Book of Common Worship* accounts for different cultural contexts, except insofar as it acknowledges the dynamic relationships between "form and freedom" and "local and universal" patterns of worship.[35] Just as the "universal masculine" language of the 1970 service book sought to emphasize our common humanity, yet obscured women's experience, it may be argued that the 1993 service book, with its strong ecumenical impulse, inadvertently perpetuated certain cultural and ecclesial biases.

The 2017 Directory for Worship reaffirmed its precursor's guidance on inclusive language for humanity and expansive language for the divine. But it added this comment on the plurality of languages in Presbyterian worship: "Since Pentecost, the Church of Jesus Christ has been a community of many nations and cultures, united by the power of the Holy Spirit. Therefore our churches worship in many languages. The words we use in worship are to be in the common language or languages of those who are gathered, so that all are able to receive the good news and respond with true expressions of their faith. Through the rich variety

---

[33] Ibid., W-1.2006.

[34] *Book of Common Worship* (1993), 10.

[35] Ibid., 6–7, 9–10.

of human speech we bear witness to God's saving love for all."[36] The 2017 directory makes a similar observation about the multiplicity of cultural contexts in the Church: "God has poured out the Holy Spirit on all flesh; scripture promises that everyone who calls on the name of the Lord will be saved. The book of Acts and the New Testament epistles record the challenges and controversies of an emerging Church that would be 'no longer Jew or Greek' (Gal. 3:28), but one in Jesus Christ. As the Church has grown and spread over two thousand years, it has taken root and flourished in cultures and lands all around the globe— bearing witness to the love of God for all the world and Christ's sovereignty in every place. Finally, from the book of Revelation, we know that the company of the redeemed will be a great multitude from every nation, tribe, and people, singing praise to the Lamb of God."[37] With respect to the latter, the 2017 Directory for Worship borrows language from the 1996 Nairobi Statement on Worship and Culture from the Lutheran World Federation, detailing the "contextual," "cross-cultural," "transcultural," and "countercultural" dimensions of Christian worship.[38] This is an example of how a directory for worship may introduce new nuance and complexity in the church's understanding and practice of the liturgy (see second principle: strength of the compass, and third principle: independence of compass and map).

The 2018 *Book of Common Worship* took further strides to expand the linguistic and cultural horizons of Presbyterian service books. It introduced languages other than English—namely Spanish and Korean, the two other most commonly spoken languages among members of the Presbyterian Church (U.S.A.). A fully bilingual (Spanish/English) Service for the Lord's Day is provided; in this case, the English is a translation of the original Spanish.[39] Other services offered in Spanish include the sacrament of Baptism, Ordination and Installation, Reception of New Members, the Service of Marriage, and the Funeral. Common liturgical texts, such as creeds, the Lord's Prayer, and the Decalogue, are published in English, Korean, and Spanish. The preface to the 2018 *Book of Common Worship* features a lexicon of other familiar phrases (such as "The Lord

---

[36] Directory for Worship (2017), *Book of Order* (2019), W-1.0302.

[37] Ibid., W-1.0304.

[38] Ibid.

[39] *Book of Common Worship* (2018), 33–53.

be with you" and "Lift up your hearts") in the same three languages, along with illustrations of liturgical gestures.[40] A new section on the mission of the Church includes a service for justice and peace, as well as prayers that lament the evil of systemic racism and confess the sins of prejudice and privilege; other new texts give voice to the experiences of indigenous people, immigrants, and refugees.[41] There is much more work to be done, of course, but with these modest steps the service book becomes an icon of the multilingual and intercultural church envisioned in the directory for worship (see first principle: using compass and map together).

The Ongoing Renewal of Presbyterian Worship

How might these traveler's tools—the compass and the map—be used to navigate emerging challenges in the twenty-first century? In the final section of this chapter, I will give brief consideration to three possibilities: daily prayer, collaborative ministry, and technology and new media.

Daily Prayer

Decades of vital and valuable liturgical reform around the order of worship and the frequency of communion, as described above, have had an unintended and unfortunate consequence. Our emphasis on the Service for the Lord's Day as a service of Word and Sacrament has eclipsed other patterns and possibilities for ordering worship—particularly that of the daily office. How might this matter be addressed in future directories for worship and service books?

The 2017 Directory for Worship provides a brief description of services of daily prayer, But it could benefit from a more extensive discussion of the theology of the daily office and its usefulness in personal devotion, household worship, congregational assemblies, and

---

[40] Ibid., xviii–xxvi.

[41] Ibid., 591–632.

councils of the church.[42] The 2018 *Book of Common Worship* actually has much to offer in this regard (third principle)—material that might be better suited to a directory for worship (second principle).[43] The 2018 service book also reorganizes the liturgy for daily prayer around a baptismal rhythm of dying (evening) and rising (morning) with Christ.[44] Until these insights are reflected in the directory for worship (first principle), however, they will likely escape the notice of many Presbyterians.

Collaborative Ministry

Despite our emphasis on the priestly vocation of all believers, our esteem for the ordered ministries of deacons and ruling elders, and our eschewal of distinctions between clergy and laity, there remains a strong focus on the role of the preacher and presider in Presbyterian worship. How might we encourage more collaborative forms of liturgical ministry in new editions of the directory for worship and the denominational service book?

The 2017 Directory for Worship and 2018 *Book of Common Worship* have both attempted (first principle) to delineate appropriate roles for deacons and ruling elders in the Service for the Lord's Day, even as they confirm and clarify the responsibilities of the pastor as presider.[45] Yet more formation and empowerment will be required if these recommendations are to take root and bear fruit. It would be helpful to have similar discussions around other church vocations, such as musicians, artists, and educators—who may or may not be deacons, elders, or pastors. Finally, as notions of church membership are becoming more fluid and diffuse, further reflection is needed on the leadership and participation of people who are not formally affiliated with the church. Directories for worship could explore the implications

---

[42] Directory for Worship (2017), *Book of Order* (2019), W-5.0202.

[43] *Book of Common Worship* (2018), 827–829.

[44] Ibid., 834–907.

[45] Directory for Worship (2017), *Book of Order* (2019), W-2.03, W-3; *Book of Common Worship* (2018), 3–156.

for the church's theology and polity (second principle); service books could outline forms for liturgical action (second principle).

Technology and New Media

Technological change is advancing rapidly in the twenty-first century church. Especially in the midst of the 2020 coronavirus pandemic, with the suspension of in-person worship and a proliferation of online services, many congregations have begun to offer liturgical events by way of live-streaming, pre-recorded, and video conference platforms. How might forthcoming directories for worship and service books help us to reckon with this new reality?

The Presbyterian Church (U.S.A.) Directory for Worship offers an intriguing set of reflections on "time, space, and matter" in Christian worship.[46] In its current form, however, it fails to account for situations in which these physical phenomena are divided—for instance, people worshiping at the same time in different spaces (as in live-streaming or video conference services), people participating in the same service of worship at different times (as in pre-recorded services), and people worshiping in different places with different matter (as in bring-your-own-sacrament services). Our service books, too, are at something of a loss in responding to these concerns. Their texts and rubrics were not written with such circumstances in mind. At present, congregations are working out these questions in their practice; documents of the church will catch up at their own pace and in their own time (third principle). But future directories must find ways of addressing these emerging questions. And future service books may not be books at all. They may be web-based systems or interactive applications for devices we cannot yet imagine.

There is a sense in which ecumenical and liturgical leaders—such as Horace Allen—must be time travelers. They are compelled to haunt the catacombs, to stalk the saints, to search the archives of antiquity, always trying to tap the wellsprings of our traditions. At the same time, they are

---

[46] Directory for Worship (2017), *Book of Order* (2019), W-1.02.

called to scan the horizons, to venture into the unknown, to entrust themselves to the future, always hungering for the heavenly banquet.

As Allen concluded in his 1965 article for *Reformed Liturgics*: "Because the unique nature of the Church is that [it] lives in time and in eternity, and looks both forward and backward in time, all these new forms of life and of worship must be similarly informed. To inform, to experiment, to excite ... these are all part of the liturgical task which called into being the Church Service Society one hundred years ago, and which must occupy our minds and hearts and imagination anew."[47]

We give thanks that our brother Horace now stands among the great cloud of witnesses. We lay down the burdens of the past and commit ourselves to the promise of the future. And we look to Jesus, "the pioneer and perfecter of our faith" (Heb. 12:2), holding these humble traveler's tools—a compass and a map.

---

[47] *Reformed Liturgics* 2, no. 1 (1965), 12 (unnumbered).

9. A NEW HERMENEUTIC
AND AN EVOLVING PEDAGOGY
FOR PRESBYTERIAN WORSHIP

by Jonathan Hehn, OSL

Introduction

One might argue that, in a time when fewer Presbyterian congregations are able to call a full-time pastor, and when denominational loyalties are presumably of little importance to church-goers, an increased emphasis on Presbyterian worship in the context of theological education is misplaced. Should not the training of pastors, especially in seminaries, increasingly focus on their roles as ecumenical Christian leaders, or even more broadly, as evangelists, community activists, or non-profit administrators? My response is two-fold.

First, the increasing percentage of Ministers of Word and Sacrament in part-time calls cries out for a paradigm shift in the way local congregations plan worship. The assumption, ever since the time of the Westminster Directory, was that full-time pastors spend significant amounts of time and spiritual energy each week preparing for worship - - not just preaching, but composing prayer texts, selecting psalms and hymns, *et cetera*.[1] That assumption has been carried forward to some extent even in the latest revision of the Directory for Worship, in which teaching elders (Ministers of Word and Sacrament) are identified as responsible for the great majority of worship planning.[2] A part-time pastor of a congregation with modest resources will likely lack the amount of free time (or even expertise) needed to do such thoughtful planning each week. However, a pastor (either full or part-time), well trained in worship, who knows not only Presbyterian liturgical history, but who also has thoughtfully crafted denominational resources on which to draw, will be much better equipped to lead God's people in their liturgical work. They will also be able to take comfort in their knowledge that Presbyterian worship, which has historically tended toward simplicity of form and aesthetic, translates well to small, modestly resourced local communities. The people of God do not need high liturgical production value, but rather authenticity.

---

[1] The Directory for the Worship of God, *Constitution of the Presbyterian Church in the United States of America* (Philadelphia: Thomas Bradford, 1789), Chapter V, Section IV (p. 190). "It is easy to perceive that in all the preceding directions there is a very great compass and variety, and it is committed to the judgement and fidelity of the officiating Pastor to insist chiefly on such parts, or to take in more or less of the several parts, as he shall be led... But we think it necessary to observe, that altho' we do not approve, as is well known, of confining Ministers to set, or fixed forms of prayer for public Worship; yet it is the indispensible (sic) duty of every Minister, previously to entering on his office to prepare and qualify himself for this part of his duty, as well as for preaching. He ought, by a thorough acquaintance with the holy Scriptures; by reading the best writers on the subject; by meditation; and by a life of communion with God in secret to endeavor to acquire both the spirit and the gift of prayer." Instructions of the same essence are found in the original 1645 edition, though this particular wording seems to be new to the 1788 version.

[2] The Directory for Worship, online edition, website of the Presbyterian Mission Agency. W-2.0101 and W-2.0304. (PC(USA) Directory for Worship 2018), https://www.presbyterianmission.org/ministries/worship/directory-for-worship/rdfw-chapter-two/. "Those responsible for planning and leading worship are also to be guided by the Constitution of the Presbyterian Church (U.S.A.), instructed by the wisdom of the Reformed tradition, attentive to the traditions of the universal Church, and sensitive to the culture and context of the worshiping community... Teaching elders (also called ministers of Word and Sacrament) are called to proclaim the Word, preside at the Sacraments, and equip the people for ministry in Jesus' name. Specifically, teaching elders are responsible for: the selection of Scriptures to be read, the preparation of the sermon, the prayers to be offered, the selection of music to be sung, printed worship aids or media presentations for a given service, and the use of drama, dance, and other art forms in a particular service of worship."

Second, in response to the charge that denominational loyalties are of little (or at least decreasing) importance to potential church-goers, I would say this should not prevent congregational leaders from embracing their tradition. It is true, now more than ever, that many Christians feel at ease when moving across denominational lines. That is certainly true of this author. However, such freedom does not necessarily represent an erosion of a healthy denominational identity. Rather, it more likely represents the great success of the ecumenical movement over the last century. On the denominational level, there have been multiple full communion agreements which have enabled the easy and orderly transfer of membership as well as the exchange of ministers between congregations of different denominations. But more important than this from the perspective of worshipers is the amazing ecumenical convergence in the liturgy. This convergence, beginning as far back as the middle of the nineteenth century, became concretely manifest in the latter decades of the twentieth century, as various denominations produced new liturgical books that showed remarkable similarities in scope and form. Since then, the shape of worship across these same denominations has continued to converge, so that what one experiences in a liturgically-aware Presbyterian or Lutheran or United Methodist congregation today looks increasingly similar. This makes it easy for a Christian formed in one denomination to feel comfortable worshiping in the church of another. However, while movement across denominational lines may occur easily and frequently nowadays, it does not occur randomly. In our pluralistic religious society, adult Christians mostly *choose* to attend a certain church. While worship is certainly not the only factor involved in this choice, it is a significant factor. Leaders of Presbyterian congregations can take heart; those who have migrated into their worshiping communities from other traditions, or from no tradition at all, have *chosen* to be there. Something about the Presbyterian way of worship and life as modeled by that particular congregation is compelling to them. It is okay to embrace one's own tradition and, as the late Horace T. Allen might say, its particularities, even while celebrating the great gifts of the ecumenical movement.[3] But in order to be able to

---

[3] Denominational distinctives can remain important witnesses to the fact that unity need not equal uniformity. We might look back, in fact, to much of the medieval era, when a plethora of different rites and usages, both in the East and the West, all having developed in parallel from apostolic tradition, were seen as legitimate expressions of unity without uniformity. In more recent times, we might embrace the wisdom of the

do so, leaders of Presbyterian churches must first be edified as to what those gifts, both ecumenical and denominationally particular, are.

Thus it is incumbent upon Presbyterian seminaries and other educational venues to make sure their students are well-equipped to go out and be leaders of a Presbyterian community – not a community shackled by a narrow denominationalism, but one which celebrates its distinctive contribution to the ecumenical Church.[4] What is needed to accomplish such training is a new, more complete hermeneutic for studying the history of Presbyterian worship, and an evolving pedagogy which looks both to past precedent and to future pastoral needs for the denomination. Identifying that hermeneutic and suggesting that pedagogy is the intent of this chapter.

An Evolving Pedagogy

With few exceptions, academic writers specializing in Presbyterian worship since the middle of the twentieth century have been wonderfully descriptive, but they have shied away from offering any liturgical *pre*scriptions[5]. From a certain perspective, such hesitancy to advocate for

---

Nairobi Statement on Worship and Culture that worship should both embrace the cultures in which it is situated while simultaneously being trans- and cross- cultural. Full text of the Nairobi Statement can be found at https://worship.calvin.edu/resources/resource-library/nairobi-statement-on-worship-and-culture-full-text. For some of the ways in which Horace T. Allen approached the question of denominational particularities in his teaching, see Chapter 1 by Mark Stamm, "Magnifying Particularity: Horace T. Allen's Model of Ecumenical Liturgical Formation at the Boston University School of Theology."

[4] Though not addressed specifically in this essay, I and others have articulated some of the particularities of the Presbyterian, or at least Reformed, liturgical tradition. Many such examples can be found in the following paragraphs.

[5] The most notable example is Julius Melton, *Presbyterian Worship in America: Changing Patterns since 1787,* reprint edition (Eugene, OR: Wipf and Stock, 2001), 147-148. Melton's book is of unique importance. It is, to date, still the only detailed history dealing specifically with the worship practices of American Presbyterians. Though Melton was trained as theologian, in this book he writes primarily as a historian,

specific liturgical forms and practices is understandable. In the early and middle decades of the twentieth century, scholars were uncovering the riches of the Christian liturgical tradition at a rate unmatched since the Reformations. At the same time, they were working within a church whose identity was shifting rapidly in response to the cultural forces of the time and to the gifts of the ecumenical movement. In such a time of transition, it would be foolhardy to try to publish an authoritative prescription for Presbyterian worship; thus books of the time remained largely descriptive.[6] Julius Melton said it this way:

> Presbyterians are not unique in facing serious challenges to rethink and reform their worship to make it meaningful to a new age. The task is awesome, for there is no consensus in today's world, even on many matters formerly taken for granted -- world view, moral law, reliability of reason, to name three. Worship, which must operate through commonly understood metaphors and symbols, has few stable ones on which it may build. . .

---

describing the various social, political, and theological influences on the denomination's liturgical practices from colonial times through the middle of the twentieth century. The 1967 edition was reprinted with an addendum in 1984, and it remains an important though increasingly dated pedagogical resource for those training as leaders in the Presbyterian family of churches today. Other notable books in this descriptive vein from the 1960s and 70s include James Nichols's *Corporate Worship in the Reformed Tradition* (Philadelphia: Westminster Press, 1968), and John Leith's *An Introduction to the Reformed Tradition: a way of being Christian community* (Atlanta: John Knox Press 1977/1981). Nichols's book is another important pedagogical source from the post-Vatican II era. A reworking of lectures given initially in the 1950s, it is much broader than Melton's. He defines the Reformed family of churches in North America as including the "Episcopalian, Methodist, Presbyterian, Congregational, Baptist, [and] Disciple" denominations. The main focus of the book, after tracing the origins and structures of early Reformation-era liturgies, was to trace the theological currents over the centuries which gave rise to these various denominations. It is not so much a liturgical history as a social-political history of Reformed denominations vis-à-vis their worship life. Leith's is a well-known introduction to Reformed Christianity which contains a substantial and well-written chapter on worship.

[6] One European writer of the time, Jean Jacques von Allmen, does actually provide a fair number of prescriptions for Reformed worship in his book *Worship: its theology and practice* (London: Lutterworth Press, 1965). The broad perspective from which he writes, however, prevents him (by his own admission) from making any prescriptions which would apply across all Reformed denominations.

Present-day liturgical forms must be tentative. Liturgies cannot be *made* in any case; if meaningful, they, like symbols, are *begotten* out of group experience. But a disunited group can never hope to beget a unifying expression of devotion. This is true of Christianity as a whole; it is true of Presbyterianism in particular. Several branches of American Presbyterianism are, therefore, taking a step toward enabling their members to achieve the kind of unity of experience which can enable them to give birth, in time, to a form of Christian worship which will express the faith of a new age while maintaining the Church's fellowship with all ages and with its Lord as revealed in the scripture.[7]

There is, of course, the seemingly ever-present conviction, held by many Presbyterians, that a fixed liturgy will always be anathema to Presbyterian church polity and local pastoral or evangelical needs. Whether stemming from North American culture, or perhaps from earlier Puritan and separatist movements in Britain, or a mixture of both these and other factors, such an individualized, congregationally-based understanding of liturgical freedom has remained prevalent in many sectors of the denomination. Perhaps sensitivity to this segment of the church has rendered authors hesitant to push too hard for a common form of liturgy. Charles Baird witnessed to the well-known Presbyterian debate over liturgical freedom as early as 1855 in his collection *Eutaxia*.[8] David Douglas Bannerman gave detailed accounts of the same debate in both Britain and North America in his book *The Worship of the Presbyterian Church: with special reference to the question of liturgies* in 1884.[9] The Canadian minister Robert Johnson sums up the general feelings regarding fixed liturgies and liturgical freedom in 1901 thus:

> To Presbyterians, therefore, thankful as they are for an historic past that has in it so much to arouse gratitude to God and loyalty to the Church they love, the citing of the

---

[7] Melton, *Presbyterian Worship in America*, 147-148.

[8] A Minister of the Presbyterian Church [Charles Baird], *Eutaxia: or the Presbyterian Liturgies: Historical Sketches* (New York: M.W. Dodd, 1855).

[9] D. D. Bannerman, *The Worship of the Presbyterian Church: with special reference to the question of liturgies* (Edinburgh: Andrew Elliot, 1884).

practice of their forefathers in Reformation times, or even that of the early fathers of the Church, can never be a final argument for the acceptance of any particular method in worship. Believing in a Church in which the Spirit of God as truly governs and guides to-day [sic] as He did in Reformation or post-Apostolic times, and in a Christian liberty of which neither the practice nor legislation of holy men of the past can deprive them, they rightly refuse to surrender their liberty or to retire from their responsibility.[10]

Alongside the group of authors writing descriptive histories of Presbyterian worship in the middle of the 20th century, there has also been a significant outpouring of works of liturgical theology from within the Presbyterian tradition since 1960, many of which were non-academic in tone. These works helpfully awaken readers to the importance of worship, oftentimes explicitly calling for the reform of worship practices in the contemporary church to meet changing pastoral needs. Floyd Doud Shafer's book *Liturgy: Worship and Work* is one example of this type of work.[11] John E. Burkhart's *Worship: A Searching Examination of the Liturgical Experience* is another.[12]

---

[10] Robert Johnson, *Presbyterian Worship: Its Spirit, Meaning, and History* (Toronto: The Publishers Syndicate, 1901), 12-13. Johnson's book, primarily addressed to the Presbyterian Church in Canada, is a North American example of worship as a "living subject of discussion and practice in the Presbyterian Churches" in the late nineteenth and early twentieth centuries. (introduction, page v). Leaning hard on its preference for liberty to abstain from set forms, the book nevertheless shows how open the question of the use of liturgies was at this time. Indeed, it shows the great interest in Presbyterian worship in general and gratitude for a spirit of a Church ever reforming. A modern historian might question some of Johnson's characterizations of history, especially his claim that Knox's liturgy essentially held the people silent (23), given what we know about the use of Psalmody as well as the possible voicing of the Lord's prayer and Creed by the people in worship.

[11] Floyd Doud Shafer, *Liturgy: Worship and Work* (Philadelphia: Board of Christian Education, 1966).

[12] John E. Burkhart, *Worship: A Searching Examination of the Liturgical Experience* (Philadelphia: The Westminster Press, 1982).

There are many other fine books that have been important pedagogical sources in Presbyterian settings focusing more broadly on Reformed worship, or even more generally, on Protestant or Christian Worship. Foremost among these are the books of James F. White. Also notable and more recent are Ruth Duck's *Worship for the Whole People of God*[13] and two edited volumes: *Christian Worship in Reformed Churches Past and Present,* edited by Lukas Vischer,[14] and *To Glorify God: Essays on Modern Reformed Liturgy,* edited by Bryan Spinks and Iain Torrance.[15] An excellent but older bibliographic resource is volume four of Nelson Burr's *Critical Bibliography of Religion in America,* which lists many influential books and other works pertaining to worship renewal in the United States up to the year 1960.[16]

Some Presbyterian-focused books mix theological reflections with historical practices in a more purposeful way. Works by Hughes Oliphant Old come to mind, such as his book *Worship: Reformed According to Scripture.*[17] However, few of the authors in this vein take the extra step of offering advice on how such theological musings might translate concretely into current or future worship practices. Those that do, tend to do so by applying a rather conservative interpretation of the regulative principle. The resulting suggestions often end up looking like a reworked Genevan pattern or the order from the Westminster Directory.[18]

---

[13] Ruth Duck, *Worship for the Whole People of God: Vital Worship for the 21st Century* (Louisville: Westminster John Knox, 2013).

[14] Lukas Vischer, *Christian Worship in Reformed Churches Past and Present* (Grand Rapids: Wm B. Eerdmans, 2003).

[15] Bryan Spinks and Iain Torrance, eds., *To Glorify God: Essays on Modern Reformed Liturgy* (Grand Rapids, Wm B. Eerdmans, 1999).

[16] Nelson Burr, *Critical Bibliography of Religion in America.* Volume 4, Part 4, Section III (Binghamton, NY: Vail-Ballou Press (for Princeton University Press), 1961), 795-808. One additional, particularly important example to note is Horton Davies's *Christian Worship: Its history and meaning* (New York: Abingdon Press, 1957). Davies was a long-time professor of Christian history at Princeton University who also taught regularly at Princeton Theological Seminary. He was highly respected as a historian and theologian, and was a prolific author.

[17] Hughes Oliphant Old, *Worship: Reformed According to Scripture,* revised and expanded edition (Louisville: Westminster John Knox Press, 2002).

[18] For example, see Philip Ryken, Derek Thomas, and J. Ligon Duncan III, eds., *Give Praise to God: A Vision for Reforming Worship* (Phillipsburg, NJ: P&R Publishing, 2003). Another example is D.G. Hart and John R. Muether, *With Reverence and Awe: Returning to the Basics of Reformed Worship* (Phillipsburg, NJ: P&R Publishing, 2002).

Standing in contrast to these conservative efforts is one book, Donald Macleod's *Presbyterian Worship: its meaning and method.*[19] Of all the texts on Presbyterian worship published in the twentieth century, Macleod is perhaps the most prescriptive in tone. Unlike many other books of earlier eras, Macleod does not offer orders of worship which are based in the preaching service model stemming from the nineteenth century evangelical and liturgical movements. Nor does he offer a sort of ecumenical conflation of liturgies as did Scott Francis Brenner in his 1944 book *The Way of Worship.*[20] Nor does he offer a conservative renewal of Genevan or Westminster Directory pattern. Rather, MacLeod's writing is marked by an implicit yet very strong advocacy for *The Worshipbook* (1970) and the UPCUSA's 1961 Directory for Worship. And while he frequently moves into the realm of liturgical theology, the bulk of Macleod's book is meant as a "source of encouragement and a handy guide" to Presbyterian worship practices.[21] A notable series of recent additions in this vein of works mixing theological musings with historical practice has been Paul Galbreath's collection of books, especially *Re-Forming the Liturgy: Past, Present, and Future.*[22]

A highly influential genre spanning the nineteenth and much of the twentieth centuries has been the so-called "ministers manual." These are practical works aimed at offering guidance to local ministers on matters of worship. They often pay special attention to the needs and practices of the presider, as one would expect. There are far too many examples

---

[19] Donald MacLeod, *Presbyterian Worship: its meaning and method,* revised edition (Atlanta: John Knox Press, 1980). MacLeod's book is intentionally denominationally focused but also ecumenically aware. Though UPCUSA resources are primary for him, he also explicitly draws on the PCUS's *Directory for Worship and Work* (1963) and a number of other Reformed service books from North America, Britain, and India.

[20] Scott Francis Brenner, *The Way of Worship: A Study in Ecumenical Recovery* (New York: The MacMillan Company, 1944). Brenner was an ordained minister of the United Presbyterian Church. In seeking to promote continued renewal of Reformed worship in an ecumenical context, Brenner provides an historical treatment of liturgy and sacramental theology. He also provides a sample ecumenical order for worship (with eucharist) that synthesizes both Western and Eastern terminologies, showing the extent to which his ecumenism embraced the entirety of the Christian liturgical tradition.

[21] Macleod, *Presbyterian Worship,* foreword.

[22] Paul Galbreath, *Re-Forming the Liturgy: Past, Present, and Future* (Eugene, OR: Cascade Books, 2019).

in this genre to list.[23] Their abundance and long life span not only suggests that they have been a valued resource among Presbyterian ministers, but also hints at the fact that many ministers, despite their seminary training, either found their personal expertise in the area of worship lacking or at least needed ongoing support in worship leadership beyond seminary.

What insights can one glean by surveying this literary corpus on worship in the Presbyterian tradition? First, there is a rich and varied history of resources within the tradition on which to draw, but the overarching approach to worship pedagogy in the Presbyterian realm has been thoroughly descriptive, not prescriptive in tone. Second, since the 1980s there has been no general-use academic work particular to Presbyterian worship at all.

A Prescription for Presbyterian Worship

Worship in Calvin's Geneva was marked by a system of discretionary liturgy which differed markedly from the system as it is commonly understood by Presbyterians to exist today. In Calvin's Geneva, while the exact words of the liturgy were never prescribed, both the order of worship (that is, the liturgical structure) and the basic tenor of the prayers were expected to be followed.[24] However, the obligation to follow these certain structures extended only as far as the authority of those creating it. Thus, for Calvin's Geneva, the liturgy he created, and which was edited and approved by the city council, was the *de facto* liturgy for the entire

---

[23] For example, see Albert W. Palmer, *The Art of Conducting Public Worship* (New York: MacMillan, 1939). These types of manuals were still being published into the early 1960s. Scott Brenner, in addition to his book *The Way of Worship*, also wrote a manual called *The Art of Worship* in 1961. Julius Melton's Ph.D. dissertation (Princeton University, 1966) has an extensive discussion of Manuals (237-.)

[24] Many of the following ideas were confirmed and/or refined during a phone conversation in April 2020 with Elsie Anne McKee, who at the time of this writing is the Archibald Alexander Professor of Reformation Studies and the History of Worship at Princeton Theological Seminary. Many thanks to Dr. McKee for sharing her wisdom on this portion of the chapter.

city. Such was Calvin's model of "discretionary" liturgy. This contrasts sharply with the contemporary understanding, which seems to have emerged only in the nineteenth century, but which often is read backwards into earlier eras.[25] In this contemporary understanding, liturgy is usually understood as both as structure (form/order) of worship and set texts within that structure. The discretion to use or disregard liturgies, in that understanding, extends both to the texts themselves *and* to the structures within which they are found. One could say that there is, in this understanding, a sense of "total" discretion. Moreover, such total discretion is granted not just to a synod or General Assembly, but to each individual pastor or session.

The Directory for Publick Worship, originally published in 1645 and known colloquially as the Westminster Directory, carried forward the essential paradigmatic elements of liturgical practice in Calvin's Geneva. This means that, according to both established Presbyterian custom and the wording of the Westminster Directory itself, the prescribed structure of worship, that is, the so-called "heads and articles," was obligatory.[26] It

---

[25] See, for example, David Douglas Banner's *The Worship of the Presbyterian Church, with special reference to the question of liturgies* (Edinburgh: Andrew Elliot, 1884).

[26] "The Estates of Parliament now convened... after the publick reading and serious consideration of the act under-written of the General Assembly... do heartily and cheerfully agree to the said Directory, according to the act of the General Assembly approving the same. Which act, together with the Directory itself; the Estates of Parliament do, without a contrary voice, ratify and approve in all the Heads and Articles thereof; and do interpone and add the authority of Parliament to the said act of the General Assembly. And do ordain the same to have the strength and force of a law and act of parliament, and execution to pass thereupon, for observing the said Directory, according to the said act of the General Assembly to al points." (Introductory paragraph) https://www.apuritansmind.com/westminster-standards/directory-of-publick-worship/. The most important source for understanding the Westminster Directory and its Americanization is Stanley Hall, "The American Presbyterian Directory for Worship: History of a Liturgical Strategy" (Ph.D. Dissertation, University of Notre Dame, 1990). Though exceedingly thorough and brilliant, Hall's work does not in fact ever address to what extent the *structures* of the Directory were considered obligatory. I believe this might be because of his tendency to conflate the idea of "set forms," a topic of frequent debate, with set liturgical texts. More careful study is needed showing the extent to which imperative language ("is to", "shall", etc.) outlines a mandatory structure of worship. This author is of the opinion that such language in both the 1645 Directory and subsequent American revisions of it does indeed make mandatory a structure for worship, if not the textual content filling out that structure. The heads and articles argument itself is

also means that, while the structures were obligatory, the actual texts of the prayers included could be modified, so long as they remained true to good doctrine and to the general "sense and scope" of Directory text.[27] The idea of the texts in the Directory being a mere "help and furniture" does go slightly beyond the level of freedom perhaps envisioned by Calvin for Geneva, but it does not disrupt the idea of set structures.[28] Additionally, and importantly, the ratification of the Westminster Directory established that it was the Parliament, along with the General Assembly of the Kirk, which had authority to establish the order of worship throughout the nation. The discretion granted to a local minister only extended to the text of prayers, selection of readings, and psalms, and other decisions such as the frequency with which the sacraments were administered. In other words, the passing of the Westminster Directory represented a geographical expansion of the discretionary liturgy model set up by Calvin and city council for Geneva. American Presbyterians, for the almost one hundred years between the founding of their earliest congregations and the signing of the Declaration of Independence, remained under the same authority as the rest of the Church of Scotland.[29] And though American versions of the Directory for Worship were significantly altered from the 1645 original and also

---

clear from reading the document, in which each "head" (heading) designates a particular part of the worship service, and the articles are the particular subjects or movements within that part.

[27] "Wherein our care hath been to hold forth such things as are of divine institution in every ordinance; and other things we have endeavoured to set forth according to the rules of Christian prudence, agreeable to the general rules of the word of God; our meaning therein being only, that the general heads, the sense and scope of the prayers, and other parts of publick worship, being known to all, there may be a consent of all the churches in those things that contain the substance of the service and worship of God; and the ministers may be hereby directed, in their administrations, to keep like soundness in doctrine and prayer, and may, if need be, have some help and furniture, and yet so as they become not hereby slothful and negligent in stirring up the gifts of Christ in them; but that each one, by meditation, by taking heed to himself, and the flock of God committed to him, and by wise (sic) observing the ways of Divine Providence, may be careful to furnish his heart and tongue with further or other materials of prayer and exhortation, as shall be needful upon all occasions." (Preface) https://www.apuritansmind.com/westminster-standards/directory-of-publick-worship/

[28] Hall outlines the concept and debates over sample prayer texts as "help and furniture" in "The American Presbyterian Directory for Worship," 55-59.

[29] Hall, "The American Presbyterian Directory for Worship", 92.

increasingly ignored through the nineteenth and early twentieth centuries, they did, at least officially via the text of the Directory itself, carry forward this particular model of discretionary liturgy until the 1960s.[30]

In the early 1960s, the United Presbyterian Church in the United States of America (UPCUSA) and the Presbyterian Church in the United States (PCUS) each drafted completely new directories for worship.[31] With regard to the idea of set structures for worship, both were double edged swords. On the one hand, they called loudly and eloquently for a fresh appreciation of the importance of worship within their respective denominations and offered a much-needed update to those denominations' official theologies of worship, especially regarding the importance of the sacraments. This would help spur many Presbyterian congregations to consider the issue of weekly celebration of the Eucharist. In fact, if there is one thing for which nearly all the authors writing about Presbyterian worship have consistently advocated, it is the more frequent celebration of the Eucharist; however, it is significant to see that call within the Directory for Worship itself. James White reflects on this late 20th century eucharistic renewal among Presbyterians when he says, "perhaps Presbyterians have still not caught up with Calvin, but efforts are certainly being made to do so, and even to go far beyond what he envisioned."[32]

On the other hand, neither of the 1960s directories set forth an order of regular Sunday worship that was in any sense obligatory. Whether embracing the idea of total discretion purposefully or not, in creating these new directories, the nation's two largest Presbyterian denominations enshrined as church law a total liturgical discretion; pastors and congregations were officially free to create any order of worship they desired, with any contents they desired, as long as those structure and contents were faithful to the general ethos of the Directory.

---

[30] There were of course some minor changes as well as arguments regarding the Directory along the way, in the late nineteenth century especially, but none of these were substantive. See Hall, "The American Presbyterian Directory for Worship," 185-199.

[31] More details of this process can be found in chapter 6 by Peter C. Bower.

[32] White, *Protestant Worship*, 78.

One important factor contributing to a more theologically rich but liturgically permissive 1961 Directory was the presence of the Book of Common Worship. Hall notes that, in fact, the UPCUSA's new directory "came about as a function of the planned revision of the *Book of Common Worship*."[33] The book "was intended to serve the preparation of a book of voluntary liturgical forms, in a rather ironic over-turning of the traditionally guarded permission for the use of aids and helps for the minister."[34] Since the publication of the 1906 *Book of Common Worship*, in fact, Presbyterian liturgists had been seeking to convince congregations and their ministers to use the liturgical books published by the denomination. However, given the fact that the understanding of liturgical discretion had shifted in the previous century to include both texts and structures, they had to do so largely by commending their usefulness as mere exemplary models. That is, over the nineteenth century, Presbyterian pastors had gradually taken for themselves full license over both the structures and texts of worship, but this was only officially affirmed in the 1960s with the publication of new directories for worship, whose careful wording left ministers free to do essentially anything that was faithful to the ethos of the new directories. It was thus not understood as necessary to abide by the clearly delineated liturgical structures of the 1961 UPCUSA directory, as it had been initially under the Westminster Directory or certainly in earlier eras under Knox or Calvin. The irony earlier pointed out by Hall is that the 1906, 1932, and 1946 editions of the Book of Common Worship were published under the assumption that ministers had total discretion over the worship in their congregations, while in fact that would not be the case according to church law until the 1960s. The 2018 Directory revised by the Presbyterian Church (U.S.A) (PC(USA)), which like its predecessors clearly suggests a set of structures for worship to be used in alignment with the Book of Common Worship, carries that (now codified) assumption forward to the present day, granting to the local minister and/or the session a "total" discretion:

> The order of worship offered here for the Service for the Lord's Day is rooted in Scripture, the traditions of the universal Church, and our Reformed heritage. In

---

[33] Hall, "The American Presbyterian Directory for Worship," 316.
[34] Hall, "The American Presbyterian Directory for Worship," 344.

particular, it seeks to uphold the centrality of Word and Sacraments in the Church's faith, life, and worship. This description of the Service for the Lord's Day is presented as one commendable model, but is not intended to exclude other ways of ordering worship.[35]

It need not be so, however. The current *Directory for Worship* and Book of Common Worship already give Presbyterians a superb "compass and map" for guiding their liturgical renewal. The question is to what extent the denomination and its leadership desire and/or are willing to create firmer mechanisms for effecting change at the local level. One of the key mechanisms, I believe, will be for pedagogues in our seminaries to reclaim and begin teaching the older and more long-established idea of discretionary liturgy; that is, our pedagogy needs to move away from the basic assumption that local pastors, when push comes to shove, have always had total freedom to conduct worship however they wish. In other words, we need to craft a pedagogy for Presbyterians that is more prescriptive, even while it continues to be descriptive of practices both in our past and present. This will include a detailed and profound appreciation for the liturgical freedoms enjoyed by British, American, and Canadian Presbyterians and their ecclesial offspring over the last century and a half. However, it will do so in a way that tempers students' assumptions of "total discretion" by more purposefully teaching the Reformed church's past heritage of fixed, or at least normative, liturgical structures.

It will also include a strong call for a way of worship that is unapologetic in its Presbyterian identity and which will meet the pastoral needs of the Church moving into the future. As the late liturgist Horace T. Allen was wont to remind people, denominational particularities regarding worship are still of importance even in this ecumenical age. Leaders who are being educated and trained for service in a denominational tradition must understand the particularities of that tradition. This is especially true of worship, which is not only the foundational theological activity of the Christian community, but which is also the most visible leadership venue for ministers, musicians, and

---

[35] PC(USA) Directory for Worship 2018, W-3.0103.
https://www.presbyterianmission.org/ministries/worship/directory-for-worship/rdfw-chapter-three/.

other church leaders. If Presbyterian seminaries and other educational avenues for church leaders are not teaching the history, practices, and theology of worship in the Presbyterian tradition, then they are failing to adequately prepare leaders for their most important and visible role in the local church.

A return to normative liturgical structures across the PC(USA) is not just about historical precedent, but also about pastoral need. At present, there are no actual mechanisms for ensuring that the worship of local churches is done with integrity, including the requirement (elucidated not only in the Directory for Worship, but also by Calvin himself and countless other Reformed theologians) that Word and Sacrament are central to the liturgy.[36] Given the fact that the current Directory for Worship grants authority variously to the local minister and to the session to make decisions, one cannot simply assume that better training for ministers will accomplish change. The wording of the Directory itself needs to be clarified so that both pastors and sessions have a greater measure of accountability to the wider church.[37] If the law of prayer indeed constitutes our law of belief, as the famous *"lex credendi"* adage claims, then we owe it to our congregations to have worship which is designed and executed well enough to be truly formative. More than that, though, we owe our congregations worship which magnifies the particularities of the Reformed tradition,[38] a goal which will never be realized until 1) the formation of both teaching elders (ministers of Word and Sacrament) and ruling elders (members of session) undergoes some

---

[36] PC(USA) Directory for Worship 2018, W-3.0102, "The Service for the Lord's Day is a service of Word and Sacrament." Among other places, Calvin discusses the link between Word and Sacrament in the *Institutes* Book 4, Chapter 14. Works by many of the modern authors cited in the preceding paragraphs attest to the same idea.

[37] For instance, one might reword the second paragraph of PC(USA) Directory for Worship W-1.0103 thus: "The order of worship offered here for the Service for the Lord's Day is rooted in Scripture, the traditions of the universal Church, and our Reformed heritage. In particular, it seeks to uphold the centrality of Word and Sacraments in the Church's faith, life, and worship. This [order] of the Service for the Lord's Day is presented [as this denomination's primary] model, but is not intended to exclude other ways of ordering worship. Other patterns may be appropriate in the context of a particular congregation or culture, provided that they [maintain the centrality of Word and Sacrament on each Lord' Day], [are] open to the Spirit, and [are] dedicated to the glory of God.

[38] The phrase "magnify particularities" is taken from Horace T. Allen, Jr. See chapter 1 by Mark Stamm.

reforms, and 2) that formation includes the embrace of normative structures that safeguard and celebrate the particularities of the Reformed liturgical tradition.

I acknowledge that there are some immense difficulties with such a proposal. Presbyterian seminaries are populated more and more by ecumenically diverse student bodies, as well as a greater percentage of distance learners and part-time students. In many current M.Div. curricula, students only take a single introductory course on worship, which means that professors are simply unable to teach much that is Presbyterian-specific. Moreover, attempts at top-down change in the church, especially in an American context, are often fraught with controversy and resistance. Yet for many decades, leaders in the church have been calling for change in the way we worship. How then might we respond concretely to this call for pedagogical change? Thankfully, the work of creating distinctive and rich liturgical forms for our time has already largely happened within the Presbyterian denominations through the publication of The Book of Common Worship, or for denominations like the Presbyterian Church in America, the commonly used *Worship Sourcebook*[39]. The question now is a question of reception, and that reception is bound up in the pedagogy of our pastoral and congregational leaders.

First, I would advocate for seminaries and theology departments to require at least *two* worship courses: The first could be a survey course as exists now, rightly offering a broad overview of Christian worship history and source materials, as well as introducing key concepts of liturgical theology. The second should be a course particular to the Presbyterian tradition, required only of Presbyterian students. This should include a detailed study of The Directory for Worship, The 2018 *Book of Common Worship* and its antecedents, and perhaps offer comparative elements between the PC(USA) and other Presbyterian/Reformed denominations using the new hermeneutic outlined below. Right now, many seminaries offer a number of elective courses in worship which in many cases are well populated by students. I would suggest perhaps turning one of these

---

[39] *The Worship Sourcebook,* 2nd ed., (Grand Rapids: Faith Alive Christian Resources, 2013). Created largely by folks at the Calvin Institute of Christian Worship, *The Worship Sourcebook* has gained traction among many PCA leaders who have a connection to the CICW and/or its annual Worship Symposium.

elective courses into the required course in Presbyterian or Reformed liturgy for seminarians within that tradition.

Second, I would advocate for more frequent celebration of liturgies in seminary chapels, and ones which normally utilize the denominational worship resources. As leaders are trained in seminaries, they not only gain a knowledge of worship through coursework, but they also absorb a sense of what worship should be during seminary chapel services. This is especially true for those seminary students, ever more common, who come to seminary without having had a life-long grounding in the practice of a local congregation. There are many complicated factors at work when planning seminary chapel services, not the least of which is the need to use chapel as a preaching and presiding laboratory for students and others.[40] However, increasing the frequency of services would make room for both "regular" services grounded in the denominational tradition and "special" services altered to meet the needs of a liturgical laboratory. The increased frequency of common prayer would also foster a greater sense of spiritual unity in the seminary community.

Third, and last, one should not underestimate the great deal of influence that conferences at the national, regional, and presbytery level have on local leaders. These should not be overlooked as a source of liturgical pedagogy. Within the Presbyterian Church (U.S.A), the primary example of such a national conference is the Presbyterian Association of Musicians' Conferences on Worship and Music, held annually at the Montreat Conference Center in Montreat, North Carolina. Many Presbyteries also have annual conferences centering around meetings of the Presbytery which feature communal worship, guest speakers, and workshops. Events like these have the potential for significant theological and liturgical formation both for pastors as a form of continuing education and for congregational leaders generally.

---

[40] Siobhan Garrigan and Todd E. Johnson's book *Common Worship in Theological Education* (Eugene, OR: Wipf and Stock, 2010) outlines many of these issues in great detail by tracing the actual practices of several denominational seminaries in the United States.

A New Hermeneutic

The evolving pedagogy for which I've been advocating has to do largely with the structures of worship as received by the church moving forward. These sorts of structures can be operative independent of particular textual, non-textual, and aesthetic elements. But in addition to a shifting pedagogy, there also needs to be a new hermeneutic for Presbyterian worship moving forward that addresses such elements. The core of liturgical studies curricula in the twentieth and twenty-first centuries has been centered around text criticism. For Christian communities whose liturgical texts are fixed along with their structures -- such as the Roman Catholic Church, Orthodox churches, and various Anglican churches -- this can be a wholly appropriate approach. However, for the Presbyterian tradition, such an approach falls far short in its attempt to provide an accurate picture of historical (or even current) practice. A hermeneutic for Presbyterian worship based primarily on text criticism is problematic on two fronts. First, it requires a stable version of the texts one is seeking to work with. While that approach is feasible for examining particular rites in and of themselves, it cannot be used for Presbyterian worship as a whole, where structures have historically been fixed, but not words. Second, some of the most distinctive historical aspects of Presbyterian worship have had to do with non-textual elements and aesthetics as much as anything else. Therefore any hermeneutic geared toward Presbyterian worship must meaningfully incorporate techniques that move far beyond the realm of text criticism.

This is, in this author's view, one of the reasons why teaching Presbyterian worship effectively has been so tricky. I am far from the first person to realize the need for a more inclusive way to study worship in Presbyterian and other similarly situated Christian communities. James White, arguably the most influential scholar of Protestant worship in the previous century, outlined such a more inclusive approach in his book *Protestant Worship: traditions in transition.*

> "We shall spend little time on liturgical texts, service books, or sacramental theology, the staples of most liturgical scholarship. Eucharistic prayers will scarcely be mentioned. These are not our priorities. Rather, we are

trying to delineate the phenomenon of Protestant worship as it happens for ordinary worshipers. Our concern is with the total event of worship as it occurs in local churches, not as analyzed in textbooks."[41]

To be sure, many Presbyterian pedagogues are already aware of this need for a fuller hermeneutic and incorporate the study of non-textual elements in their seminary or theology department classrooms.[42] Thankfully, and especially through the intersection of ritual studies and liturgical studies, many new tools have developed over the past several decades to help them do so.[43] However, to my knowledge, no one has yet written any book or other substantial general history of Presbyterian worship in a way that incorporates non-textual elements.[44] In fact, while there has continued to be a gracious outpouring of books and other resources on Christian worship over the past several decades, and while there has been some good recent work done in the realm of Reformed worship, there has been no substantial textbook about *Presbyterian* worship since the 1980s. Those books that have appeared have continued to work primarily with the tools of text criticism or have been works of liturgical theology.

Edward Foley has outlined an excellent and inclusive approach to studying the worship of the ecumenical Church in his book *From Age to Age*.[45] Similarly to other scholars such as Anita Stauffer (d. 2007), Foley utilizes visual elements such as architecture, paintings, and furnishings to

---

[41] James F. White, *Protestant Worship,* 14-15.

[42] I am grateful for the many colleagues across the PC(USA) seminaries who were willing to share with me curricula for their worship courses. It was encouraging to see the obvious thoughtfulness, expertise, and care for diversity with which they were prepared.

[43] See, for example, Nathan Mitchell, *Liturgy and the Social Sciences* (Collegeville: Liturgical Press, 1998).

[44] Several important works have addressed the question of non-textual elements in Reformed Worship in a more focused way. These include Graham Hughes's books *Worship as Meaning* (New York: Cambridge University Press, 2003) and *Reformed Sacramentality* (Collegeville, MN: Liturgical Press, 2017) as well as Martha Moore-Keish's *Do This in Remembrance of Me: A Ritual Approach to Reformed Eucharistic Theology* (Grand Rapids, MI: Eerdmans, 2008).

[45] Foley, Edward, *From Age to Age: How Christians Have Celebrated the Eucharist,* revised and expanded edition (Collegeville: Liturgical Press, 2009).

give a more complete picture of the worship of a given time and place. However, Foley is relatively unique in his use of "thick descriptions," a device borrowed from anthropology. Thick descriptions are marvelous ways to synthesize various types of data about worship practice into a manageable format, one that is easily understood by a reader.

The time is right for a new, authoritative resource on Presbyterian worship that models such an expanded hermeneutic. Not only will it help students of worship gain a more inclusive understanding of their own tradition, but it will also help them gain tools for understanding the incredible significance of non-textual elements in the worship of the communities they seek to lead. The 2018 Directory for Worship already provides a fairly thorough theological exploration of non-textual elements in its section on "Time, Space, and Matter" (W-1.02) and "Language, Symbols, and Culture" (W-1.03). However, knowing the theological underpinnings of non-textual elements is nearly useless pastorally unless one has tools for analyzing them, understanding their historical context, and putting them into practice. The type of resource I envision would be one specific to the Presbyterian tradition, and thus appropriate for use either as a supplemental resource in a general course on worship, or as a primary resource for an elective course on Presbyterian worship. It would first and foremost be an historical treatment of the practices of Presbyterian worship across various epochs of the Church's life, beginning with the late middle ages and proceeding up to the current day. Among other things, users of the resource would be introduced to relevant orders of worship, architecture, congregational song, choral and instrumental music, visual art (including vestments), and other non-textual elements from each epoch. These elements, perhaps synthesized with the help of thick descriptions and other techniques from the social sciences, would be the basis for a theological engagement, where students consider the dynamic interplay between a fully inclusive *lex orandi* and the *lex credendi*.

That is not to say, however, that a hermeneutic for Presbyterian worship should not include the careful study of texts. It is true that a system of discretionary liturgy makes it nearly impossible to engage in text-critical methods of historical liturgical study generally. This may in fact be one of the reasons why so few of the books surveying Presbyterian worship look first to the rites themselves as sources for theological inquiry. But this should not necessarily be the case. Liturgical theologians have no problem looking to early church orders, such as the First Apology of Justin or the Didache, for sources of both theology and practice, even though these documents represent just one particular time and place. Yet we have not done so in any meaningful way yet with the liturgies of Calvin, Knox, A.A. Hodge, John Williamson Nevin, or others. For understanding Calvin's theological thoughts on worship, for instance, we turn not to the *Forme des Prières*, but instead to the *Institutes*, or perhaps various commentaries or sermons. Yet consider that, since the time of the Reformation in Geneva, English speaking Presbyterians have never been without an official worship structure that contained at least some example texts filling out that structure. A new, more complete hermeneutic for our tradition should include study of such texts, both historic and contemporary, alongside the various structures and non-textual elements.

Conclusion

James White once wrote that "by and large, the history in Scotland and North America among Presbyterians is that of a tradition compromised, becoming vulnerable to both political and cultural practices as it evolved."[46] That continues to be the case for Presbyterians now. Our liturgical tradition is rich, and today we have an incredibly well-written Directory for Worship and Book of Common Worship, which are there for the using. But if most Presbyterian liturgists, in their heart of hearts, think that such worship should be normative for the denomination, they have compromised such convictions by tacitly endorsing the idea of "total" liturgical discretion. Compromise is in a way, of course, the nature of the American Presbyterian system, its government comprising a diverse mixture of ruling elders and ministers of Word and Sacrament from across a large and increasingly diverse social landscape, all of whom must engage in compromise to get done the business of being Church. But compromise in the realm of worship

---

[46] White, *Protestant Worship*, 70.

cannot mean giving up what is essential and distinctive to our tradition.[47] Presbyterian worship is, at its roots, liturgical worship, by which I mean it has its origins in set forms that are corporate, belonging to the whole church, and which both influence and express the theology of the Presbyterian tradition. Because of this, the more I see Presbyterians learning about and embracing their rich denominational history, the more I believe that the arc of its liturgical history will bend, not towards greater freedom *from* liturgy, but rather towards the freedom *to* embrace liturgical structures which bind us together in a united yet diverse community of love.[48]

The essential element to consider for Presbyterians is, as I have argued, the basic structure of our common worship as articulated for each generation anew in the Directory for Worship and The Book of Common Worship. Texts themselves, and certainly many non-textual elements, should be freely and faithfully adapted according to local culture and tradition. Another way to argue the point about common structure is to insist, as the PC(USA) Directory for Worship already does, that Word and Sacrament are the central elements of Reformed worship. Presbyterian liturgical scholars for many decades, including the late Horace T. Allen, Jr., to whom this volume is dedicated, should be given credit for moving the denomination and its documents in this hopeful direction to a great extent already. If scholars and other leaders of today can continue to promote the vision of these earlier reformers to make the sacraments central -- celebrated alongside and in equal weight to the proclamation and preaching of the Word on Sundays -- then we could

---

[47] Unfortunately, there is not sufficient room here to discuss in detail what I hold as the "essential" and "distinctive" elements of Reformed worship, though I do make some suggestions in the following paragraphs. Fortunately, this topic has already been treated at greater length recently in *The Oxford Handbook of Presbyterianism* (New York: Oxford University Press, 2019). Another broad, liturgically oriented treatment of Reformed distinctives can be found in the excellent and now classic text by J.J. von Allmen, *Worship: its theology and practice* (London: Lutterworth Press, 1965).

[48] There is a parallel here to the classic definitions of Christian freedom as articulated by Aquinas and others. To be free in God is to embrace our humanity in its fullness, to embrace eternal life. Our humanity is meant also for community and ritual, and these things are made manifest to us in liturgical worship, for it is there that community is formed through ritual in communion with the Triune God. Therefore, to embrace our common rituals, our liturgical worship, is to embrace our humanity, and thus our freedom.

see a drastic shift in the worship of most local Presbyterian congregations, one which would align them more closely with the models already given in the Directory for Worship and Book of Common Worship, not to mention our ecumenical partners.

Perhaps American Presbyterians are afraid of giving up too much of their freedom because it runs counter to the Hooverian ideal of "rugged individualism." To this sentiment I might respond with the help of Michael Horton:

> As constituted "from above" by the always surprising and disruptive announcement of the gospel, the covenant community receives its catholicity along with its entire being *extra nos,* outside itself, in spite of its own history of unfaithfulness. As constituted "from below" in history ("to a thousand generations"), catholicity is mediated through the faithful ministry of Word and Sacrament, yielding a succession of faith from one generation to another across all times and places. . .
>
> . . . particular (local) churches must make "every effort to maintain the unity of the Spirit in the bond of peace" (Eph. 4:3) by ever wider and deeper solidarity that expresses itself in concrete, visible, and enduring structures.[49]

One could apply this ecclesiological argument easily to the worship of the church, and Horton in fact does so in his chapter. One of the "enduring structures" that Horton calls for, I argue, is a common worship that is grounded in the ecumenical witness of the Church but which is not afraid to magnify the particularities of the Presbyterian tradition. It should also be borne constantly in mind that ecumenical awareness as part of liturgical renewal is not just about playing nice with others; it's about healing the wounds of division within the Church. These wounds not only hurt our relationships to one another as

---

[49] Horton, Michael, "The Church," in *Christian Dogmatics: Reformed Theology for the Church Catholic* (Grand Rapids: Baker Academic, 2016), 331.

Christians; they hurt our ability to witness to the kingdom of God, a kingdom mirrored, albeit dimly, by us, the Church, in the world.

It is difficult to imagine what the future holds for the PC(USA) or any other Presbyterian denomination, or how ecumenical endeavors and church mergers will continue to change the trajectory of things. Regardless of these uncertainties, however, I am absolutely sure that the worship of the Church will remain central to its identity in whatever form it takes. I am also absolutely sure that the Presbyterian tradition has made unique and lasting contributions to the life of the ecumenical Church and is worth upholding. So long as we continue to live into our tradition, let us do so with our worship at the center, embracing a new hermeneutic and an evolving pedagogy that will lead us with faithful confidence into the future.

10. PROPOSALS FOR DIAGNOSING AND RESTORING WORSHIP IN THE KOREAN PRESBYTERIAN CHURCH

by Seung Joong Joo

Introduction

According to Marva Dawn, "worship is a total immersion in the eternity of God's infinite splendor for the sole purpose of honoring God."[1] If we were to say this in the language of the Reformed tradition, worship can be said to be an act of response that glorifies God alone. The love and grace that God has given us is so overwhelmingly amazing that, whenever we stand before God, we give God glory with gratitude and wholeheartedness, giving back our best to God; this is true worship.

However, this dignified ideal of worship has begun to deteriorate in the Korean Presbyterian Church. As a consequence of changing liturgical philosophies, so-called "worship wars," already familiar to North American Protestant churches, have begun within Korean

---

[1] Marva J. Dawn, *A Royal "Waste" of Time* (Grand Rapids: Wm. B. Eerdmans Publishing Co., 1999), 11.

Presbyterianism.[2] There is a growing tendency among leaders to view worship as a means of attracting more people into the Church; as a consequence, many such leaders have begun to think of worship as simply another pastoral program. That is, as the church begins to feel threatened by various socio-cultural changes that are infiltrating the church, it is using worship, among several other pastoral methods, as a means to deal with this issue. God, who should be the heart, center, and recipient of worship, is now being removed from that pride of place; humanity taking it instead. In particular, under the influence of postmodernism's sensational culture, worship in Korean Presbyterianism has begun degrading into a tool to satisfy people's desire for entertainment and enjoyment.

One may ask, "how ought the Korean Presbyterian Church approach this issue?" The answer is clear; we must restore the true nature of worship — an act of glorifying God alone. This article intends to analyze the worship of the Korean Presbyterian Church through the worship theology of the reformer Calvin, to discuss the current issues around worship, and to propose suggestions for a recovery of the type of true worship proper to Calvinist tradition.

The reason for using Calvin's theology to diagnose the worship of the Korean Presbyterian Church is because his worship theology provides the most fundamental standards of evaluation for Presbyterians. Of course, Calvin is not a theologian representing the whole Protestant church, and the theological and pastoral view of his worship does not represent the view of Korean church worship. Nevertheless, since seventy-five percent of Korean churches are placed in Reformed church traditions, including Presbyterian churches, the reason for using Calvin's theology of worship as a diagnostic criterion is to provide a clear evaluation standard for pastoral and theological diagnosis.[3] Therefore, even though Calvin is not a theologian representing the whole Protestant church, owing to the overwhelmingly Reformed demographic of Korean

---

[2] For more information regarding "worship wars," see Ronald P. Byars, *The Future of Protestant Worship: Beyond the Worship Wars* (Louisville: Westminster John Knox Press, 2002), 8-20.

[3] Byeong-cheol Ko, "Research Report on Religious Status in Korea" (Seoul: Institute for Religious Culture, 2008), 19-26.

Christians, I will occasionally speak more generally about the "Korean Protestant Churches" within this chapter.

Calvin's goal in reforming worship was to regain the purity of worship according to the Bible, and for this, Calvin attempted to realign every component of worship to scripture. Therefore, the most basic principles of worship that Calvin sought to reform were the warrant of scripture and the custom of the ancient Church.[4] Calvin believed that reforming worship meant restoration of the purity of the worship in the apostolic age, and for this, worship should be evaluated in the light of the Bible. Therefore, in order to restore the worship of the Korean Presbyterian Church which has gone astray, it is important to analyze the current situation, centering on Calvin's worship theology, and to present some suggestions for the restoration of worship.

Calvin's Worship Theology

As mentioned earlier, Calvin aimed to restore the purity of biblical worship through worship reform. He continually reviewed and sought to rectify all parts of worship in light of the Bible, and he believed that every aspect of worship must find its justification in the teachings of the Bible and/or in early apostolic tradition; thus, he was unable to accept any form of worship that one of these sources failed to direct. Of course, this does not mean that every sequence of worship is specified in the Bible. However, Calvin insisted, "The Lord has in his sacred oracles faithfully embraced and clearly expressed both the whole sum of true righteousness, and all aspects of the worship of his majesty, and whatever was necessary to salvation,"[5] and emphasized that every sequence of worship should at least find some implicit justification in the teachings of the Bible.

---

[4] Bard Thompson, *Liturgies of the Western Church* (Philadelphia: Fortress Press, 1961), 185.

[5] John Calvin, *Institutes of the Christian Religion* (Philadelphia: The Westminster Press, 1960), 4:10:30.

In particular, Calvin understood Acts 2:42 ("They devoted themselves to the apostles' teaching and to fellowship, to the breaking of bread and to prayer") as the "most important custom of the apostolic church."[6] In this verse he points out the four most important elements of Church worship: the proclamation of the Word (teaching), the sacraments, public prayer (including praise),[7] and fellowship (almsgiving). Calvin points out "the proclamation of the Word" as the first legitimate element offered in true worship to God, for true worship requires obedience to God's Word. Calvin claimed that this verse, "He will teach us his ways, so that we may walk in his paths" (Micah 4:2), is the provision for the Word to be a legitimate element of worship, and therefore, stressed that every worship service must have a sermon that teaches and proclaims the word of God. Then, based on Acts 2:42, Calvin emphasizes that the Sacrament, "the visible word," along with the proclamation of the Word, is another key element of worship. Calvin insisted that communion be taken every Lord's Day, as the early Church did, which reflects his thought that communion is a significant part of the worship service held every week. Calvin even stated, "This custom which enjoins us to take communion once a year is a veritable invention of the Devil. The Lord's Table should have been spread at least once a week for the assembly of Christians."[8] Although Calvin's claim later met with opposition from Geneva's administrative leaders, he eventually compromised to having communion four times a year (Christmas, Easter, Pentecost, and Thanksgiving), but he clearly stated, "at least once a week" was most ideal.[9]

When a person truly worships God, the Holy Spirit proclaims the Word of God through preaching, confirms it through the Sacrament, entrusts believers with faith in the Word, and draws humanity into union with Christ. As a result, human beings who truly worship God not only stand in awe before Him, but also accept God as the one who is worthy of faith and trust. "O who has true faith cannot be indifferent about

---

[6] "Thus it became the unvarying rule that no meeting of the church should take place without the Word, prayers, partaking of the Supper, and almsgiving." Calvin, *Institutes* 4:17:44.

[7] Calvin mentioned that the act of praise is singing our prayers to God. Cf. Calvin, *Institutes* 3:20:31.

[8] Calvin, *Institutes* 4:17:46.

[9] Calvin, *Institutes* 4:17:43.

calling upon God."[10] Therefore, along with the Word and Sacrament, Calvin says that "the chief part of his worship lies in the office of prayer."[11] In other words, through the Word and Sacraments, a person whose faith and trust has been solidified in God will ask for the grace of God through prayer. In other words, Calvin considered prayer to be the fruit of faith and trust in God and Christ, and therefore, viewed the act of praying to be a significant component of worship.

One should note that Calvin distinguishes between spoken prayer and sung prayer, including hymns in his spectrum of prayer. For this reason, Calvin emphasized congregational song and instructed that the lyrics of the congregational hymns should always be grounded in the scripture. He introduced congregational songs into worship to help the congregation pray to God with sincerity of the heart, focusing particularly (though not exclusively) on metrical psalms. He was convinced that the most appropriate form of praise,

in praying with a sincere heart, is when the whole congregation sings psalms together to simple melodies.

Finally, along with sermon, Sacrament, and prayer, Calvin included "fellowship" or "almsgiving" as the fourth essential element of worship. Warranted by Acts 2:42, "They devoted themselves to the apostles' teaching and to fellowship, to the breaking of bread and to prayer," Calvin asserted, "Thus it became the unvarying rule that no meeting of the church should take place without the Word, prayers, partaking of the Supper, and almsgiving."[12] In the 1559 edition of his work *Institutes of the Christian Religion*, Calvin interprets "fellowship" from Acts 2:42 as "almsgiving,"[13] while in his commentary, he interprets "fellowship" more generally as "the bond of brotherly fellowship,"[14] stating that both "almsgiving" and "fellowship" are essential parts of worship. The reason why Calvin claimed "fellowship" or "almsgiving" as one of the fundamentals of worship is because those who truly worship God

---

[10] Calvin, *Institutes* 3:20:1.

[11] Calvin, *Institutes* 3:20:29.

[12] Calvin, *Institutes* 4:7:44.

[13] Calvin, *Institutes* 4:7:44.

[14] Calvin, *Commentary on the Acts of the Apostles*. Vol. 1 (Louisville: Westminster John Knox Press, 1958), 48.

through the proclamation of the Word, the Sacrament, and prayer cannot help but to live the Christian life of communion and generosity. Here we can see that worship does not end in a vertical relationship with God, but extends horizontally to our neighbors, as we "offer [our] bodies as a living sacrifice" (c.f. Romans 12:1 NIV).

Issues in Korean Church Worship
in light of Calvin's Theology of Worship

Considering the four most essential elements of worship according to Calvin, what is the main issue in the Korean church worship? Regarding the first fundamental component of worship, the proclamation of the Word, the Korean church does not initially seem to have any major problems. However, when looked upon more deeply, one sees that the problem is, in fact, severe. The most serious problem in the sermons that are being preached in Korean church services is that they have degraded into messages of materialism and successism. As one theologian looked upon the deteriorating pulpit of the Korean church, he stated, "Populism is prevalent in today's pulpit. The danger that the Korean church is facing today is that its pulpit is being polluted by populistic preaching."[15] His term, "populistic preaching," to put it simply, refers to a sermon that conforms to the congregations' belief in the prosperity gospel, and is analogous to what I mean by "materialism and successism." Once the church begins to put its utmost interest and goal in raising its congregational numbers, what follows is sermons that are preached according to what satisfies their tastes. In other words, when preachers become obsessed with populism, the sermon changes to messages that delight the ears of the congregation. As a result, instead of "kneeling down and asking God of His message to His people today, and trying to focus on researching and understanding the heart of the text,"[16] they give themselves over to things that attract the congregations' interests and make them feel comfortable. This is a clear marker of the corruption of

---

[15] Eui Hwan Kim, "What is the Problem in Current Church's Concept of Blessing: Let Us Return to God-Centered Preaching" *Monthly Ministry* (2009. 3), 37.

[16] Eui Hwan Kim "What is the Problem," 38.

the pulpit, a dangerous trend in the proclamation of the Word in the Korean Presbyterian Church that reminds one of the eighth chapter of the Book of Amos. While witnessing the spiritual fall of Israel, the Prophet Amos explained that the cause was "...not a famine of food or a thirst for water, but a famine of hearing the words of the Lord" (Amos 8:11). If this is what has been happening in the Korean church, we must be fearful and return to the Word of God as soon as possible, for only when the Word of God is witnessed and properly proclaimed can the Church be restored to its original form.

There is a second, more serious problem in the worship services in Korean Protestant churches, which is the loss of sacraments — specifically, the Eucharist. The majority of Protestant churches in Korea have communion about twice a year, which according to Calvin's way of speaking, means that most Protestant churches in South Korea have been fooled by the "devil's plot[17]" without even knowing it. As pointed out above, when we offer true worship to God, the Holy Spirit proclaims the Word of God through sermons *and* the Sacrament; the Sacrament confirms the Word and entrusts faith while drawing us into union with Christ. As the "visible word of God" (Augustine), the Eucharist is a significant and fundamental part of worship; however, the Korean Presbyterian Church seems to have forgotten it. Presently, several churches from a few denominations have restored communion monthly to their services, but it can be said that the graceful means of the Sacrament has all but disappeared from the worship of most Korean churches.

There is at least one historical cause for this issue. In the late nineteenth century, American churches sent out missionaries to South Korea who were strongly influenced by the Frontier tradition of worship, part of the aftermath of the two Great Awakening movements in the United States.[18] These missionaries focused mainly on evangelical preaching; therefore, while they in many ways excelled at proclaiming the Word, they all but ignored one of the most significant elements of early

---

[17] C.f. Calvin, *Institutes* 4:17:46.

[18] For resources on the frontier tradition in American Christianity, see Nathan O. Hatch, *The Democratization of American Christianity* (New Haven, CT.: Yale University Press, 1989). For frontier worship specifically, see James F. White, *Protestant Worship: Traditions in Transition* (Louisville, KY: Westminster John Knox Press, 1989).

Church and Reformation-era worship — the Eucharist. As a result, the majority of Protestant churches in South Korea were born of an ecclesiastical culture that downplayed one of the most important means of grace.

Third, Korean church worship has some problems with prayer, specifically regarding what Calvin stated as the matter of praying in song, or in other words, congregational singing. For many decades, Korean Protestant churches have emphasized the singing of gospel songs during more than the classical style of strophic hymns.[19] Since the 1990s, the term "worship and praise" has been very actively used in Korea to describe such songs. Various other types of "contemporary Christian music" are now being used as well, some churches even incorporating genres such as rock and rap music into worship. Many, including this author, consider songs in these popular idioms inappropriate for worship music. One of the reasons these newer genres of songs are problematic is that they have supplanted the tradition of congregational Psalm singing, a tradition which Calvin and other reformers worked diligently to recover. Admittedly, there are still traces of psalmody, such as in responsive readings, present in Korean Protestant church worship today. However, believers who faithfully participate in such vestiges of psalmody on a regular basis remain ignorant of the history of Psalm-singing in their tradition. Most Reformed denominations in the United States, whose missionaries brought passionate gospel songs along with the Gospel in the nineteenth century, have since then at least partially restored their beautiful heritage of sung psalmody. However, the Korean Presbyterian Church continues to sing the same gospel songs in worship services that were brought from the United States in the nineteenth century. The absence of congregational Psalm singing, which was embraced by the Church in the patristic era and again by the reformers of the sixteenth century, is perhaps one indicator that Korean Presbyterians are more interested in using music to gather more people in for their services than they are in embracing the truest form of worship.

Fourth, the Korean church is not living out a lifestyle of worship, that is, a life-giving worship through service to the world, by engaging in the

---

[19] Those familiar with C. Michael Hawn's seven streams of congregational song might refer to these two genres as "Revival/Gospel Songs" and "Classical Hymnody."

fellowship and almsgiving pointed out as essential by Calvin. The critical issue here is that church worship services are being separated from a lifestyle of worship in the congregation. In other words, while many people in Korea go to church on Sundays to worship, that worship does not seem to prompt the congregation to act as living sacrifices through acts of service in the world. True worship depends on how Christians respond to God throughout their lives as a whole because worship is a response of faith and action toward God. Therefore, if Christians do not specifically obey God and respond in faith in their daily lives, the worship of Christians will be in vain, no matter how good and godly they may act during the services. Thus, Paul said, "...offer your bodies as a living sacrifice, holy and pleasing to God—this is your true and proper worship" (Romans 12:1). Only when worship in the church service coincides with life in the world will Christians offer their bodies as a "holy living sacrifice" to God. This is one of the most crucial concerns of Korean church worship — when worship and life are not aligned together.

Four Suggestions for Restoration of Korean Church Worship

Restoration of the most essential content for worship

First, in order for the worship of the Korean church to be "a living sacrifice, holy and pleasing to God," the Word of God must be fully restored in worship (Romans 12:1). Only the Word of God should be witnessed and properly proclaimed, and only the gospel should be preached on the pulpit. In the words of the reformer John Calvin, the preacher is the "mouth of God." Therefore, a preacher who is the "mouth of God" must speak only the Word of God in the pulpit. If a preacher speaks of private matters or states one's opinions instead of preaching the gospel on the pulpit, or if one preaches the prosperity gospel, this is clearly a corruption of the pulpit, which will eventually lead to the downfall of worship.

Second, the Korean church needs to reestablish the Eucharist as a normal part of its worship. As Calvin pointed out, and as the early

Church had done, there must be a balance of the Word and the Sacraments in the worship of the Church. In this sense, the Korean church is losing one essential aspect of worship. Although it may not always be possible to have communion on a weekly basis like the early Church, the Eucharist should be celebrated at least once a month during Sunday worship service, as some Korean churches are attempting to do. One suggestion, which would add a deeper meaning to the church service, would be to celebrate the Eucharist according to the church calendar. As Horace Allen stated, "The Christian year is the annual rehearsal of the history of our salvation accomplished in the birth, death, resurrection, and return of Jesus Christ."[20] In other words, the Church recreates the events of the birth, life, death, resurrection, coming of the Holy Spirit, and the Lord's Second Coming in the seasonal worship cycle. Thus, in a similar way to the regular celebration of the Sacraments, "the liturgical year is a constant means of grace through which we receive God's gift to us."[21] The church calendar helps us to continue to experience annually the complete process of salvation through the birth and ministry of Jesus Christ, His suffering, dying and resurrection, coming of the Holy Spirit, and His second coming. In this sense, the church calendar is "one of the constant means of grace" through which we are able to receive the grace of God.[22] There are at least six occasions in the church calendar: Advent, Christmas, Epiphany, Lent (or a day during the Passion Week), Easter and Pentecostal Sunday, as well as other significant and meaningful holidays like Thanksgiving and National Liberation Day, during which it would be remarkable for the Church to experience the amazing love and grace of God, with every fiber of one's being, through the celebration of the Eucharist.

Third, the Korean church must continue to recover proper prayer and praise during worship. Regarding prayer, a prayer of penitence (which Calvin emphasized) and the prayer of intercession (otherwise known as pastoral prayer) in response to hearing the Word of God are currently lacking and must be restored to worship. With regard to praise, there must be a restoration of congregational psalm singing. The reformers

---

[20] Horace T. Allen, Jr., *A Handbook for the Lectionary* (Philadelphia: The Geneva Press, 1980), 25.

[21] James F. White, *Introduction to Christian Worship*, 3rd. ed. (Nashville: Abingdon Press, 2000), 68.

[22] White, *Introduction to Christian Worship*, 68.

desired for the entire congregation to confess their faith through song, and praise God as one. According to Calvin, the Word of God must be sung in praise, since the most precious form of praise is when it is sung through the voice of humanity, which has been created in God's image. Calvin valued sung Psalmody especially because it represented the marriage of sung praise and the very Word of God. The Korean church must restore this forgotten practice of singing the psalms. By all means, the Korean church must consider responding to the needs of the younger generation in developing new hymns and using various musical genres of praise. However, we must always be reminded that the praise during worship is not for humanity, but for God.

Fourth, fellowship and acts of service through almsgiving must be restored in the worship of Korean Presbyterian churches. As mentioned above, the separation of worship and life is a fatal trend seen in Korean church members. In Mark 10:45, we hear that "even the Son of Man did not come to be served, but to serve, and to give his life as a ransom for many." Jesus came to the world to serve and to do God's will in the world, and even obeyed to the point of death (John 4:34). Thus, Jesus gave our Heavenly Father the greatest glory. If the ultimate purpose of worship is to bring glory to God, then a life of service and obedience in this world can never be separated from worship. For this reason, worship should always be offered in a way that is oriented toward serving the world, and serving in the world can be said to be a continuation of the worship that brings glory to God — this is the spiritual worship that believers should offer to God. Accordingly, the Korean church should further educate and emphasize the life of worship through fellowship, service and almsgiving for its restoration of worship.

Suggestions for elements of worship to be changed in a changing culture

Thus far, we have analyzed the worship of the Korean church while giving some suggestions of biblical worship and the fundamental elements of apostolic worship as Calvin has insisted. Lastly, from this point on, we will address the issue of the relationship between worship and culture.

When we look at the history of worship, we find that worship has always been a history of cultural exchange. For instance, early Christian worship was heavily influenced by Jewish traditions, including elements of synagogue worship, Jewish annual festivals (seasons), and weekly Sabbath gatherings, continuing to develop simultaneously alongside Jewish liturgy for many centuries. After Christianity became a state religion under Constantine, it increasingly brought the framework of Roman culture into worship. In a related way, in what became the Churches of the East, Byzantine culture greatly influenced the character of Christian worship for those regions. In this way, Christian worship has maintained its dynamism when encountering different cultures to this day (this is known as inculturation or contextualization). In the history of worship, whenever this dynamism faded, a new transformation was always attempted. This shows us that the cultural adaptation of worship is as old as the history of Christianity itself. In other words, Christianity, regardless of nationality or culture, has developed into the church of each country and nation while accommodating its unique culture; the representative cultural expressions are displayed in worship. Therefore, the endless task of the Korean church is to accept the ever-changing culture and to incorporate it into its ministry.[23]

Conclusion

As mentioned earlier, Calvin sought to restore the worship of his day according to scripture and early church tradition, often arguing for a return to what he perceived to be the simplicity of early church worship. Calvin's goal was a restoration of worship largely as the apostolic Church had known it, and for this reason, he concluded that worship should be evaluated in light of the biblical witness and early apostolic tradition. He

---

[23] In this regard, I suggest that readers read the paper published in "The 2nd Underwood International Symposium" hosted by Saemoonan Presbyterian Church, the mother church of Korea, in 2009. At this symposium, the main lecturer, Professor Thomas G. Long of Emory University, listed the fundamental elements of worship that the Korean church must keep and never lose sight of, and he further made a few suggestions for the aspects of worship that must change in the midst of the rapidly changing culture. The contents he presented are issues that should be pondered continuously for the renewal and development of Korean church worship.

particularly understood Acts 2:42 to elucidate the most important customs of the apostolic Church,[24] and he pointed out that the elements mentioned in this verse -- the proclamation of the Word (teaching), the Sacraments, public prayer (including praise), and fellowship (fellowship/almsgiving) -- are the most fundamental for the worship of the Church. These elements must be preserved even into the future. Therefore, it is necessary for the Korean Presbyterian Church to be cognizant of the essentials of worship, while still being able to consider how other content can be added as well as variably expressed in worship within a rapidly changing culture.[25]

We must sustain our efforts to renew our worship. However, in relation to the renewal of worship, we must be reminded, through the legacy of the reformers' faith, that our worship reforms must strive to echo the pure worship of the apostolic Church, and for this, the worship must be evaluated in light of the Bible. Therefore, the Korean church must reject any type of worship that attempts to please people in the church, and rather constantly strive for the restoration of true worship — one that will immerse the entire congregation in the infinite splendor of God and glorify Him as they are deeply moved in His presence — for the sole purpose of exalting God.

"Ascribe to the Lord the glory due his name;
worship the Lord in the splendor of his holiness" (Psalm 29:2).

---

[24] "In this way, the teaching and prayer of the Word, participation in the sacrament, and almsgiving were incorporated into church services." Calvin, *Institutes* 4:7:44.

[25] Regarding the aspect that worship should attempt to change in the midst of a rapidly changing culture, Professor Thomas G. Long mentioned a few crucial points. In this lecture, the aspects of worship that he mentioned are: 1) Rediscover and recover the intrinsic sense of drama in an active Christian worship 2) A variety of different excellent musical styles 3) Moving the energy of worship away from the clergy into the people 4) Giving more attention to the actual physical space of worship 5) A palpable sense of the mystery of God at the center of worship. Thomas G. Long, "Something Old, Something New: Worship in a Time of Change" *The 2nd Underwood International Symposium.* (Saemoonan Presbyterian Church, 2009), 15-21.

11. UNITY AT THE TABLE OF THE WORLD:

THE UNFOLDING FUTURE
OF PRESBYTERIAN WORSHIP

by Kimberly Bracken Long

Visitors to the 1964 World's Fair in Flushing, New York, were treated to an exhibit called "Futurama," where they could see what life would be like in the decades to come. They saw happy families smiling from the windows of cars that looked like rockets and homes that looked like hermetically sealed pods standing on stilts above barren landscapes. People were introduced to strange new machines called "computers," and the message was clear: life would never be the same. It would be better, sleeker, and faster. Some of those predictions turned out to be pretty close to the truth. Others now seem just plain silly.

Writing an essay on the future of Presbyterian worship feels a bit like mounting a Futurama exhibit for the Church. Perhaps some predictions will turn out to be pretty close to the truth. And others, in hindsight, may seem just plain silly. Especially in these times of global pandemic, protests for racial justice, and ecological crisis, times when the Church and its worship is in a constant state of flux, writing about the future strikes this author as a proposition that is doomed to fail.

What I offer in this essay, then, are some observations of where we find ourselves these days and the influences that have brought us to this point. From there, I will suggest what trends I see continuing and propose practices—and questions—that I believe will lead to faithful and vital worship in the Presbyterian Church, worship that participates in God's mission in the world.

In the first decade of the 21st century, Horace Allen reflected on the influence of the lectionary on Protestant worship in "Common Lectionary and Protestant Hymnody: Unity at the Table of the Word-- Liturgical and Ecumenical Bookends."[1] In that essay, Allen pointed to the increasingly widespread use of the lectionary, along with a surge in recently-composed hymnody, as elements that enabled further unity between Presbyterians and other Christian communities. The title of this essay borrows from Allen's own title, as well as from his own hope for the unity of the Church. Certainly, increased use of the Revised Common Lectionary and the availability of numerous lectionary-based worship planning resources have led to great similarities in the worship of historic Protestant denominations, including the Presbyterian Church (U.S.A) and, to some extent, between Protestant and Roman Catholic worshiping communities as well. Among those who rely on lectionary-based worship resources, there is an unprecedented sharing of liturgy, psalmody, and congregational song.

Various musical movements have also affected the Church's worship—Presbyterian and otherwise—over the last several decades. Methodist scholar Michael Hawn argues that seven streams of song have influenced Christian worship.[2] In additional to Roman Catholic liturgical song and newly-composed hymns (what he terms "classic contemporary Protestant hymnody"), Hawn identifies five other significant influences on the Church's music: African-American congregational song; gospel and revival songs; folk hymnody; praise and worship music; and global and ecumenical congregational song, which includes perspectives on African, Caribbean, Central American, South American, Asian, and European hymns and songs. One needs only to look through the indices

---

[1] In James Puglisi, *Liturgical Renewal as a Way to Christian Unity* (Collegeville, MN: Liturgical Press, 2005).

[2] C. Michael Hawn, editor and compiler, *New Songs of Celebration Render: Congregational Song in the Twenty-First Century* (Chicago: GIA Publications, Inc., 2013).

of *Glory to God*, the Presbyterian hymnal published in 2013, to see this whole range of congregational song represented.

The lectionary and hymnody are not the only significant unifying factors in worship in the early 21st century. For the last quarter of the 20th century, Protestants watched with interest as Catholics reformed their liturgical practices. Because of their appreciation for documents that emerged from the Second Vatican Council—particularly *Sancrosanctum Concilium,* or the Constitution of the Sacred Liturgy—Presbyterians along with other Protestant communions revised their worship books. The 1993 *Book of Common Worship* (to which Horace Allen contributed) represented the culmination of nearly two decades of learning from the liturgical renewal movement in its reclaiming of both Word and Sacrament as central to Lord's Day worship; a baptismal rite that reflects ancient forms; the introduction of the Great Prayer of Thanksgiving, a form of prayer based on the earliest known eucharistic prayer (once thought to be composed by Hippolytus, Bishop of Rome); attention to the Christian year and the three-year Revised Common Lectionary, and the four-fold pattern of Gathering / Word / Eucharist / Sending. Through years of teaching and modeling in churches, presbyteries, seminaries, conferences, and workshops, the patterns reflected in the Book of Common Worship became normative for many (though not all) PC(USA) churches. We took more seriously Calvin's insistence that Word and Sacrament are both equally essential to faithful worship.

In 2002, the 214th General Assembly authorized the appointment of a group of pastors, elders, and scholars to undertake "a full and substantive study of the sacraments both within the Reformed tradition and in the ecumenical context, in order to help the church discern the history and theology of Baptism and the Lord's Supper, as well as their appropriate relationship."[3] The resulting study, *Invitation to Christ: Font and Table,* was sent to churches for a three-year period of study and reflection around five simple practices:

1. Set the font in full view of the congregation.
2. Open the font and fill it with water on every Lord's Day.
3. Set cup and plate on the Lord's Table on every Lord's Day.

---

[3] Presbyterian Church (U.S.A.), A Corporation, Louisville, Kentucky, on behalf of the Office of Theology and Worship, *Invitation to Christ: Font and Table,* 2006.

4. Lead appropriate parts of weekly worship from the font and from the table.

5. Increase the number of Sundays on which the Lord's Supper is celebrated.[4]

This landmark study—described more fully by Tom Trinidad elsewhere in this volume—enabled churches to consider more intentionally and deeply the role of the sacraments in worship, as well as the relationship between Baptism and Eucharist. More than a decade later, the evidence of this study can be seen even in churches that do not know the document. Fonts are visible and filled with water; communion tables are no longer bare but hold a plate and chalice to remind us of the meal, even if we are not eating it. Portions of worship services are being led from the font and table, and communion is celebrated more often than in the previous generation, with most churches reporting monthly celebrations in addition to festival days. A small percentage of churches even offer weekly Eucharist during at least one of their services, a practice which John Calvin encouraged. The 2018 revision of the *Book of Common Worship*, which is described in greater detail by David Gambrell in chapter nine, reflects this sacramental deepening in its forms, prayers, and rubrics.

Along with this increased emphasis on the sacraments has come an awareness of the embodied nature of worship. We understand that we are not just worshiping minds—as important as that is for Presbyterians—but we are also worshiping bodies. We are more inclined to walk forward to receive communion from the table (although passing the elements to one another in the pews is also an embodied act!); we are more apt to gather around the baptismal font for confirmations, ordinations, and receiving new members; we lift water from the font so we can be reminded that we are baptized; we raise a hand in blessing from where we stand; worship leaders move around the liturgical space rather than doing everything from the pulpit. We have also left behind the iconoclasm of the reformation era and are embracing the role of visual arts in worship. And the inclusion of a wide range of musical forms means that we might even be caught swaying or clapping while we sing.

---

[4] *Invitation to Christ: Font and Table*, 5.

In addition to all of these changes in the ways we worship, Presbyterians are being affected by larger social and ecclesial trends as well. We are witnessing less concern about denominational affiliation on the part of worshipers. For some, this signals a decline in denominational loyalty; however, it may also be considered an indication of increased unity between churches when it comes to liturgical practice. As established congregations continue to experience a decline in membership, experimental worshiping communities continue to spring up. In both established congregations and new worshiping communities, there seems to be less interest in doctrinal agreement and more emphasis on missional action—a focus on moving outward rather than looking inward. If the old model of "joining a church" meant believing and then belonging, the new model focuses on giving people an experience of belonging so that they may then have the experience of believing.

In order to do this, new worshiping communities of the Presbyterian Church (U.S.A.) organize themselves around common causes, such as feeding the community; common interests, such as running or art-making; or common cultural backgrounds, as is found in immigrant communities.[5] These new worshiping communities begin small and local; many of them are neighborhood-based. Many of the usual markers of 20th-21st century Presbyterian worship are noticeably, and intentionally, absent. Few sermons are preached, and there is little, if any, organ music. Few communities meet in sanctuaries or use printed worship orders. Instead, space is often borrowed or rented. Conversation replaces preaching. Leadership is shared among pastors and participants.[6] And there is food, always food, very often with the Lord's Supper as well; making meals is often at the heart of worship. Since many participants have little or no experience with the liturgy of established churches, new practices arise from shared experiences and cultures. One leader of a new worshiping community describes how he once talked about breaking

---

[5] 1001 New Worshiping Communities is a movement within the Presbyterian Church (U.S.A.). It is an outgrowth of a commitment made by the 220th General Assembly (2012) to create 1001 new worshiping communities in the United States within ten years.

[6] Angie Andriot and Perry Chang, "1001 NWC Leader Interviews: Report from 2019 Perspectives Conference," published by Research Services of the Presbyterian Church (U.S.A.), 2020. Accessed at file:///C:/Users/Admin/Downloads/Report-1001-Interviews-2019%20(1).pdf on June 8, 2020.

bread, and then raised his hands to do so. Those present, not knowing what to do, saw him break the bread and so lifted their own bread and broke it as well. What started with people simply copying his actions has turned into a meaningful practice. Now each time bread is broken, they all break it together.[7]

New worshiping communities often experience a different relationship to their gathering space than do more traditional churches. On the one hand, there are challenges that arise from not having control over a borrowed or rented space. On the other hand, however, new worshiping communities are freed from concerns associated with maintaining properties. Their spaces are often more flexible with fewer traditional Christian visual symbols, and participants have a role in creating worship space.

While sustainability continues to be a concern of new worshiping communities, paying attention to their practices can inform more established churches as we lean into the future. Not a few congregations are finding that taking care of older buildings, some of which are quite large, is a drain on their resources. Some of those churches are leaving their buildings behind and finding creative ways to share space. One Detroit area church moved out of its massive structure and is now sharing space with a nearby Lutheran church. A church in Arlington, Virginia tore down the building it no longer filled so affordable housing could be built in its place; the congregation now worships in the new apartment building or in its community garden.[8] As the Presbyterian Church (U.S.A.) continues to gray, and memberships decline, more congregations may make similar choices, and newer worshiping communities may opt to avoid owning property at all.

New worshiping communities tend to decentralize leadership, lessening the focus on ordained ministers while empowering and equipping participants to share in the planning and leading of worship. In the context of a new worshiping community, where some participants

---

[7] Andriot and Chang, 7.

[8] Ashley Goff, "The Eucharist and an Ecological Crisis: Arlington Presbyterian's Call to Love the Body of God," *Call to Worship: Liturgy, Music, Preaching, and the Arts* 52, no. 4 (2019), 8-13.

may be wary of ecclesial authority—or have suffered trauma because of it—this democratizing is especially important. In more established churches, the decentralization of leadership may be seen as an expression of the priesthood of all believers. In the 2018 *Book of Common Worship*, expanded rubrics suggest parts of the service where it is particularly appropriate for a ruling elder or deacon to share in leadership. This is a fitting reflection of the Presbyterian understanding of ordered ministry in which ministers of Word and Sacrament, ruling elders, and deacons are all ordained to particular tasks and functions. Yet we need not stop with ordained offices; many people, including children and teenagers, have gifts for leading worship. One of the most effective and compelling readers of scripture I ever heard was a seven-year-old girl. Presbyterians have traditionally valued an educated clergy, a value that persists, but valuing the role of educated clergy does not imply that we should ignore the charisms of all the members of the worshiping body.

Having quickly sketched a picture of the developments seen in Presbyterian worship over the last few decades, I now turn to how I see them continuing, and to propose how we might move into our future most faithfully.

First of all, I believe there are some characteristics of Presbyterian worship that will remain constant; these defining elements do not belong solely to this denomination but nevertheless serve as markers. Presbyterian worship will be trinitarian. Presbyterian worship will be doxological. Presbyterian worship will be rooted in scripture, and will continue to reflect "faith seeking understanding," to quote Anselm's famous phrase. If we are faithful, Presbyterians will still understand that we are "Reformed and always being reformed," even while remaining ecumenically involved. Finally, we will remain grounded in eschatological hope as we pray, "your kingdom come, your will be done on earth as in heaven."

We have observed that the Presbyterian Church (U.S.A.) has experienced a deepening of sacramental life over the last decade or two. The 2018 revision of the *Book of Common Worship* reflects this growing emphasis. For example, the 2018 edition includes 51 eucharistic prayers, nearly twice the number found in the 1993 book. While all are trinitarian, they take different forms and use language in a variety of ways. A stronger emphasis on Baptism is visible throughout the 2018 book as well.

Rubrics indicate that various parts of the liturgy may be led from the font. Both liturgical texts and rubrics draw connections between Baptism and related rites, such as confirmation, the reception of new members and the blessing of members departing, weddings, and funerals.

Similarly, the range of hymns, songs, and psalms found in *Glory to God* (2013) shows increased attention to the sacraments. More than twenty hymns and songs are related to Baptism, and over forty are related to the Lord's Supper. Additionally, a "Service Music" section includes numerous options for sung portions of the communion liturgy, offering a far more expansive array of options and musical styles than the 1990 *Presbyterian Hymnal*.

In addition to a general deepening, recent decades have also seen changes in the frequency of eucharistic celebration. Surveys done in 2000, 2009, and 2012 indicate that, as of this writing, nearly three-quarters of churches in the PC(USA) celebrate communion monthly, a significant change from a generation ago, when quarterly communion was the norm. Although there is a small but committed number of Presbyterians advocating for weekly Eucharist, fewer than ten percent of churches report celebrating weekly. There is evidence, however, that a growing number of churches include the Sacrament during at least one weekly service, even if it is not the most-attended service of that congregation.

Presbyterians have always valued the life of the mind, and I imagine we always will. Yet we are discovering, more and more, that the sacraments enable us to encounter God in ways that we cannot quite understand or articulate. By the power of the Holy Spirit, Christ is made present to us in the proclamation of the Word and also in water, bread, and wine. We hear the Word; we see, touch, smell, taste, and share the sacramental elements. This sacramental awakening is part of our becoming more attentive to the embodied nature of worship. We are finding out that we do not only worship from the neck up, but with the swaying of our bodies as we sing, by gathering around font and table, by extending our hands in blessing, by sharing a kiss of peace, by lifting our hands in prayer and praise.

Part of this embracing of bodily worship is a newfound appreciation for the visual arts in worship. The iconoclasm of the Reformation era responded to one concern: what was perceived as an overabundance of idolatrous images. The burgeoning of interest in liturgical art in our time is a response to a different concern: our over-intellectualized ways of worshiping. A decade or so ago it was the rare church that paid much attention to visual art, apart from aging felt banners and flower arrangements. Now, worship and music conferences have included artists on their faculties, and great care is taken with arranging and adorning the worship spaces at those events. Churches are seeking out liturgical artists to create installations, make art during worship services, and lead workshops on art-making. Artists in congregations are offering their gifts to the liturgical life of their churches. One collaborative effort between four young women—three of them seminary classmates—has grown in just four years to provide visual art, videos, liturgy, and other resources to churches in the United States, Canada, the United Kingdom, Australia, New Zealand, and South Africa.[9] The rapid growth of this collective, A Sanctified Art, attests to the power of graphic design, visual art, and film to speak to Christians in a visual age.

This sacramental, embodied deepening reveals that worship is physical as well as internal; visual as well as aural; emotional as well as intellectual; creative as well as didactic. Yet it is not only about the experience of worshipers; sacramental worship has implications for the life of the world. Presbyterian theologian Paul Galbreath asserts that the Lord's Supper—and the way we pray at the Lord's table—gives us "a template for how to live our lives."[10] We give thanks to the triune God, remembering not only the death and resurrection of Christ, but also his earthly ministry. To mention "Jesus' care for the poor is to insert and reassert the basic biblical claim that God has a particular interest in the plight of the poor," he explains. To recall Jesus' healing ministry and exorcisms is to urge us "to tend to the needs of the sick and to fight the forces of evil and oppression in our society." Remembering Jesus' feeding ministry, and the meals he shared with sinners and those rejected by society, "is to challenge us to share our food with those we sometimes judge or ignore."[11] Through the words we pray, we are schooled in what

---

[9] A Sanctified Art is Lisle Gwynn Garrity, Lauren Wright-Pittman, Sarah Are, and Hannah Garrity. www.sanctifiedart.org.

[10] Paul Galbreath, Re-Forming the Liturgy, Past, Present, and Future (Eugene, OR: Cascade Books, 2019), 77.

[11] Galbreath, 77.

it means to follow Christ. Furthermore, the acts we share around the eucharistic table anticipate the new creation and form us for seeking economic justice, racial equality, and intercultural understanding. Our earthly tables may not look quite like the heavenly banquet table, but we can live as if they should, and work until they do.

These concerns are expressed in the 2018 *Book of Common Worship*, which includes a new section called "Justice and Reconciliation." The orders of worship and additional prayers in this section are provided to enable the church to worship "in the wake of acts of violence, denials of justice, bitter debates, or contested decisions," when "it is fitting for us to seek the abiding presence and transforming power of the liberating Lord."[12] Similarly, *Glory to God* lists some seventy hymns, songs, and psalms related to justice and/or reconciliation. Both of these books, produced in the second decade of the 21st century, reflect the denomination's focus on living as a missional church, turning the focus from nurturing those inside the church (although that still happens, and should) to one of serving those in need and joining in the *missio Dei*.

As I noted earlier, our deepening sacramental life also includes a greater emphasis on Baptism as a way of life rather than a singular event. When we are baptized, we are claimed by God in Christ and empowered by the Holy Spirit to live the baptismal life, which is complete only in our death (cf. Rom. 6:1-11). The prayers we say at the font, baptistry, or river—like the prayers we pray at the Lord's table—are trinitarian. We remember what God has done through water, we recall Christ's own baptism and how we are joined with him in it, and pray for the Spirit's work in the water before us. We only baptize a person once in a lifetime, but we have created ways to continually remind ourselves that we live as baptized people. Whenever we pour water into the font, we remember that we have been cleansed and forgiven. Whenever we welcome new members by the font, we recall that we are all made one in Christ Jesus. Whenever we sprinkle water on a coffin or urn, we proclaim that we live eternally with the risen Christ. In all these ways, we are formed for "walking wet," practicing forgiveness, relating all people as equal in the sight of God, and living free from the fear of death.

---

[12] *Book of Common Worship* (2018), 591-592.

The waters of Baptism also remind us of the life-giving waters all around us, our responsibility to ensure that everyone has access to clean water, and our charge to care for the health of the planet. As French Reformed scholar Louis-Marie Chauvet puts it, "Sacraments present the world to us as something that we may not use in an arbitrary fashion; they demand that we make of reality a 'world' for all, and not simply for the well-off....They reveal to us the 'sacramentality' of the world as creation."[13]

Here again, the 2018 *Book of Common Worship* and *Glory to God* reflect significant themes in contemporary life, in this case, the growing understanding among Presbyterians that our worship is tied to ecological concerns. A new section in the *BCW* titled "Creation and Ecology" offers a service for the care of creation, an order for the blessing of the animals, and ways of praying after natural disasters. Furthermore, intercessory prayers for the Service for the Lord's Day and services of daily prayer frequently ask God for the healing of the planet and the wherewithal to care well for all of creation. *Glory to God* features scores of hymns devoted to creation and the care of creation.

In an age of global warming, the sacraments will be essential to remind us to care for the waters in which we baptize and the fields that produce grapes and grain. If we attend to them, they will continue to form us for living as a community of faith and shape us to be the body of Christ in the world. We need the sacraments in a time when the United States, along with much of the rest of the world, is struggling toward a more just society, calling for deeply-   engrained racism to be exposed and expunged, working for the equal treatment of women and girls in both the academy and the workplace, and seeking to eliminate poverty. If Presbyterian worship is to be faithful in the future to God and God's mission, we must continue to seek a balance between Word and Sacrament, both for our sake and for the sake of the world.

At the time of this writing, I am watching as artists and volunteers paint "Black Lives Matter" on city streets, from Washington, D.C. to towns all around the country. In my own little town of Cambridge,

---

[13] Louis-Marie Chauvet, *Symbol and Sacrament: A Sacramental Reinterpretation of Christian Existence,* trans. Patrick Madigan and Madeleine Beaumont (Collegeville, MN: Liturgical Press, 1995), 553. Quoted in Galbreath, 100.

Maryland, those words, along with portraits of Harriet Tubman, Frederick Douglass, and local civil rights leader Gloria Richardson Dandridge, have been painted on the very street that was home to the white business district in the 1960s, a street along which the town's black citizens did not walk and were not welcome in stores. The Black Lives Matter movement, resurging after a string of deaths of African American men and women at the hands of white police officers, coincides with the Matthew 25 initiative in the Presbyterian Church (U.S.A.), which includes as one of its three goals the dismantling of systemic racism. This work is long overdue, and necessary for the continued life and health of the church and world. Presbyterian worship must also exhibit awareness of, and involvement in, this work—not to be politically correct, but to participate in the justice-making that God is doing in the world.

The Presbyterian Church (U.S.A) remains a predominantly white denomination with Scottish roots. About one-third of PC(USA) churches have prioritized "the goal of becoming more racially and ethnically diverse," and research indicates that such an emphasis has led to an increase of intercultural or multiracial congregations in the denomination.[14] Yet this is just a first step. At present, 88% of PC(USA) pastors are white, as are 91% of church members. It is worth noting here that 60% of leaders of new worshiping communities are white, and 46% participants are people of color. Furthermore, 29% of new worshiping communities speak a language other than English.[15] Within the next thirty years, the white population of the United States is likely to be less than 50%.[16] If congregations want to live and serve faithfully in a changing world, they cannot expect people of color to simply want to join them and worship in the way white congregations have always worshiped. Churches must decide to be intentional about calling non-

---

[14] Mike Ferguson, "PC(USA) Surveys: MLK's 'One of the most segregated hours in Christian America slowly giving way," January 29, 2019. Accessed at https://www.presbyterianmission.org/story/pcusa-surveys-mlks-one-of-the-most-segregated-hours-in-christian-america-slowly-giving-way/ on June 19, 2020.

[15] PC(USA) Research Services, 1001 NWC Leaders Report, February 2017. Accessed June 28, 2020 at https://www.presbyterianmission.org/resource/2016-leader-survey-report/.

[16] Dudley Poston and Rogelio Sáenz, "The US White Majority Will Soon Disappear Forever," *The Chicago Reporter*, May 16, 2019. Accessed on June 10, 2020 at https://www.chicagoreporter.com/the-us-white-majority-will-soon-disappear-forever/.

white pastors and musicians, which likely means being open to other styles of worshiping, listening "to the voices of people long silenced,"[17] and being willing to be changed.

Well-established Reformed principles provide a strong foundation for these necessary changes. Our concept of form and freedom allows for flexibility and creativity in ordering worship.[18] Our identity as a priesthood of all believers calls for "the full, conscious, and active participation of the whole body of Christ," and insists that "the ordering of worship should reflect the richness of cultural diversity in the congregation and the local context in which it ministers."[19] Our understanding of what constitutes "prayerful participation" allows for all sorts of ways of praying: "listening and waiting for God, remembering God's gracious acts, crying out to God for help...Prayer may be spoken, silent, sung, or enacted in physical ways." Our Directory for Worship makes it clear that there is room for all kinds of participation in worship: "singing...kneeling, bowing, standing, lifting hands; dancing, drumming, clapping, embracing, or joining hands; anointing and laying on of hands."[20] There is room in God's house for everyone. How will we break down the barriers that keep us apart?

Musical style has long been a source of conflict in the church, but employing a broad range of musical styles could just as easily be a unifying force. Although churches have begun opening themselves to new musical genres—some more than others—the continued future of Presbyterian worship depends on including an ever-increasing spectrum of musical forms. Singing songs from other countries, sung in original languages (or a close approximation!) signals that we truly are one body. Including gospel music and spirituals in our regular song repertoire says that we sing one another's songs with gratitude. Knowing the stories behind the hymns and songs we sing enable us to understand more deeply both the suffering and the faith of people whose lives may look very different from our own. Incorporating jazz, folk, hip hop, and even some popular songs broadens the range even farther, allowing Christ to

---

[17] Brief Statement of Faith. https://www.presbyterianmission.org/what-we-believe/brief-statement-of-faith/. Accessed December 8, 2020.

[18] *Book of Order*, 2019-2021, W-2.0102.

[19] *Book of Order*, 2019-2021, W-2.0201.

[20] *Book of Order*, 2019-2021, W-2.0202.

be made present to those who may not apprehend the divine in hymns from centuries long past. Singing the songs of contemporary hymn writers allows us to express the concerns, hopes, and prayers of this generation. Calling forth the gifts of drummers, guitarists, brass players, harpists, dulcimer players, fiddlers, and bassists enlivens the church's song and broadens the circle of musical leadership. All of this is not simply for the enjoyment of worshipers, or to create an enhanced aesthetic experience. The point is to draw the circle ever wider, making room for any and all who would worship. It means relinquishing control over our perceived right to order worship the way we choose, sharing the responsibility for choosing music so that all the members of the body of Christ may join in song.

Expanding the breadth and role of music raises the challenge of both training and paying musicians for the church. As the number of large churches dwindles, and as more and more smaller churches find themselves unable to support a full-time or even part-time musician, we need to get creative about how to nurture the musical life of churches. Might the church become the site for community music academies? Could we develop online training courses for local, amateur musicians? How might larger churches partner with smaller churches to enable a rich and vital musical life for everyone? These are just a few of the questions that will help us lean into the future of Presbyterian worship in the context of a rapidly changing world.

One of the difficult questions pertaining to the future of Presbyterian worship involves the use of printed liturgies. This is, of course, not a new question; one might say our denomination was founded because of a tug-of-war between those who wanted a prayer book and those who did not (hence, our Directory for Worship).[21] We have now had a *Book of Common Worship* for more than a century, but there are still those who eschew printed liturgies—whether previously published or newly composed, favoring clergy-centered services that feature extemporaneous or newly composed prayers. As we move into the future, however, the question grows even more complex. Whether a congregation makes use of the *BCW* or not, it likely uses an order of worship printed on paper and/or projects elements of a service on a screen. Both methods enable

---

[21] For more details of this "tug-of-war," see chapters 6, 8, and 9 by Bower, Gambrell, and Hehn, respectively.

congregational participation, and both methods have an ecological impact. Sustainability will be part of the conversation as we move into our future.

Furthermore, some have made the critique that our denomination's published worship book is steeped in white theological and liturgical history. Although the 2018 *BCW* includes liturgies in Spanish, as well as common liturgical phrases in both Spanish and Korean, this is just a first step. As Brazilian-American theologian Cláudio Carvalhaes argues:

> …theology has mainly been a white project. Worship has been a white project over the bodies of people, in order to teach them to pray in white performative and content-heavy ways. Historically, white churches have learned to discern faith and live in white terms….Very few people prayed for people of color, with colored people, or concerning colored people and their histories![22]

These are difficult words to hear, as someone who devoted five years to the revision of the 2018 *Book of Common Worship*. And yet, they are necessary words to hear, and our future forms of worship must take into account this critique and build upon it. As homiletician Gennifer Brooks said in her 2020 address to the North American Academy of Liturgy, "In order to gain wisdom, we must learn, understand, and use those activities that embody justice and equity in our relationship with all human beings, as a mandate from Holy Wisdom."[23] As our nation and our denomination face up to the hard truth that we live in a hierarchically racist society, we dare not move into our worshiping future without listening to, and collaborating with, those in our church (and in other churches) who have not had dominant voices.

As I write, our world is also living through the COVID-19 pandemic, which has caused churches to consider entirely new ways of worshiping. Stay-at-home orders and quarantines have forced us to keep physical

---

[22] Cláudio Carvalhaes, *What's Worship Got to Do with It? Interpreting Life Liturgically* (Eugene, OR: Cascade Books, 2018), 107.

[23] Gennifer Benjamin Brooks, "Irrelevant Wisdom: NAAL at the Margins" in *Proceedings of the North American Academy of Liturgy*, Annual Meeting, Atlanta, January 2-4, 2020, 7.

distance from one another, and we are working hard to figure out how to worship God and maintain community through virtual means. Will online worship replace in-person worship? No. We are an incarnational people—the body of Christ—living an incarnational faith, following Jesus Christ, who ate with people, laid hands on people, and washed their feet. Yet, this time of online worship has revealed to us how many people there are who cannot physically gather with their worshiping communities due to age or mobility issues who are now delighted to be able to be part of worship again. Children and teenagers, who may not have been given leadership roles when churches were meeting in person, now read scripture and play music and lead the body of Christ virtually. Even when we do eventually return to in-person worship, we are likely to take these technological gifts and insights with us.

Worshipers have always known that God speaks to us through scripture; we have learned that God also speaks to us through sacraments. We have always known that singing and hearing music is an essential part of praise, prayer, and proclamation; we are realizing that the triune God is also revealed to us through graphic design, textiles, film, and other visual arts. Now that we know that we do not need to remain anchored in one spot, scarcely moving our bodies (although some of us may prefer to continue to do just that), we are free to worship with the hands and feet and hips that God gave us. As Presbyterians anticipate the future of our worship, it seems likely that this movement toward more embodied, sacramental worship will continue.

As I imagine our future, I see a blurring of lines between "in here" and "out there." I see a bursting forth from the doors of the church into public places and private homes. I see a breaking down of dividing walls between people who until now have been kept apart by social, racial, and cultural prejudices. I see hands raising and feet dancing. I see water splashing. I smell bread baking. I feel the touch of oil on my skin. And I hear singing, so much singing, as we worship with an active, earthy eschatology.

What is the future of Presbyterian Worship? Only God knows. But we can be sure that, however imperfect and messy it may be, it will be all to the glory of God.

12. OUR BAPTISMAL LIMINALITY:

THE CHURCH'S
BETWIXT AND BETWEEN

By Jennifer L. Lord

<u>Liminal Panorama</u>

I write this essay during what some say is only the second of nine innings of COVID-19, a global pandemic.[1] In the early days of COVID-19 many of us kept a strict shelter-in-place rule and tracked the daily reports of infection rates and deaths. We watched Wuhan, Italy, Brooklyn. Soon after that, we monitored failing businesses and unemployment numbers and saw food lines. We teeter-tottered between health and economic alarm. We are still balancing. And all of this has been politicized.

Some are using the word *liminal* to describe our time: the unrest, the instability, the very blurring of much that seemed normal for commerce and life.[2] *Liminality* has entered many church/academic/cultural lexicons

---

[1] https://www.cidrap.umn.edu/osterholm-quotes?page=1. Accessed July 1, 2020.
[2] Austin Presbyterian Theological Seminary students serving on the Worship Committee chose "Thresholds" as the faculty preaching theme for Fall 2020, directing faculty members to apply liminality as a frame for interpreting Christian faith and

as a way to describe just this sort of in-betweenness. It is a way to say that things are no longer the way they were and that how things will be is not yet clear. Liminality, used this way, focuses on describing the "betwixt and between" as not normal, as a threshold between worlds, as a time of chaos. The term liminality references *limen* (Latin, threshold) and in current conversations is used to label the felt sense of being adrift, of unending unknowing, and of a world-weariness (*ennui*) in this in-between time.

I write this during COVID-19 pandemic, but I also write this essay days after the murder of George Floyd on May 25, 2020. We are again in the midst of vast unrest and instability, yet of a different sort than that funded by COVID because it entails explicit injustice/moral evil. Can we use this same word —"liminal"— to describe the cultural milieu surrounding the most recent murder of yet another black life and the ensuing swell of protests demanding justice? Is the term adequate to invoke our upended experience of public space: Citizens converging to protest, crowding into parks and city streets; American infantry simultaneously present, carrying out the abnormal task of guarding America from Americans? I write now, sheltered in North Austin, while armed, uniformed military personnel stand in formation alongside SWAT and police forces in Minneapolis and Washington D.C. discharging rubber bullets and tear gas. These reoccurring scenes are indivisible from the ongoing distortions of our U.S. political leadership. We wonder about our government, whether it *is* what we have become accustomed to thinking it is.

Although it does not seem that liminality—as we have defined it thus far—is the right word for revolution, social scientists would have us apply the concept of liminality exactly to such a time as this. They invite us to use it as a framework to describe, diagnose, and act in the midst of large-scale social events. They propose, for instance, that "political

---

world events. See too Susan Beaumont, *How to Lead When You Don't Know Where You're Going: Leading in a Liminal Season* (Lanham: Rowman and Littlefield Pub. Group, Inc., 2019).

revolutions represent clear-cut liminal situations in large scale settings."[3] And they differentiate this liminality from its original usage:

> The liminal state, in its classical anthropological usage as referring to life-crisis ritual passages, for example from boyhood to manhood, is always clearly defined both temporally and spatially: there is a way into liminality and a way out of it. Members of the society are themselves aware of the liminal state: they know that they will leave it sooner or later, and they have masters of ceremony to guide them through the rituals. Compared to liminality in ritual passages, two evident differences appear when the concept is applied to large-scale situations of wholesale collapse: (1) the future is inherently unknown (as opposed to the initiand whose personal liminality is still framed by the continued existence of his home society, awaiting his re-integration); and (2) there are no real masters of ceremony, since nobody has gone through the liminal period before.[4]

Already we have before us multiple definitions of liminality.

"Thinking with liminality"[5] is helpful as we navigate life in such unprecedented times. Yet if we only attach a sense of unknowing and *ennui* to liminality, then liminal is too soft a word to describe the urgency of these days. However liminality did not always mean troubled drift. Originally it was a descriptor for rites of passage and as such it always included both *a way in* to the liminal time as well as *a way out* of the liminal time. It is critical that we hold this understanding of liminality alongside these other uses. Christians have a particular connection with liminality. This connection with liminality begins with the sacrament of Baptism.[6]

---

[3] Bjørn Thomassen, *Liminality and the Modern: Living Through the In-Between* (Surrey, England: Ashgate Publishing Ltd., 2014), 201.

[4] Thomassen, *Liminality and the Modern,* 210.

[5] Thomassen, *Liminality and the Modern,* 1.

[6] See Gordon W. Lathrop "baptismal death and . . . baptismal reorientation in the world" in *The Pastor: A Spirituality* (Minneapolis MN: Fortress Press, 2006), 117.

I propose that Christian baptismal liminality is a litmus test to other forms of liminality and that thinking with a baptismal liminality can orient us during such a time of disorientation. In this essay I review the origins of the term. I describe a liminal understanding of Christian corporate worship and what I mean by baptismal liminality. I introduce key intellectual permutations of the concept and conclude by suggesting ways that a baptismal liminality reframes these other forms of liminality. Here is an invitation to live out our baptismal liminality fully even as we yearn to gather together again corporately for worship.

Liminality: Provenance

A perhaps overly simplistic image for liminality that I have long held is this: the decorated three-foot-long Styrofoam bridge that I, at age eight, ceremonially crossed over to move from Firefly to Camp Fire Girl status. (I'd also moved from Brownie to Girl Scout but without a bridging ceremony!) Any of us who have cast even a cursory glance at the works by Arnold van Gennep or Victor Turner know that my image is merely a prompt to think about liminality, that transitional phase for an individual or social group as they pass from what was to what will be regarding their new identity or status.

Arnold van Gennep introduced the concept and coined the word *liminality* in his 1909 publication *Les Rites de Passage.*[7] Through his study of ethnographic data from a global variety of tribal rites he noticed a common three-fold pattern: rites of separation (the pre-liminal), transitional rites (the liminal), and rites of incorporation (the post-liminal rites). He distinguished between rites dealing with personal/group identity transitions, which he deemed rites of passage, from rites dealing with the passage of time (harvests, the change of seasons, etc.). Liminality for van Gennep was the betwixt and between phase for an individual or a group as they made passage to a new status.

---

[7] Arnold van Gennep, *The Rites of Passage: A Classical Study of Cultural Celebrations* (Chicago IL: Chicago University Press, 1960 [1909]).

My memory of the bridge is my shorthand for this transition between what was and what is to be. It does not evoke the complexities of van Gennep's account such as the individual's or group's (often lengthy) ritualized phase of separation from their community before the event of re-aggregation. Nor does this bridge suggest an intrinsic link between the passage and the natural world, referencing the rhythms and cycles of nature and human life. My memory presumes but does not elaborate on leadership as trustworthy, experienced, and wise. It does not complexify the experience of the three-fold movement, allowing for the fact that each phase may not be equally important or elaborated or clearly distinct.

Yet such a prompt for thinking about liminality is useful because it provides a starting place. These days the conceptualization of liminality has shifted multiple times; the concept continues to mutate as it were, yet it is still critical for us to encounter it as the in-between that is *headed somewhere at some time.*

Liminality Grounded in Worship

My orientation to Christian corporate worship includes understanding it as a liminal event. Once I decide to go to church,[8] cross the threshold to join with others in our corporate worship of the triune God, I willingly place myself in a position to be changed in ways distinct to what happens in the worshiping assembly. "Thus human beings become new beings, are continually in the process of becoming new beings, as they are called out of their propensity to chaos and nothingness and given a new identity in God's reconciling purposes."[9] Whether we call this process of change sanctification or growth in holiness or even *theosis*, we are being changed. I am gathering with others to do those things whereby the Spirit of the risen Christ promises action on me-as-member-of-Christ's body. Call

---

[8] Alexander Schmemann, *For the Life of the World* (Crestwood: St. Vladimir's Seminary Press, 1973), 27. Here I speak about the physical, in-person assembly (pre-COVID-19).

[9] David Willis, "The Sacraments as Visible Word," *Theology Today* 37, no. 4, (January 1981): 455.

this "growing in the likeness and image of Christ."[10] Author Annie Dillard memorably describes this connection between worship and change.

> On the whole, I do not find Christians, outside of the catacombs, sufficiently sensible of conditions. Does anyone have the foggiest idea what sort of power we blithely invoke? Or, as I suspect, does no one believe a word of it? The churches are children playing on the floor with their chemistry sets, mixing up a batch of TNT to kill a Sunday morning. It is madness to wear ladies' straw hats and velvet hats to church; we should all be wearing crash helmets. Ushers should issue life preservers and signal flares; they should lash us to our pews. For the sleeping god may wake someday and take offense, or the waking god may draw us to where we can never return.

Dillard speaks of conditions: the condition of our life before God, the condition of our worshiping assemblies. Her words, especially the need for "crash helmets," evoke danger and urgency in the presence of God who means to change us. Liturgical theologian Aiden Kavanagh also gives us the liturgical language around this dangerous process of change.

> Liturgy leads regularly to the edge of chaos, and . . . what results in the first instance from such an experience is deep change in the very lives of those who participate in the liturgical act. And deep change will affect their next liturgical act, however slightly. . . the church is caught in the act of being most overtly itself as it stands faithfully in the presence of the One who is both object and source of that faith. The liturgical assembly's stance in faith is vertiginous, on the edge of chaos. Only grace and favor enable it to stand there; only grace and promise brought it there; only grace and a rigorous divine charity permit

---

[10] See II Corinthians 3:18; Colossians 3:9-10 (NRSV).

the assembly, like Moses, to come away whole from such an encounter. . .[11]

Worship as liminal event, cumulative in its power, means that it is an event of change and that it is dangerous in that it does not sanction status quo but regularly positions us for such a transformational encounter.

However, we are likely more familiar speaking of ourselves as the object of such transformation, of worship as liminal because it begets *our* continued becoming in Christ. But the liminality of corporate worship is not only about the *me* or the *us* of assembly, it is also about the world (and all that dwells therein) being made new according to God's promises: "In this view, the liturgical assembly *is* the world being renovated according to the divine pleasure – not as patient being passively worked upon but an active agent faithfully cooperating in its own rehabilitation. What one witnesses in the liturgy is the world being done as the world's Creator and Redeemer will the world to be done.[12]

In corporate worship we repeatedly re-enter that transformational, liminal time and space of being made new, whole, liberated and reconciled in Christ for the life of the world. As liturgical theologian Gordon W. Lathrop says, all of this is world-making: "The world that is thereby suggested is not the status quo, but an alternative vision that waits for God, hopes for a wider order than has yet been achieved or than any ritual can embody, but still embraces the present environment of our experience."[13]

It is important to clarify that recognizing corporate worship as a liminal event is different than feeling liminal *about* corporate worship because I am separated from what it was before the pandemic. Clearly many feel we are in a liminal state these days *regarding* corporate worship. In the midst of the pandemic-necessitated isolation, many of us wonder how to be the worshiping Church. For those of us who have not worshiped *virtually* before, we have been figuring out how to gather, sing,

---

[11] Aiden Kavanagh, *On Liturgical Theology* (Collegeville, MN: Liturgical Press, 1992), 73.

[12] Aiden Kavanagh, *Elements of Rite: A Handbook of Liturgical Style* (New York: Pueblo Publishing Co., 1982), 46.

[13] Gordon W. Lathrop, *Holy Things: A Liturgical Theology* (Minneapolis MN: Fortress Press, 1993), 210.

pray, read, preach, bless, and commune in ways mediated by electronic technologies. Some have now re-opened church buildings and assembled again for in-person worship, though in abridged ways (physical distancing, masks, restrictions on singing, spaces cleaned *and* sanitized, limited number of persons gathering, some counties permitting only outdoor church gatherings).

Liminal questions continue: For those of us who think of corporate Sunday worship as the ongoing centering act of the Church (with dependable encounter with the means of grace), what does it mean if we cannot fully do the things that enact our core identity in Christ? If worship is a liminal event, then what does it mean *not* to enact that liminality as fully as we normally do? Is corporate worship still world-making if worship is less than it was? Is it less than it was? Are we still being drawn out by the waking God?[14]

I find myself thinking a great deal about baptismal liminality because it is a central way that we remain tethered to the liminal meanings of the worshiping assembly. And I am thinking about baptismal liminality because it critiques other liminalities that, in baptismal terms, need to be renounced.

Baptismal Liminality

Though the sacrament of Baptism is on my mind these days it is not the singular act of Baptism, though our churches are figuring out ways to baptize in this time. But, rather, I think about the living out of our Baptism. While our churches—and some of us within our churches—are of differing opinions with regard to holy communion (Done virtually? How distributed if in-person?), we can ask how we are faithfully living out our identity as table people. This is a way of asking how we are living as those who are baptized into Christ. "The wiping away of tears has

---

[14] See Gordon W. Lathrop, "Thinking Again About Assembly In a Time of Pandemic," *Cross Accent* Association of Lutheran Church Musicians 28:1 (Summer 2020).

begun in the resurrection, and that beginning is washed over us in Baptism. God's grace for the world is washed over us, and we are made a witness of the coming."[15] In other words, while we are waiting to fully enact all of our beloved ways of worshiping God together, we can focus on living as the very people that corporate worship has shaped—and continues to shape—us to be: God's own for the world. Baptism is our initiation into, among other things, God's reconciling mission of love and righteousness for the life of the world. As Reformed theologian David Willis writes while commenting on the Lord's Prayer, "They need continually to be corrected and balanced by the conviction that God's kingdom ultimately, definitely means a change in the order of this *present* world and the quality of life lived in *it*."[16] Elsewhere Willis says:

> When Jesus speaks of the implications of his baptism, it is in terms of the ordeal he had to undergo (Luke 12:50). Hearing his word and being yoked with him in his ministry means that the disciples share in his suffering servanthood. As he fulfills the messianic hope in a very selective way, after the stamp of the suffering servant, they too are entered into a service which involves taking up the cross and following him as the cost of discipleship. To receive the Spirit is to be thrust into a mission which brings them into deadly conflict with the structures of the religion and society in which they operate.[17]

It seems to me this COVID-19 and protest-for-justice time is a good time to dwell on this question: How is the symbol of Baptism and the baptized life now so very clearly turned inside out for the life of the

---

[15] Gordon W. Lathrop, *Central Things: Worship in Word and Sacrament* (Minneapolis, MN: Augsburg Fortress, 2005), 62. Not all ecclesial traditions practice baptism before table (and therefore would not necessarily express the same orientation to sacramental inter-relatedness I state here); decisions to do otherwise normally center on discussions of welcome and hospitality. Here I emphasize the covenantal nature of coming to the table: How do we respond to such gracious feeding? How do we live out our thanksgiving for such hospitality? To live in relation to the table is to live as those baptized. See *Central Things*, 58.

[16] David Willis, *Daring Prayer* (Atlanta: John Knox Press, 1977), 79.

[17] Willis, "Sacraments as Visible Words," 452.

world?[18] While we discern how to worship in the time of plague and protests, let us also give disciplined thought to living as those baptized into Christ *for* the time of plague and protests. Baptism and baptismal liminality challenge the sense of a liminal episode as only a time of unknowing, drift, *ennui*. We are called to be changed and to change the world.

Baptism is not only a liminal event in its punctiliar sense but also is the beginning of a Christian liminality that sees our corporate life in Christ as a life of growth and change. *Baptismal liminality* points to that robust quality of liminality that is inherent in the baptismal journey. *Baptismal liminality* is the *journey or process of change* of each Christian's life until our death in Christ and a mark of our corporate identity in Christ for the life of the world. This is a liminality that is active, engaged, communal, well-led, and with the clarity of "a way in and a way out."[19]

In all of this I think and write as a middle-class, American, white woman. I am mindful that change looks different for different persons and different communions. Part of our change, our growing in the wholeness of God, is discerning what it means for our particularity. My journey of growth in the likeness of Christ will involve, for instance, my increased learning, knowing, and practice of anti-racist ideas and anti-racist policies.[20] It will also, for instance, necessitate my continued growth in valuing my voice-as-woman while negotiating patriarchal systems. The journey is toward God's promised wholeness and it is not only other worldly, it is for now.

---

[18] Here I reference the schematic used by Thomas Schattauer to speak about the relationship between worship and mission. See Thomas H. Schattauer, ed., *Inside Out: Worship in the Age of Mission* (Minneapolis: Fortress Press, 1999). I apply his "inside out" category to worship and justice, arguing that the central actions and symbols of worship are inherently symbols of biblical justice shaping us through corporate worship for life in the world. Keynote lecture, *Just Worship Conference*, PC(USA), Decatur, Georgia, 2018; Austin, Texas, 2019.

[19] Thomassen, *Liminality and the Modern*, 210: "There is a way into liminality and a way out of it."

[20] I am using these terms viz. Ibram X. Kendi's work, *How to Be An Anti-Racist* (New York: One World, 2019) in which he describes anti-racist work as dismantling racist ideas and racist policies.

Liminality is a rich concept that is useful to many theoretical disciplines such as ritual studies, religion, and political science. The following overview summarizes the origins and key developments of the term.

The Establishment of Liminality as an Idea

Arnold van Gennep and Liminality

Arnold van Gennep's (1873-1957, born Ludwigsburg, Württemberg) legacy is both complex and clear. Complex highlights of his life include: his conviction about the importance of his 1909 book, *Les Rites de Passage,* but his subsequent, ongoing, and never resolved relationship with the French academy, especially Emile Durkheim, Marcel Mauss, and neo-Kantian thought of the times; his emphasis, especially important for connections to liturgical studies, on understanding liminality and all phases of passage primarily as *faits naissants* - that we know of them first in their "concrete coming to life" rather than knowing first by theory; his conviction that rites work simultaneously on an individual and societal level, and that they are intrinsically bound with imitation.[21] He spent his life studying peoples, customs, and cultures. He was a remarkable German-born fellow, spoke twenty languages and read twice as many, wrote twelve books and over a hundred articles, but a rift with sociologist Emile Durkheim meant his work was never well-received in his lifetime. Even into the twentieth century van Gennep's theories were understood, in anthropological and sociological circles, as a mere supplement to those of Durkheim. But in fact, van Gennep's key work was an attempt to counter the errors he saw in Durkheim's approach as he broke with the functionalism of Durkheim's sociology and emphasized rites working at both the individual and societal levels.[22]

In his insistence on the centrality of liminality for humanity, van Gennep left a clear legacy: "Durkheim established a framework of analysis positing ritual as a timeless *consolidation* of society, whereas van

---

[21] Thomassen, *Liminality and the Modern,* 24.

[22] Thomassen, *Liminality and the Modern,* 22.

Gennep had proposed a more open-ended framework of analysis focusing on patterns, and positing *transition* as the central 'fact of life.'"[23]

Liminality, then, by its origin is not simply the time of undoing, change, transformation, nebulousness, shift, chaos, but it is this state of things precisely because the change is occurring as a person or persons moves from one state of being to another. It is greatly important to retain this sense that there is movement toward something else and that goal, that something else, is something clear. "If it is not about transition, it is not about liminality."[24] It will also be very important to return to what van Gennep has said about a trusted guide through the liminal state.

Victor Turner's work shifted this understanding of liminality in ways that popularized the concept for the American context with our interest in innovation, exploration, and adrenaline.

Victor Turner and The Liminoid

In 1960 *Les Rites de Passages* was translated into English which allowed for Victor Turner's (1920-1984, b. Scotland) discovery of van Gennep's work and a rediscovery, and eventual re-conceptualization, of liminality. "In terms of reception and development of Turner's work and the concept of liminality, it is certainly not irrelevant that Turner's ideas first started to spread around the late 1960s in America, a period so heavily marked by a taste for transgression and the celebration of out-of-the-ordinary experiences to break with everything 'traditional.'"[25]

Turner's ideas grew from his study of the African Ndembu tribe while on college grant funding. His evaluation of the Ndembus' rites initially followed the functionalist/structuralist paradigm of his supervisors, but he began moving away from that paradigm even before discovering van Gennep. His analysis of social life as theatrical and his introduction of the term "social drama" came about because he recognized that the Ndembu peoples' rites unfolded in a processual form: there was a

---

[23] Thomassen, *Liminality and the Modern*, 59.

[24] Thomassen, *Liminality and the Modern*, 15.

[25] Thomassen, *Liminality and the Modern*, 83.

dramatic arc to the rites. In 1957, the year of van Gennep's death, Turner wrote on ritual but he would not read van Gennep until 1963. When he did, he wrote the essay "Betwixt and Between: The Liminal Period in Rites of Passage."[26] His subsequent development of related concepts like the *liminoid* (1982) explored the emancipatory quality of the liminal phase.

In "From Liminal to Liminoid,"[27] Turner claimed that modern societies had replaced liminal experiences with liminal-like moments which he called the *liminoid*: practices of art and leisure events that are creative, playful, even fantastical as they engage uncertainty.[28] Modern societies, Turner noted, did not practice the sorts of rites of passage per van Gennep but, instead, engage liminal-like qualities through art, theatre, and leisure. Liminoid, then, describes the way these modern out-of-the-ordinary events function to give us an experience outside of ourselves, an "as if" time. Such liminoid performative out-of-the-ordinary experiences create "life in the conditional."[29]

According to Turner, Carnival was a prime example of the liminoid: it is a lived-out spectacle, large scale, and all-encompassing. There is no life outside of this event for its duration; no division between performer and spectator as all are caught up in the event. The liminoid, whether large or smaller scale, provides a break from normal life, a playful "as if," but without the personal crisis of the self undergoing change to a new status with repercussions to a larger society.[5] The liminoid helps us get out of a rut, do something different, have an experience that makes us forget about things for a while, lift our spirits. Turner observes that these liminoid experiences are optional and their meaning is individually determined rather than obligatory acts carrying communal meaning.

---

[26] This article became a chapter in his book *The Forest of Symbols* (New York: Cornell University Press, 1967).

[27] V.W. Turner "From Liminal to Liminoid, in Play, Flow and Ritual: An Essay in Comparative Symbology," Rice Institute Pamphlet–Rice University Studies 60, no. 3 (1974).

[28] Thomassen, *Liminality and the Modern,* 82.

[29] Thomassen, *Liminality and the Modern,* 82.

With his work on Christian pilgrimage,[30] Turner anticipated our next re-conceptualization of liminality in the connections between pilgrimage and liminality. In pilgrimage the temporal and spatial morph to a fixed liminal state, physical passage becomes a sustained reality, and transition becomes a permanent condition as participants take on a new status while they are distanced by former/other structures/identities and participate in that which demands the same of all of them (*communitas*). He had previously identified this suspended or sustained liminal state as a way of speaking about monastics and mendicants.[31]

Turner's ideas are distinct from van Gennep's sense of liminality. With Turner's work we see framings of societal explorations into "life as if," social dramas such as Carnival, experiences that are optional and individualized rather than obligatory for a group. For Turner these liminoid moments of modernity replace the liminal times of transition in rites of passage. This is Turner's best-known theory of liminality. However it is his observation about the fixed quality of pilgrimage that, along with the liminoid, clearly carries over to our twenty-first century context.

Liminality Becomes Permanent

Turner's shifts anticipate what is probably our primary connection to liminality in the twenty-first century: the transitional has become permanent. While we can readily identify liminoid events (and even liminoid worship events), we are additionally helped by understanding this permanent quality of our liminal state.

At the turn of this century one leading theorist, Arpad Szakolczai, in Ireland, coined the term *permanent liminality* to describe the quality of life or circumstances where transition is an ongoing condition. Critical social

---

[30] V.W. Turner and E.L Turner, *Image and Pilgrimage in Christian Culture* (New York: Columbia University Press, 1978).

[31] Thomassen, *Liminality and the Modern*, 83.

theorists use this term as a diagnostic tool to describe the modern age.[32] As a result, liminality studies have been taken up by over twenty academic disciplines, branching out in ways van Gennep could not have imagined.

These theorists agree that whereas liminality had functioned precisely as van Gennep described in small-scale rites of passage, they also know it is central to all human experience. "Liminality refers to moments or periods of transition during which the normal limits to thought, self-understanding and behavior are relaxed, opening the way to novelty and imagination, construction and destruction."[33] But this centrality comes with a caution that can be seen in descriptions of permanent liminality.

- Many of us live in societies/cultures that are shaped by an endless fascination with the innovative—and have adopted a celebratory stance toward anything that disrupts. The aspect that becomes permanent is "a fascinating and necessary shaking of routines."[34]
- Persons and societies constantly end up in liminal periods for a variety of reasons and for varying lengths of time. Critically, they are not emerging from these liminal spaces due to the nature of the precipitating event (illness, wars, asylum seekers, etc.). They are stuck in a permanence due to larger, often uncontrollable events. This is what COVID-19 causes. Many of us, especially those with an abundance of privileges, are experiencing this version of permanent liminality for the first time whereas for others COVID-19 is a permanent liminality layered on another (e.g., those in prisons or refugee camps, those with metastatic cancer). Sang Hyun Lee, writing about Asian-Americans and liminality, speaks of this type of permanence as "coerced liminality," a racialized inequality and oppression.[35] I understand Black Americans to live in multiple

---

[32] These theorists see the term post-modernity as unnecessary in these descriptions and make the point that modernity itself was about exploration and the new.

[33] Thomassen, *Liminality and the Modern*, 1.

[34] Thomassen, *Liminality and the Modern*, 2; see also Ilina Aristarkhova, "The Tyranny of the Possible," *Leonardo* 38, no. 1. (February 2005).

[35] Sang Hyun Lee, *From a Liminal Place: An Asian American Theology* (Minneapolis: Fortress Press, 2010), 33. Lee, as well as Thomassen, distinguish between marginality and liminality. While both are boundary concepts, liminality is interstitial rather than

permanent liminalities including this coerced liminality alongside the specificity of liminal instances such as COVID-19 and Black Lives Matter protests.[36]

- Permanent liminality is also the condition whereby those experiences that were formerly considered marginal or on the outer limits or only for the boundaried-liminal space of a passage *are now all the time everywhere.* For instance: gaming and the popularity of boundary-breaking leisure activities (e.g., Bungee jumping). Thomassen dubs these *limivoid* events; they are "because why not" events in an age of "ontological excess."[37]

It is critical to note that permanent liminality also includes political revolutions—those "drastic moments in which previously existing structures crumble and collapse, where norms and hierarchies are turned upside down."[38] Political uprisings and revolutions are in-between and an example of permanence because they are without the final frame of incorporation. In Turner's four-fold view, they have experienced breach and crisis but still press toward redress and reintegration. The future is inherently unknown.[39] Political uprisings and revolutions have a double aim: "to delegitimize the existing order (as non-representative of the 'people') and to legitimize themselves as carriers of the new order (of the 'people')."[40]

The liminality of political revolutions includes crowds and leadership and is particularly resonant as I write just prior to the 2020 elections: "By

---

outside/excluded. Lee also speaks to a theological (baptismal) liminality: "The redemption of fallen creation, especially humankind, involves the transformation of fallen humanity into persons who can participate in God's own work of repeating in time and space the inner-trinitarian community of love" (p. 36).

[36] See Resma Menakem, *My Grandmother's Hands* (Las Vegas, NV: Central Recovery Press, 2017) for his discussion of racialized trauma which I understand as connected to such coerced, permanent liminalities.

[37] Thomassen, *Liminality and the Modern,* 169, "Thomassen coins and defines the *limivoid* as "the inciting of near-death experiences, a jump into nothingness, a desperate search for experience in a world of ontological excess."

[38] Thomassen, *Liminality and the Modern,* 191.

[39] Thomassen, *Liminality and the Modern,* 210, ". . . revolutions do not announce themselves with end-dates."

[40] Thomassen, *Liminality and the Modern,* 202.

political revolution we mean not only an overthrow of a regime or state but also an overthrow that involves a popular movement. The 'masses' must somehow be involved."[41] Yet the masses need leadership for the movement to be successful, otherwise the movement remains a social uprising that does not bring about lasting change in institutions and structures. Most often these leaders have first been a part of the crowd but then, as van Gennep underscored regarding the centrality of a trustworthy guide in rites of passage, they become those who navigate the liminal period on behalf of the initiand. In the permanent liminality of political upheaval, the master may be missing (since no one has been through this before) or there is a false master of ceremony: the trickster figure.

It becomes clear that there is a difference between the trickster figure who disrupts with the aim of truth, of unveiling falsehoods, and tricksters who are only *out for themselves*, perpetuating conditions of confusion and ambivalence for purposes of self-attention and self-gain.[42] They live for the attention of the public, play with words and images, and they disregard the real nature of their own acts. They think they are the originators of a new world but have no sense of measurement and disregard social effects.[43]

> Trickster figures . . . are professionals in creating and escalating division up until violence or destruction breaks out, at which point they manage to represent themselves as saviors. When trickster figures are mistaken for saviors, then emotions will be continually and repeatedly incited.[44]

We should not underestimate the disruptive sway of a trickster figure, especially at a societal level during an experience of permanent liminality. It is devastating. And Christian ministers do our work in this context, against this backdrop.

---

[41] Thomassen, *Liminality and the Modern*, 203.

[42] See Charles L. Campbell and Johan H. Cilliers, *Preaching Fools: The Gospel as Rhetoric of Folly* (Waco, TX: Baylor Univ. Press, 2012).

[43] Thomassen, *Liminality and the Modern*, 208.

[44] Thomassen, *Liminality and the Modern*, 208.

A final observation about liminality in times of political upheaval (I linger here because this describes aspects of American society) is that a society can be stuck for a long time in a state of schismogenesis, meaning the *previous unity was broken*, and yet the schismatic components are forced to stay together, producing an unpleasant, violent, harrowing, truly miserable existence.[45] Sometimes the original ruling powers or the subverting powers have it in their best interests to keep the society guessing, in the state of unknowing. Enforced or coerced liminality is always for someone's gain. To say that we do *liminality, permanently* (italics mine) is to acknowledge that we've lost our frames of Separation/Incorporation. And to lose these frames is, as we have seen, another definition for schizophrenia: "no culture would be foolish enough to devise a ritual sequence that stops at the liminal. . . individuals go crazy and societies become pathological."[46] Again, to name this dynamic here is to offer another diagnostic tool as we strive to understand why our current context is wearying and destructive.

Our current liminal context is more than a time of listlessness, drift, *ennui*. Instead, we live in *a collision of liminalities*, multiple versions of permanent liminality: the imposed permanence due to COVID-19, economic failing, political uprisings in response to police murders of black persons, trickster leadership, and schismogenesis. For many persons these liminalities are layered over others including coerced liminality. Our liminal context is complex.

The Church's Liminal Stance: A Way Out

What shall we say of the Church's relationship with liminality, especially in light of these ideas and permutations? This essay is preliminary work, setting the stage for longer and more detailed work on this topic elsewhere. By way of conclusion I focus on one aspect of baptismal rites and offer initial thoughts on what is at stake when thinking with this baptismal liminality.

---

[45] Thomassen, *Liminality and the Modern*, 208.
46 Thomassen, *Liminality and the Modern*, 216.

Horace Allen, in "Liturgy as the Form of Faith," spoke about "Losing connections." "Vast and historic traditions of Christian worship have. . . actually destroyed the forms they inherited, including the vital relationships among those forms."[47] Baptism still seems to be one of those lost connections, at least for many members and churches of the PC(USA). We have lost the fullness of its form[48] and the connection between the one-time act and its lifelong claim on our lives. Still today many churchgoers see the baptismal rite as a social nicety (perhaps more so in places which asperge rather than affuse, let alone immerse or submerse). "When persons are baptized in communities which appear to be only minimally aware of the content and momentum of the faith, the question is raised whether the act is much more than the self-perpetuation of a religiously-inclined association."[49] Annie Dillard, with her call for crash helmets, signal flares, and life preservers, would have us see otherwise in this rite of the church.

My ongoing work with baptismal liminality will include making connections between the baptismal rite, the Sunday assembly as continued instantiation of Baptism, and Baptism or baptismal liminality as the pattern of our days: our life in the world as Christ's own for the life of the world. But one example follows.

I am heartened by the fact that my denomination, the Presbyterian Church (U.S.A.), includes the Renunciations before the Affirmation of Faith in the Rite of Baptism. However, not all ministers include this portion of the rite. When the renunciations are excluded, we undermine an aspect of the newly sealed covenantal relationship, avoiding this personal-societal pledge and the meanings they hold for those baptized in Christ.

By comparison, this pledge is emphasized, heavily, in eastern orthodox baptismal rites:

> *The ones to be baptized turn about and face West, with their backs to the priest. The priest then asks the following question three times:*

---

47 Horace T. Allen, Jr., "Liturgy as the Form of Faith," *Liturgy* 12, no. 1 (1994), 9.
48 See Lathrop, *Central Things*, for a description of baptism "unshrunk" (p. 63).
49 Willis, "Sacraments as Visible Words," 456.

Priest: Do you renounce Satan, and all his works, and all his angels, and all his service, and all his pride? (*three times*)

Candidate: I do renounce him.

Priest: Have you renounced Satan? (*three times*)

Candidate: I have renounced him.

Priest: Breath and spit upon him.

The ones to be baptized now turn about back to the East, and they stand facing the priest. The priest asks them three times:

Priest: Do you unite yourself to Christ? (*three times*)
Candidate: I do unite myself to Christ.
Priest: Have you united yourself to Christ (*three times*)
Candidate: I have united myself to Christ.
Priest: Do you believe in Him?
Candidate: I believe in him as King and God.

The candidate/s kneel to recite the Creed.[50]

I remember the first time I saw baptismal candidates turn and spit out as they stood at the very threshold of the front doors of the church during this rite in the eastern orthodox church. It is a dramatic moment

---

[50] https://www.oca.org/files/PDF/Music/Baptism/baptism-service.pdf. Cf. the Renunciations from the PC(USA)'s *Book of Common Worship* (1993), p. 407:

Do you renounce all evil,
and powers in the world
which defy God's righteousness and love?
I renounce them
Do you renounce the ways of sin
that separate you from the love of God?
I renounce them.
Do you turn to Jesus Christ
and accept him as your Lord and Savior?
I do.

even if you know what is coming. Standing again after reciting the creed, they answer the three affirmations one final time: Do you unite yourself. . . have you united yourself to Christ? One translator says that *align* is the better word, because align indicates the active nature of what the baptized must do as we continually work to be in step with Christ, with Christ's commandments and teachings, with Christ himself in his *kenosis* as the Way, Truth, and Life. This rite includes a literal turning, *metanoia*, embodying in that ritual moment our lifelong turning away from all that corrupts and destroys the life God has given all creatures, and our lifelong turning to Christ.[51]

If I think about those renunciations and connect them with ways they are continued throughout our baptized life, I think of them giving guidance, orientation, even discipline to our thoughts and actions in the world. They are why we are discerning with our thoughts, words, and deeds. For example:

- As the baptized, we challenge contentment with the liminalities of *ennui* and of incessant drive for innovation that serve to keep us stuck without a way out.
- As the baptized we attend to the plank in our own eye even as we strive to change the permanent liminalities of unjust systems, governments, institutions.
- As the baptized those of us with privileges call out and change those dynamics that perpetuate coerced liminalities like anti-black racism.
- As the baptized we shun allegiance to "trickster" leadership and ways that perpetuate permanent liminalities that aid the powerful.
- As the baptized we are mindful concerning our consumption and our consumer-based enticement with "amusing ourselves to death."

Baptism initiates us into this life of aligning ourselves with the God we know in Jesus Christ and God's new creation. *Baptismal liminality is this lifelong work of alignment, of change.* We do not perpetuate a "religiously-inclined association" but are changed and work to change the world

---

[51] The Greek word is μετάνοια (metanoia).

around us to align with God's purposes. Alignment involves ongoing renunciation and turning.

In this essay I engage "thinking with liminality" as a helpful way to diagnose these unprecedented times yet caution against a sole definition of liminality as a state of weariness, chaos, and drift. I acknowledge the uprootedness of our lives especially with regard to corporate worship during a pandemic. I call us to think with a baptismal liminality. Finally, with an eye turned to my home denomination I know that we need, in Horace Allen's wording, to recover this liturgical form and its "vital relationships" so that faith shapes our daily lives. Our baptismal liminality, even during this pandemic, discloses *a way out* which, simultaneously is *The Way* we are to live until our dying day.

III. EPILOGUE

by Martha Moore-Keish

I never had the joy of meeting Horace Allen face to face. In editing this volume, therefore, I have rejoiced to learn more about this legendary figure through the stories of his students Barbara Thorington Green, Mark Stamm, and Heather Josselyn-Cranson, as they celebrate Allen's impish wit and liturgical wisdom. Together they offer a portrait of a man who taught through story and example more than lecture, whose preaching and presiding in chapel and church was as formative as his role in the classroom.

I never had the joy of meeting Horace Allen face to face, yet since the beginning of my professional life, I have benefited from his work. Like David Gambrell and Kimberly Bracken Long, I have worked on the staff of the PC(USA)'s Office of Theology and Worship, where Allen's books formed the core of the worship library that he began while he was the first Director of the Joint Office of Worship and Music. Like Tom Trinidad, I was a member of the Sacramental Study Group (2003-2006) that developed "Invitation to Christ," continuing the work of sacramental renewal that had begun decades earlier in the Presbyterian church under Allen's leadership. Like Lisa Weaver, Jennifer Lord and many other contributors, I now teach in a theological school, seeking to shape students into strong, loving, and wise worship leaders as Allen did for so many years at Boston University. Like most of the writers in this volume, I am a member of the North American Academy of Liturgy, the ecumenical liturgical guild of which Allen was an early and important member. In all these places, I am indebted to Allen's groundbreaking work as an ecumenical, Reformed liturgical scholar.

In compiling a volume like this one, we are not only looking back to celebrate the moment of a life, but also around to the present liturgical moment and ahead to emerging developments, flowing from Allen's work, that are leading us into the future. In this way, we are mirroring the insight that David Gambrell describes in his essay about ecumenical and liturgical leaders in general:

> "There is a sense in which ecumenical and liturgical leaders—such as Horace Allen—must be time travelers. They are compelled to haunt the catacombs, to stalk the saints, to search the archives of antiquity, always trying to tap the wellsprings of our traditions. At the same time, they are called to scan the horizons, to venture into the unknown, to entrust themselves to the future, always hungering for the heavenly banquet."[1]

So too in this Festschrift. Looking back, we see the passionate brilliance and idiosyncrasy of a teacher, scholar, and storyteller who inspired generations of students and colleagues, especially in North America and South Korea. In Horace T. Allen, Jr., we see a liturgist who delighted in breaking the bread and in breaking open the word, ever finding new life in these ancient ways of worship.

From his own restless dynamic life of worship and teaching, we are pushed to look around at the new ways God is breaking things open today. For liturgy is indeed restless work, the work of people always on the move, straining forward to what lies ahead. This is the shared eschatological vision of all Christians, and it has particular resonance in the Reformed tradition of which Horace Allen was an unapologetic member, a tradition that affirms that the Church is "reformed and ever

---

[1] See chapter 8, 151-152.

being reformed (according to the Word of God)." The essays of this book testify in various ways to how understanding earlier traditions can empower contemporary liturgical leaders to try new things—like the "Lectionary Year D" (Heather Josslyn-Cranson). We also see how new worshiping communities, even without planning or preparation, might freshly illumine ancient practices—like all members of a gathered community spontaneously breaking the eucharistic bread together (Kimberly Bracken Long).

The interplay of past and future is not the only tension at work here. Many of the essays in this collection celebrate the dynamic tension that drove Horace Allen's own ecumenical vision: the tension between celebrating commonality and "magnifying particularity" (Mark Stamm). Clearly, Allen did not see these as opposing values, but as complementary ones. To read common texts, as he called the Church to do, was not to erase diversity but to cultivate a genuinely catholic vision. The example of the Revised Common Lectionary itself embodies this vision, as it invites Christians to direct their attention to the same texts at the same time, while recognizing that their interpretations will be specific to each time and place.. The unity thus embodied is the living unity of relationships among people and churches who share common commitments, not oppressive uniformity dictated from above. In addition, the formation of the Revised Common Lectionary itself reveals the interplay between these two aspects of Allen's ecumenical vision, as Fritz West discusses in his essay on the two "canons" governing the reading of scripture. All heirs of the sixteenth century reformations might well learn from Allen's emphasis on being "Reformed" rather than being simply "protestant" (as if our identity is based on unending protest against an ecclesial institution that has itself also been reformed). To be Presbyterian, in this way, is to embody an "evangelical catholicity" that seeks the unity of the church even as it also maintains its own particular emphases and honors its specific history. Jonathan Hehn persuasively argues that we should follow this path of magnifying particularity even as we celebrate ecumenical unity in our formation of pastors and other worship leaders in the Presbyterian church.

In attending to the particularity of Presbyterian worship in this volume, we have sought both to honor Allen's own work in the history of Reformed worship (especially around the reading of the Scriptures and the unity of Word and Sacrament) and to attend to aspects of

Presbyterian worship history that were not part of his field of vision. As Jonathan Hehn notes in the preface, the essay by Lisa Weaver for the first time invites attention to the history of Black Presbyterian worship in the United States, exposing the systemic racism that has been part of the Presbyterian Church in this country from the beginning, (mis-)shaping its worship practices. This contribution may be the farthest from Allen's own scholarly work, but it invites us to wrestle with one of the most important issues facing American Presbyterian worship today. Seung Joong Joo continues Allen's commitment to nurturing worship life in Korean churches by confronting challenges in the contemporary Korean Presbyterian church, and calling for a return to the principles that guided Calvin's liturgical reforms rather than a capitulation to entertainment culture. Peter Bower, David Gambrell, and Kimberly Bracken Long all address the distinctive Presbyterian balance of "form and freedom" that characterizes a tradition that has both a Directory for Worship and a service book. Long offers particularly lucid and wise observations about where we are presently and where we are going, based on analysis of where we have been, with illuminating attention to emerging research about new worshiping communities and their worship lives. And finally, Jennifer Lord eloquently ponders worship "in a time of plague and protests" through the lens of baptismal liminality.

As Mark Stamm and others have noted, Horace Allen publicly declared his disillusionment with the ecumenical movement in 2002, proclaiming it to be "dead, finished, done," particularly because of some developments in the Roman Catholic church at that time.[2] The end of his life thus leaves us with a challenge. Is the vision of common texts unifying the Church indeed defunct? Is his vision of evangelical catholicity that magnifies particularity a naïve dream? Or, granting the challenges that still impede the unity of the Church, might we yet press ahead to realize in new ways the ecumenical vision that drove him? Could it be that even when some institutions falter and fail in their progress toward God's kin-dom, other movements arise that embody the unity of the Church in unexpected forms? Could it be that even now — in bars, around kitchen tables, on the streets — the liturgy that Horace Allen so loved is emerging anew, drawing unlikely people together to encounter

---

[2] See chapter one, 19-20.

the word and share the bread and cup, proclaiming the coming of God into this weary world? We, the editors and authors in this book, yet have hope that it may be so.

ABOUT THE AUTHORS

Peter C. Bower serves as Editor in Chief of Studia Liturgica and also as Interim Pastor of Boiling Springs Presbyterian Church in Spring Church, Pennsylvania. He is the author of several books on Presbyterian worship, including The Companion to the Book of Common Worship (Geneva Press, 2003)

David Gambrell is Associate for Worship in the Office of Theology and Worship of the Presbyterian Church (U.S.A.), as well as an ordained presbyter in that tradition. He was the co-editor of the most recent edition of the *Book of Common Worship* (Westminster John Knox Press, 2018) as well as the coordinator of the 2017 revision of the PC(USA)'s Directory for Worship.

Fred Graham is Associate Professor (Emeritus) of Emmanuel College of Victoria University in the University of Toronto. In 2008 he was successful in establishing Canada's only graduate program in Church Music. He has been a representative of The United Church of Canada since 1988 on the Consultation on Common Texts, and was the CCT Convener for two terms. Graham worked collaboratively with Horace Allen, Jr. on many CCT projects, including the *Revised Common Lectionary*.

Barbara Thorington Green is an ordained presbyter (retired) in the United Methodist Church and a former doctoral student and graduate assistant to Horace T. Allen at the Boston University School of Theology. Green is the author of *Calling God She?: Reflections and Insights of a great-grandmother, retired clergywoman, and doctor of theology* (2014).

Jonathan Hehn is a Choral Program Director and Organist as well as term assistant professor of sacred music at the University of Notre Dame. As well as a prominent practitioner, he is an interdisciplinary scholar, having been oft published in the areas of Presbyterian liturgy as well as sacred music. He serves as the editor of *Doxology: a journal of worship and the sacramental life.*

Seung Joong Joo is Senior Pastor of Juan Presbyterian Church, Incheon, South Korea and Adjunct Professor of United Graduate School of Theology, Yonsei University, Seoul, Korea. He formerly served as Professor of Liturgy/Preaching at Presbyterian University and Theological Seminary, Seoul, Korea (1998-2012), and is a former chair of the Korea Academy of Liturgy.

Heather Josselyn-Cranson is Associate Professor of Music and Humanities at Regis College, where she holds the Sister Margaret William McCarthy Endowed Chair in Music. She earned a Th.D. in liturgical studies from the Boston University School of Theology as a student of Horace T. Allen. She is the author of *The Reason Why We Sing* (OSL Publications, 2016).

Kimberly Bracken Long is the editor of *Call to Worship* and former Associate for Worship in the PC(USA)'s Office of Theology and Worship. She taught for several years at Columbia Theological Seminary in Decatur, Georgia as a professor of worship. She is a widely published author, including the book *From This Day Forward—Rethinking the Christian Wedding* (Westminster John Knox, 2016), and was the co-editor for the 2018 *Book of Common Worship*.

Jennifer Lord is the Dorothy B. Vickery Professor of Homiletics and Liturgical Studies at Austin Presbyterian Theological Seminary in Austin, Texas, and is an ordained presbyter in the PC(USA). Lord is a past president of the North American Academy of Liturgy and is an interdisciplinary scholar working in both liturgical studies and homiletics. She is the author of several books and lectionary resources and recently served as Editorial Board Member for *Connections: A Lectionary Commentary for Preaching and Worship* (Westminster John Knox Press).

Martha Moore-Keish is the J.B. Green Professor of Theology at Columbia Theological Seminary in Atlanta, Georgia, having previously served as teaching faculty at Yale Divinity School and as an Associate for Worship in the Presbyterian Church (U.S.A.) Office of Theology and Worship. She is an ordained presbyter in the PC(USA), has been the author of several books, including *Karl Barth and Comparative Theology* (Fordham University Press, 2019), and is a notable leader in the ecumenical movement, especially as Reformed co-chair of the fourth phase of dialogue between the World Communion of Reformed Churches and the Pontifical Council for Promoting Christian Unity.

Mark Stamm, OSL is Professor of Worship at Southern Methodist University's Perkins School of Theology. He is a Th.D. graduate from the Boston University School of Theology, where he was a student of Horace T. Allen. Stamm is an ordained presbyter in the United Methodist Church, the author of several influential books on worship and the sacraments, and a former abbot of the Order of Saint Luke.

Tom M. Trinidad is an ordained presbyter in the Presbyterian Church (U.S.A.) and pastor of Faith Presbyterian Church in Colorado Springs, Colorado. He holds a Ph.D. in liturgical theology from the University of Notre Dame and has published a number of articles in the realm of liturgy. Among others, one of his prior leadership roles has been as chairperson of the PC(USA)'s Committee on Theological Education.

Lisa M. Weaver is Assistant Professor of Worship at Columbia Theological Seminary in Decatur, Georgia. She is an ordained clergyperson in the American Baptist Churches USA and holds a Ph.D. from The Catholic University of America. In addition, she serves as a worship grants advisory board member of the Calvin Institute of Christian Worship. Her research interests are in the areas of Christian initiation and African American liturgical practices.

Fritz West, is an ordained minister in the United Church of Christ. A liturgical scholar, he is the author of many works on liturgy and the Revised Common Lectionary and two books, including *The Ecumenical Hermeneutic of the Three-Year Lectionaries* (Liturgical Press, 1997).

Made in the USA
Coppell, TX
13 February 2021